DOSTOYEVSKY AND THE JEWS

Dostoyevsky and the Jews

By David I. Goldstein

Foreword by Joseph Frank

University of Texas Press, Austin and London

Originally published as *Dostoïevski et les Juifs*
(Paris: Editions Gallimard, 1976). English
translation by the author.

LIBRARY OF CONGRESS CATALOGING IN PUBLICATION DATA
Goldstein, David I
  Dostoyevsky and the Jews.
  (University of Texas Press Slavic series; no. 3)
  Bibliography: p.
  Includes index.
  1. Dostoevskiĭ, Fedor Mikhaĭlovich, 1821–1881—Criticism and interpreta-
tion. 2. Jewish question. 3. Antisemitism in literature. I. Title. II. Series.
PG3328.Z7J4513   891.73′3   80-15154
ISBN 0-292-71528-5

TO MY FATHER, NATHAN E.,
IN LOVING MEMORY

Contents

Foreword

DAVID GOLDSTEIN has written a valuable and indispensable book on a subject that cannot help being of interest to any reader of Dostoyevsky and that goes a long way in lighting up one unhappy aspect of this complex, baffling and self-contradictory genius. One may fear, at first sight, that it is the type of book that gave rise to the old story about the mythical Academy of Sciences that, offering a prize for a scientific study of the elephant, was mildly astonished to receive an entry entitled: *The Elephant and the Jewish Question*. But Goldstein does not unduly inflate the importance of the Jewish question for Dostoyevsky, and he happily makes no attempt to endow it with more significance than it actually has in the body of the novelist's work.

In point of fact, Dostoyevsky depicted only one Jewish character at any length (Isai Fomich Bumstein in *The House of the Dead*). The minor figure of Lyamshin in *The Possessed*, a member of Pyotr Verkhovensky's revolutionary "five," is, as Goldstein demonstrates, probably a converted Jew; but his Jewish traits are so minimal that they have hardly attracted any critical attention. There is also the passing glimpse of the Jewish fireman, incongruously rigged out in an Achilles helmet (Matthew Arnold might have been pleased by this combination of the Hebraic and the Hellenic), before whose disbelieving eyes Svidrigailov shoots himself in *Crime and Punishment*. Goldstein's analysis of this fleeting encounter is the only place in the book where a trace of the elephantine can, perhaps, be detected.

Nonetheless, Goldstein is perfectly justified in maintaining that a study of Dostoyevsky's relation to the Jews and Judaism is by no means arbitrary or superfluous. Dostoyevsky himself felt it necessary publicly to take a stand on "The 'Jewish Question'" in his important article with this title in *The Diary of a Writer*, and he constantly makes stylistic allusions, invariably uncomplimentary, to Jews and Jewishness in his novels and stories and, most of all, in his *Diary*. Yet, at the same time, he exchanged frank and courteous letters with at least two Jewish correspondents (one of them serving a prison term for theft) and made efforts to help them personally. Moreover, he vigorously denied that he was a "hater of the Jewish people" and declared "there has never been such a hatred in my heart." Clearly, he was preoccupied with this problem himself and raised it in such a way as to justify devoting to it the close scrutiny that Goldstein has finally provided.

I have now read his book twice and each time have been impressed by the thoroughness of the documentation, the rigor of the analysis and the scrupulous impartiality that Goldstein maintains in presenting the evidence. None of the facts are left out so far as my knowledge goes; opposing points of view are invariably given; and Goldstein always firmly distinguishes between Dostoyevsky's opinions as a polemicist and public figure and his genius as a novelist. All the same, his book adds up to an implacable indictment, and I must confess that it left me each time with an unrelieved sense of dismay. Let me hasten to add that I would by no means wish to conceal or distort the facts to which Goldstein calls attention or refuse to look them in the face; far better to know and accept the truth, however painful, than to struggle at all costs —even at that of intellectual integrity—to preserve a cherished illusion about a cultural idol.

Nothing seems to me more ridiculous, if not ignominious, than the perennial efforts of Marxists to refuse to admit the obvious and virulent anti-Semitism of Marx's own *The Jewish Question*, which anticipates by thirty years Dostoyevsky's identification of Jews with the lust for gold, merciless usury and the unscrupulous exploitation of others and which, moreover, states this identification with much less uneasy equivocation than we find in Dostoyevsky. Nothing has been more abject, to take a more recent example, than the linguistic acrobatics of devout Heideggerians trying to deny that Heidegger was an active Nazi sympathizer in the early years of Hitler's accession to power. Such an attitude smacks of hagiography rather than history and really does no service (quite the contrary) to the cause it seeks to advance. Those who believe blindly will have continued to believe in any case; those with some critical sense will hardly be persuaded and will only be exasperated by what, at best, can be considered obtuseness and, at worst, outright falsification. No, every admirer of Dostoyevsky should be willing to test his or her admiration against the evidence presented by Goldstein with such compelling force.

As I read and reread his book, I realized that my own discomfort at its conclusions was a result of having to confront such a challenge; and I kept asking myself whether it could really be met. Must one admit that Dostoyevsky was bitterly and blindly prejudiced and that all the appeals in his work for Christian love, and for sympathy for the oppressed and the suffering, ring false in the light of what seems to be his deep-rooted anti-Semitism? Or is there some other perspective that can be proposed that, without false apologetics, allows us to see Dostoyevsky in a slightly more sympathetic light? Some of the mental notes that I made in the course of my reading seemed to me to indicate the possibility of such an alternative, and I should like to sketch these reflections here briefly as a tribute to the stimulus provided by Goldstein's treatment of the subject.

Dostoyevsky's anti-Semitism, in my opinion, should perhaps not be taken to be as much all of one piece as Goldstein tends to assume. He never admits the possibility that Dostoyevsky might have had conflicting feelings over the issue or be caught up, regarding the Jews, in the same sort of inner conflict that we know him to have wrestled with on so many other important matters. Goldstein inclines to discredit—or to consider unimportant and even deceptive—any trace of ambiguity and uncertainty in Dostoyevsky's attitude toward the Jews and to accept as genuinely felt *only* those aspects of this attitude that reveal a marked anti-Semitism.

For example, Goldstein notes himself that Jews were invariably depicted in Russian literature of the nineteenth century, from Pushkin to Chekhov, in the most uncomplimentary fashion and solely as objects of ridicule, contempt and derision. Dostoyevsky follows this tradition, for the most part, in his portrayal of Isai Fomich; but the effect, nonetheless, is not only one of caricature.

There are passages characterized by "warmth and goodwill" and "it is with sympathy, if not affection" that Dostoyevsky evokes "the blissful countenance of my prison comrade and barracks' mate, the unforgettable Isai Fomich." These are Goldstein's own words or those he quotes from Dostoyevsky's text; yet he passes over them very rapidly and returns to the other side of the picture (admittedly much more extensive). Still, there is evidence here of something else besides the usual contempt or disdain, and it indicates that Dostoyevsky was capable of *both* reactions at the same time.

Similarly, Dostoyevsky's magazine *Time*, arguing against the Slavophile *Day* early in the 1860s, defended an extension of certain legal rights to educated Jews. Why does Goldstein take for granted that the motive was exclusively tactical, and only so that the journal might appear to have a more "liberal" coloring? Could Dostoyevsky, as editor, not have been expressing an honestly held opinion? Certainly, in view of the shading given to Isai Fomich, such a possibility cannot be excluded. And the words used in the article, written either by Dostoyevsky or a close collaborator, jibe with some of the novelist's deepest convictions: "The teachings of peace, love and concord," the article declares "should have prompted other thoughts and other words" from the supposed defenders of Christ.

Dostoyevsky's anti-Semitic posture becomes much more pronounced during the 1870s; but even here, and particularly in his sensational article on "The 'Jewish Question,'" we can find manifestations of a profoundly ambiguous and divided sensibility. The first two sections, as Goldstein rightly points out, are a handy compendium of anti-Semitic slurs and slanders, some dating from time immemorial and others slightly more up-to-date (it is very difficult to be original on the Jewish question). But then, suddenly, the tone changes, and after one particularly vicious passage, Dostoyevsky unexpectedly declares: "I am, nevertheless, in favor of full and absolute equality of rights because that is Christ's law, because that is a Christian principle."

Even more, the last section of the article, chapter 3, seems to have been written by a different person. Here Dostoyevsky faithfully cites a long letter from one of his Jewish correspondents (a young girl named Sofya Lurye, the daughter of a well-to-do Jewish family in Minsk) who had described to him the funeral of a German Protestant doctor in her community that had been celebrated by Jews and Christians alike. The saintly doctor had come to the aid of everyone who appealed to him for help; he had made no distinctions because of religion; and both communities had joined together in prayer and sorrow over his tomb. This was only an isolated case, Dostoyevsky says, but perhaps in this example is the beginning of an answer to the Jewish question. Dostoyevsky thus ends his article, written in his usual impassioned, probing and jabbing manner, with Jews and Christians united in a community of love, stirred by their common reverence and gratitude for the doctor's memory and forgetting their age-old enmities and resentments.

What are we to make of such a text, which ends up at exactly the opposite ideological pole from which it started? Goldstein discounts this last section entirely because he is convinced that, by stressing such an individual moral exemplar, Dostoyevsky was actually arguing insidiously against demands for legal action on behalf of the Jews; a change of heart in relation to them, he seems to be implying, would really be enough. Certainly this is one inference that may be drawn; but it should also be kept in mind that Dostoyevsky took up exactly the same position in relation to advocates of a Russian constitution that would have granted more legal rights to the Russian peasant.

For Dostoyevsky, legal rights made no sense unless they were already grounded in the moral feelings of the people; and no matter how extravagant it may seem (but is it really any more extravagant than the Populist doctrines of the Russian left at this time?), Dostoyevsky could only conceive of Russia as a Utopian community of love, not as a constitutional state in the Western legal sense. In the last analysis, as we see, he could not bring himself to exclude the Jews from this community despite all the evident strength of his anti-Semitic prejudices. No more on this question than on any other should the restless, tormented, incredibly volatile Dostoyevsky, whose greatest characters so often express the very views he most hated and feared, be reduced to any single or simple point of view.

Dostoyevsky was thus unquestionably anti-Semitic, just as he was anti-French, anti-German, anti-English and, particularly, anti-

Polish—indeed, anti-everybody who was not Russian, and Great Russian at that. To tell the truth, he was probably more fiercely anti-Polish than anti-Semitic, and he portrays the Poles much more extensively in his work than he does Jews. He speaks of the Poles who were his fellow prisoners in Siberia much more respectfully than he does of Isai Fomich; they were, after all, educated men, and among the few fellow prisoners with whom he could carry on an intelligent conversation. But he finally ended up by quarreling with them all the same, and he is quoted by a Polish fellow inmate as saying that, if he thought he had a drop of Polish blood in his veins, he would instantly have himself bled. In *The Gambler*, he portrays various anonymous Poles as crooks, cheats and swindlers of incredible pretentiousness and vanity, who conceal their mendacities under a thin veneer of gentility and punctilio. The same type of characterization, on a much larger scale, is given to the two Poles in *The Brothers Karamazov*, one of whom is Grushenka's ex-lover; they are both shown to be completely despicable and irredeemable scoundrels.

Dostoyevsky's anti-Semitism, it seems to me, should be placed in this larger context of a more general xenophobia; and what distinguishes his anti-Semitism from all his other national, ethnic and religious hatreds is that, here and here alone, he appears to betray a certain sense of guilt. Perhaps in this respect also, as in the case of his novels, it is necessary to invent a new category for Dostoyevsky—the category of *guilty* anti-Semite. In relation to the Jews, I would suggest, he could never reconcile himself inwardly to his own violation of what he knew very well were the commands of the Christ in whom he believed (he may have had doubts about the existence of God, but never about the divinity of Christ), and the contradictions in his anti-Semitism faithfully reflect this struggle within himself. From such a point of view, his anti-Semitism should certainly not be overlooked or excused; but at least it need not be considered ignoble or humanly repugnant. Others (Richard Wagner for one, to select only a single name from a distressingly long list) had felt no such qualms. And one can thus continue to read Dostoyevsky's work, where both guilt and the love ethic of Christ play so large a part, without any gnawing doubt as to whether his anti-Semitism does not really turn all this into a fraud and a sham.

These few remarks indicate how I should meet the challenge posed by Goldstein's book; but all who feel the same need to come to terms with Dostoyevsky's anti-Semitism will have to find their own solution. One thing, however, is certain: the place to start from is the pages they are about to read.

Joseph Frank

Acknowledgments

Anent the French edition:

Nombreux sont ceux qui m'ont aidé à mener à bien ce travail. Je les remercie tous—et en tout premier lieu Pierre Pascal, qui n'a cessé de guider mes pas dans cet univers dostoïevskien qu'il connaît comme nul autre.

Je m'exprime ici dans un idiome qui n'est pas le mien: je dois à l'amicale vigilance de Pierre Andler d'avoir évité bien des maladresses.

Last but not least, *je nommerai ma femme, dont la patience à toute épreuve m'a permis de passer tant d'heures en compagnie d'un écrivain qui est, à lui seul, tout un monde.*

Anent the American edition:

The same, save that any maladroitness of language is the author's alone.

Note on Transliteration and Basic Source Material

AMID THE DIVERSITY of transliteration systems, I have adopted, by and large, the one used by the United Nations; it is simple and straightforward and renders smoothly the natural pronunciation of the transliterated words in English.

As the basic source for all quotations from Dostoyevsky's literary works, I have used the latest Soviet critical edition of his complete works: *Polnoye sobraniye sochinenii v tridtsati tomakh* (Leningrad, 1972–). To date (November 1979), nineteen volumes, the first seventeen of which contain all of Dostoyevsky's purely literary works, variants and "Notebooks," have appeared. I have employed Roman numerals to refer to the volumes in this edition followed by the page number. While Constance Garnett's translations of Dostoyevsky's novels (London: William Heinemann) have provided some guidance, all translations are mine and all references are, accordingly, to the aforementioned Soviet edition.

For *The Diary of a Writer*, I have used as my original source volumes 11 and 12 (*Dnevnik pisatelya*) of B. V. Tomashevsky and K. I. Khalabayev (eds.), *Polnoye sobraniye khudozhestvennykh proizvedenii* (Moscow-Leningrad, 1929). For references to this edition, I have used Arabic numerals. Boris Brasol's translation of *The Diary* (New York: George Braziller, 1954), has been helpful. My source for various articles written by Dostoyevsky between 1845 and 1878 is volume 13 (1930) of this same edition.

Lastly, I have made extensive use of F. M. Dostoyevsky's *Pisma* (*Letters*), A. S. Dolinin (ed.), vols. 1–3 (Moscow-Leningrad, 1928, 1930, 1934), vol. 4 (Moscow, 1959).

And finally, a brief word about dates. For internal Russian events, I have used the Old Style dating of the Julian calendar, which, in the nineteenth century, ran twelve days behind the Gregorian calendar employed in the West.

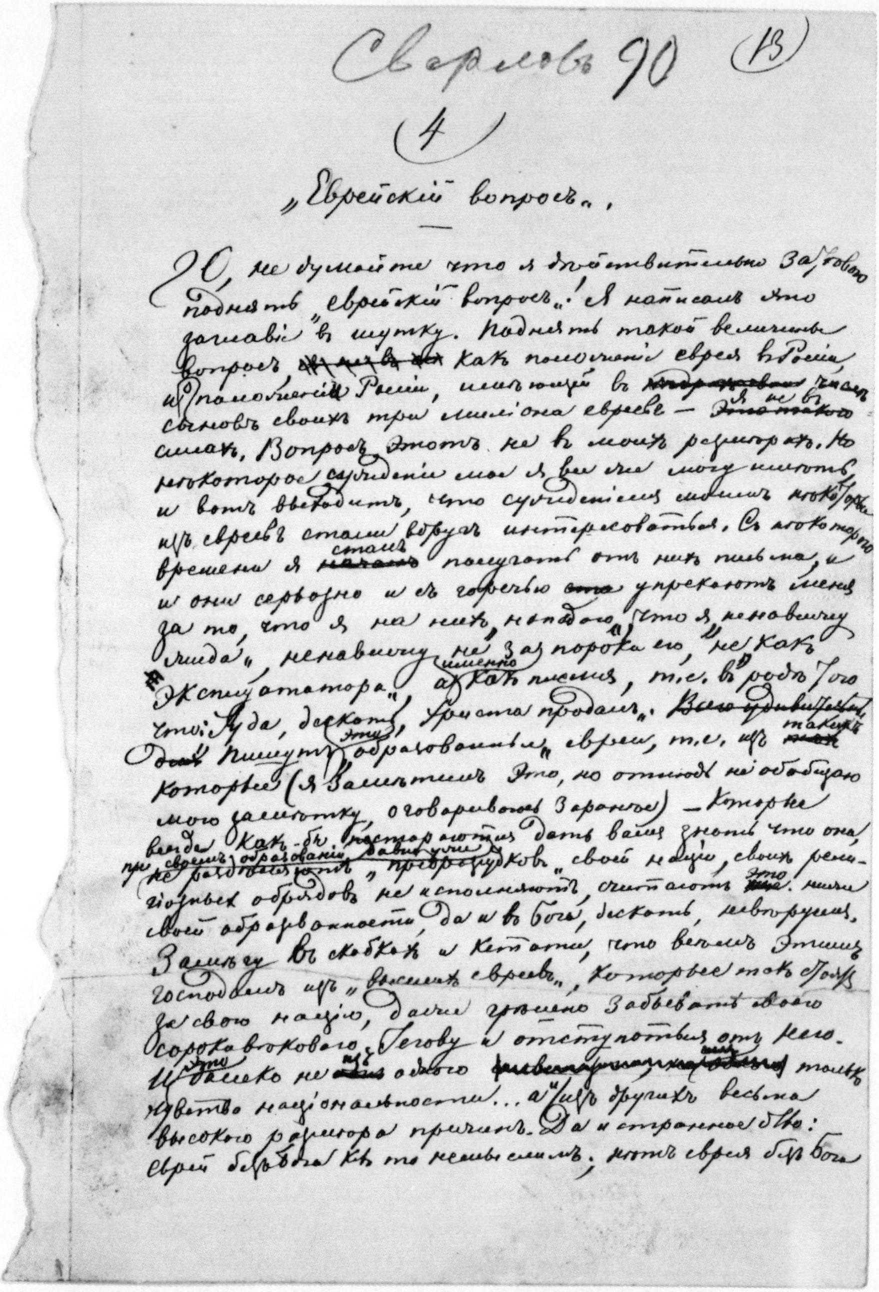

4

„Еврейскій вопросъ."

[handwritten manuscript text]

"Title page" of "The 'Jewish Question,'" chapter 2, section 1, *The Diary*, March 1877

Introduction

EVER SINCE the publication of *Poor Folk* in 1846 and its enthusiastic reception by Belinsky, who hailed "the extraordinary and original talent" of the author, Fyodor Mikhailovich Dostoyevsky (1821–1881) has not left the forefront of the literary scene, first in Russia, and later in the world at large. The number of critical studies that have grown up around both the man and his works for more than a century staggers the imagination: the bibliography of materials devoted to Dostoyevsky in Russian alone fills several volumes.[1] In this respect as in so many others, he is unequaled: no other writer of nineteenth-century Russia—not even Pushkin or Tolstoy—has so fired the imagination and held the attention of successive generations of scholars and readers throughout the world.

In the face of such a superabundance of source materials and critical literature, it would seem that few facets, if any, of Dostoyevsky's art remain that have not been revealed or reflected in their full intensity. And yet, this is not so. Since 1956 and the partial "rehabilitation" of the "great Russian writer" in the Soviet Union, the study of Dostoyevsky has been significantly enriched by the publication of hitherto unpublished documents and materials, essays and monographs, and it is also known that a considerable body of material is extant that awaits further research and elaboration. Indeed since 1956, the year that marked both the seventy-fifth anniversary of Dostoyevsky's death and his return to favor after more than two decades of near oblivion, Soviet scholarship has, as we shall see, produced a number of remarkable works that shed new light on various aspects of his writings as well as on obscure elements of his biography. Moreover, the commemoration of the 150th anniversary of the writer's birth in 1971 gave

further impetus to the publication of his works and to Dostoyevsky studies in general.[2]

In the preparation of the present work, the new materials that
have appeared have been of invaluable assistance. To be sure, before deciding to undertake a full-length study of Dostoyevsky and
his attitude toward the Jews, I had been struck, perplexed and in-
trigued by the hostility he displays toward them in his belles let-
tres. But it was only after delving into his journalistic writings and
discovering the same leitmotif that I recognized the importance
he attached to the "Jewish question." Had he not, for example,
devoted an entire chapter to it in his *Diary of a Writer?* The fact
that Dostoyevsky felt impelled to speak out publicly on this question and that he did so in the pages of his *Diary*, an organ enjoying
wide influence in its day, persuaded me that the subject of Dostoyevsky and the Jews warranted an exhaustive study.

And yet, if such a study was valid, why had it never been attempted before? Why had Russian literary critics before 1917
avoided the subject altogether except for Maksim Gorky,[3] A. G.
Gornfeld[4] and Dmitry Merezhkovsky?[5] Why the persistent silence
of the critics after the Revolution, broken only rarely by the short
but penetrating analyses of Leonid Grossman,[6] Aaron Steinberg[7]
and Pavel Berlin[8] (the last two writing in emigration) or by articles of secondary interest from the pen of David Zaslavsky[9] or
merely by a fleeting allusion here and there? More surprising still
was the extreme reserve of Arkady Dolinin, whose immense contribution to Dostoyevsky studies in the Soviet Union is, perhaps,
equaled only by Leonid Grossman's. And finally, outside of Russia itself, the subject of Dostoyevsky and the Jews had received
but scant attention.[10]

As to this neglect, not to say embargo, a number of reasons
for it may be advanced.

The first that comes to mind is the very richness, the prodigious universality of Dostoyevsky's works, the myriad of major
themes they contain. Why, then, dwell on the minor themes or on
such an incidental question as the place of the Jews in the universe
of Dostoyevsky? Furthermore, the constant development of the
principles and methodology of literary criticism in the Soviet
Union, the emergence of new schools, had placed new demands on
scholars, compelling them to give priority to the reinterpretation

of major themes of enduring value at the expense of others deemed of less consequence.

Another plausible constraint was the lack of sufficient documentation that was felt until quite recently. I have already mentioned the significance of source materials—manuscripts, notebooks, letters, memoirs—in adding to our knowledge of Dostoyevsky, materials that during the last twenty years or so have become increasingly available to researchers.

Last but not least, there is the matter of censorship and the role it has played in discouraging, if not prohibiting, the exploration of the subject of Dostoyevsky and the Jews. It has taken two forms: either the direct and constant censorship exercised by the authorities or the less rigorous but equally insidious restraints that the critics imposed on themselves out of prudence, discretion or opportunism.

In tsarist Russia, it was undoubtedly the first two factors that were determinant, that is, the priority given to major themes and the unavailability of adequate source materials. As for censorship, there is little to suggest the interference of the imperial censors, and, although there is some evidence of self-censorship, it was certainly not of decisive importance.

The phenomenon of self-censorship is perceptible in the collection of Dostoyevsky letters published by Miller and Strakhov in 1883.[11] Soviet critics have judged it severely, taking the editors to task not only for their choice of letters, but also for the liberties they took with the texts.[12] Such blanket condemnation is hardly warranted: the publication of an imposing number of the writer's letters only two years after his death was, in itself, quite an achievement. And the criticism is all the more unjustified when it comes from Dolinin, who, as editor of the fourth and final volume of Dostoyevsky's *Letters* (1959), must, despite extenuating circumstances, bear some responsibility for the deletions made in the texts of a number of letters.[13]

The case of Vladimir Solovyov provides another example. The great religious thinker, and intimate friend of Dostoyevsky in the latter period of the writer's life, an avowed Judeophile well-versed in Jewish history and thought, delivered *Three Speeches in Dostoyevsky's Memory*.[14] They contain not even the slightest allusion to Dostoyevsky's sentiments toward the Jews, a question to which we know Solovyov was not indifferent.[15] How is this lacuna to be explained if not by the phenomenon of self-censorship?

Since the advent of the Soviet régime, the study of Dostoyevsky has been subject to the vagaries of Soviet literary policy.[16] But the balance sheet is definitely positive. In the field of source materials alone, we are indebted to Soviet scholars for having made available documents of major importance. Some were published between 1918 and 1935, the latter year marking the time when Dostoyevsky and Dostoyevsky scholars fell out of favor; others, in the period that followed his "rehabilitation," from 1956 to the present. Suffice it to mention here the thirteen-volume critical edition of Dostoyevsky's *Complete Works* (1926–1930), his *Letters* in four volumes (1928–1959), the "Notebooks" for *Crime and Punishment* (1931), for *The Idiot* (1931), for *The Possessed* (1935), for *The Brothers Karamazov* (1935) and for *A Raw Youth* (1965), his *Notebooks and Copybooks—1860–1881* (1971) and the ambitious thirty-volume critical edition of Dostoyevsky's *Complete Works* (1972–). Moreover, the Dostoyevsky archives have become more readily accessible to Soviet researchers, making it possible for them not only to probe more deeply into the study of what I have called the major themes, but also to treat a gamut of narrow and more specialized subjects.[17]

What differentiates the Soviet from the pre-Soviet period is the profusion of primary source materials that have become available. It is understandable that scholars before the Revolution, handicapped by a lack of documentation, hesitated to venture into certain areas of inquiry. The same is not true for Soviet scholars: their avoidance of the theme that interests us here can no longer be justified on the grounds that the documentary evidence is lacking or that the subject is too narrowly specialized. What, then, is the reason for this abstention? Is it not to be attributed to the interference of the censorship or, perhaps even more, to the action of self-censorship?

At the risk of oversimplification, let us review a few facts that may throw some light on the problem.

Until 1928, students of Dostoyevsky in the Soviet Union enjoyed—under control of the Party, though not under its tutelage—a rather large measure of freedom. "Non-Party" scholars like Dolinin, Grossman and Bakhtin were in the ascendant. They worked unsparingly as if they were the executors of Dostoyevsky's literary estate and had a presentiment that the days of free literary criticism were numbered. Their achievements over the decade were exceptional—quantitatively and qualitatively. They uncovered and sifted through a huge volume of material and produced a number of remarkable and original studies concerned with major aspects of Dostoyevskyan thought. To be sure, the censors remained vigilant: more often than not, scholarly works were limited to editions of two or three thousand copies. But other than that, the effects of the censorship were marginal, while self-censorship was scarcely perceptible.

It was during this initial period that David Zaslavsky published "Dostoyevsky and the Jews" in the *Jewish Herald*, and Leonid Grossman his "Dostoyevsky and Judaism," as an addendum to *The Confession of One Jew*.[18] Strictly speaking, both of these essays lay outside the mainstream of Russian literary criticism and were more a part of Jewish literature in the Russian language in which these two authors got their start.

From 1929 to 1935, the position of the non-Party critics became more and more precarious. They succeeded, nevertheless, in bringing to completion several important works. During this transitional period, the régime seemed willing to tolerate Dostoyevsky studies so long as they bore some relationship—no matter how tenuous—to the principles of dialectical materialism and placed increasing emphasis on the reactionary aspects of Dostoyevsky's writing.

The non-Party critics reacted variously to the hardening of the line. Leonid Grossman managed to adapt himself to the new directives without sacrificing his integrity. In an important study dealing with the last ten years of Dostoyevsky's life entitled "Dostoyevsky and Government Circles in the Seventies," he set out to demonstrate, on the basis of irrefutable facts, that Dostoyevsky had clearly and unmistakably drawn close to the reactionary elements of the court during that decade. Moreover, and for the first time since 1924, Grossman reopened the question of the writer's attitude toward the Jews, bringing new light to bear on the question.[19]

Arkady Dolinin, however, refused to toe the line. He steadfastly maintained that, following a period marked by conservatism

(1867–1873), Dostoyevsky again veered to the left between 1874 and 1876. How else, Dolinin asked, could one account for the theme of *A Raw Youth* or the fact that it had been published in *Notes of the Fatherland*, the journal of Nekrasov and Saltykov-Shchedrin? But the adamance with which he defended this position gives rise to a number of questions. Did Dolinin feel that Grossman's thesis was an effort to undermine his own? Or did he feel that it placed Dostoyevsky, the man to whom he had dedicated his literary life, in jeopardy? Whatever the case, the fact remains that in the last work Dolinin published before being reduced to silence for a period of ten years he resolutely defended Dostoyevsky's reputation and, at the same time, his own thesis according to which the writer had definitely broken with the reaction (Aksakov, Pobedonostsev, Meshchersky) by 1874 and had returned to the ideals of his youth (Belinsky, Nekrasov) to which he remained faithful for the rest of his life.[20] Dolinin rejected almost disdainfully the arguments of Grossman, even though he refrained from mentioning him by name. He summarily dismissed the allegation that Dostoyevsky was anti-Semitic and sought to discredit it by associating it with the names of individuals who were vilified and proscribed by the new intelligentsia: "The Merezhkovskys and the Rozanovs appropriated Dostoyevsky, they made him in their own image and likeness and used him as a weapon of the class struggle, actually defending obscurantism, anti-Semitism and the clerics."[21]

Can one imagine a more eloquent manifestation of self-censorship than this? For at the time that Dolinin published these lines, scarcely one year had passed since the appearance of volume 3 of Dostoyevsky's *Letters*, published under his editorship and containing the writer's ringing reply to A. G. Kovner, a Jewish correspondent who had invited Dostoyevsky to take a public stand on the "Jewish question."[22]

The above notwithstanding, it should not be forgotten that the events I am describing relate to the year 1935. Though materials were available on Dostoyevsky and the Jewish question, there were still many lacunae; besides, the moment was anything but propitious for the investigation of such a theme. Powerful and influential voices were clamoring for the pure and simple proscription of Dostoyevsky. Quite understandably, his defenders were reluctant to play into the hands of his detractors.

But with all due respect to Dolinin for his remarkable contribution to Dostoyevsky studies and for his courageous defense of the beleaguered author, the fact of the matter remains that the eminent scholar's assessment of Dostoyevsky in the last ten years of his life is highly debatable.

I shall not dwell upon those twenty years beginning in 1935 when Dostoyevsky was consigned to near oblivion in the Soviet Union. These were, by and large, years of sterility for Dostoyevsky literary criticism. The writer did, nevertheless, enjoy a brief revival during World War II when the authorities exploited those elements of his writing that could be used to enflame the patriotic ardor of the nation. This "liberalism" lingered on until 1948, the year of the *zhdanovshchina*, which counted Dostoyevsky among its numerous victims. There followed a long and cruel Russian winter that lasted until 1956, the year of the "Thaw," which fortuitously coincided with the seventy-fifth anniversary of the death of the "great Russian writer," as he was acclaimed during this jubilee period.

As noted earlier, the years since Dostoyevsky's literary resurrection have been exceptionally productive. This is not to say, however, that the censors have disarmed. The inordinate delay in the publication of volume 77 of the *Literary Heritage*, devoted entirely to Dostoyevsky, can only be explained by the intervention of the censors: completed in 1959 (as we know from an announcement in the *Bulletin of the USSR Academy of Sciences*), this imposing tome did not appear until 1965.

So long as the situation remains as it is—unstable and tense—we may anticipate that certain aspects of Dostoyevsky's *oeuvre* will remain taboo to the Soviet scholar. Research into the question of Dostoyevsky and the Jews is, apparently, one such area. The subject is admittedly a delicate one for both the orthodox and the non-Party critics. No matter how ambiguous the policy of the Soviet régime toward its Jewish citizens, it seems that the censorship has orders to prevent the publication of materials it considers prejudicial to a national minority. It was undoubtedly for this reason, among others, that the ten-volume edition of Dostoyevsky's *Collected Works* (1956–1958) included only a selection of articles from *The Diary of a Writer*, solely those of a literary character. This would also explain why the fourth volume of Dostoyevsky's *Letters*, published in 1959, that is, twenty-five years after the third, was mutilated by the censors. Although only nine of the more than three hundred letters contained in that volume suffered mutilation (as far as one can judge), what is particularly significant is that *all* of the censored passages, without exception, contain disparaging references to the Jews.[23] Dolinin, I now know, was compelled by the censors to accept these textual disfigurations. In any event, this bungling attempt to obscure an aspect of Dostoyevsky's personality provided additional justification for the present study: one doesn't resort to dissimulation unless there is something to hide.

A final example of the mistrust of Soviet literary authorities vis-à-vis Dostoyevsky's legacy that also bears relevance to our area of inquiry may be cited: the treatment reserved for *A Description of F. M. Dostoyevsky's Manuscripts*, a work of inestimable value.[24] It is the most complete catalogue to date of materials and documents concerning the life and works of the author that are conserved in Soviet libraries and archives. It contains a wealth of information for the researcher. And yet, this key reference work was published in an edition of 800 copies! How is this ludicrous number to be explained if not by the willful intent of the régime to limit access to the heritage of a still controversial writer.

The *Description* provides significant bits of information on the question of Dostoyevsky and his attitude toward the Jews. It reveals for the first time the existence of numerous letters from Jewish correspondents to Dostoyevsky discussing his position on the "Jewish question." My request for copies of some thirty such letters conserved in the Institute of World Literature (Pushkin House) in Leningrad was turned down by the Institute's director on the grounds that they were scheduled for publication.[25] But the knowledge that these letters were extant and, particularly, the marginal notations made by Dostoyevsky (quoted in full in the *Description*) afforded new and precious insights into the subject of my investigation.

This study is, then, an attempt to determine the evolution of Dostoyevsky's ideas and feelings about the Jews as they emerge from his novels, his journalistic articles, his letters and his notebooks. I endeavor, too, to situate these varied elements of his writing in a meaningful context and determine the interrelationship and interaction between them.

The present study is, therefore, meant as an essay in clarification, an attempt to investigate, as exhaustively as possible, a theme that up to now has eluded the elaboration I believe it merits. Needless to say, it is not intended as a work of denigration. It is nothing more than an effort to reveal in its plenitude one particular aspect of Dostoyevsky's *Weltanschauung* without which his art, his genius, cannot be fully understood.

DOSTOYEVSKY AND THE JEWS

1. The Emergence of a "New Talent"

THE PUBLICATION of *Poor Folk* in Nekrasov's *St. Petersburg Miscellany* in 1846 marked Fyodor Dostoyevsky's entrance on the Russian literary scene. Until then, he had published nothing except a translation of Balzac's *Eugénie Grandet* that had appeared two years earlier in *Repertoire and Pantheon*. But before choosing the novel as a form of expression, the young Dostoyevsky—like a number of his contemporaries—was first attracted by the drama. No traces—plans or outlines—remain of his experiments in this field except for three titles: *Maria Stuart, Boris Godunov* and *The Jew Yankel*.[1] The first two plays were never finished, as we know from Riesenkampf,[2] who, moreover, is the only one to have made mention of them; they undoubtedly owed a great deal to Schiller and Pushkin.

But it is *The Jew Yankel* (*Zhid Yankel*), with its intriguing title, that interests us here. Its existence is known from Dostoyevsky's letter of January 1844 to his brother Mikhail, the sole reference he ever made to it by name. He had just then completed his translation of *Eugénie Grandet* and was anxious to share the good news with his brother:

> My translation is superb. They'll give me 350 paper rubles for it at the very least. I'm dying to sell it, but the potential millionaire that I am doesn't have the money to get it copied; or the time either. For the love of the angels on high, send me 35 paper rubles (the cost of copying). I swear by Olympus and by my Jew Yankel (my finished drama, and by what else? By my mustache, perhaps, that I hope will grow one day) that half of whatever I make on Eugénie will be yours. *Dixi*.[3]

Even though the jocular tone of the letter might suggest that it shouldn't be taken too seriously, Alekseyev finds in a subsequent letter from Dostoyevsky to his brother (September 30, 1844) confirmation that the earlier reference was, indeed, to the play *The Jew Yankel* inasmuch as that was the only play that Dostoyevsky had finished. "You say," wrote Dostoyevsky, "that the play is my salvation. But you know it takes time to produce it. . . . (I'll definitely put on the play. It will be my bread and butter.)"[4]

Again, according to Alekseyev, Dostoyevsky was undoubtedly indebted to his literary mentor Gogol for the subject of his play. It is even quite possible that Gogol's Jew Yankel in *Taras Bulba* served as the model for Dostoyevsky's hero. At any rate, Alekseyev is convinced that the Yankel of the young Dostoyevsky was patterned on the Jewish stereotype that one finds in the Russian literature of the first half of the nineteenth century and, later on, in the works of Dostoyevsky himself: Isai Fomich Bumstein in *The House of the Dead*, Lyamshin in *The Possessed* and other nameless Jews who make a fleeting appearance elsewhere.[5] This stereotype was already present (to cite just a few examples) in Pushkin (*The Covetous Knight, The Black Shawl, Songs of the Western Slavs*) and in Lermontov (*Sashka, The Spaniards*) and would be found later on in the writings of Turgenev, Nekrasov, Pisemsky, Saltykov-Shchedrin, Leskov and even Chekhov.[6] The Jew is the object of ridicule, derision, repulsion. He is the spy, the traitor, the informer, the thief, the usurer, the swindler. He is greedy, grasping, dirty, servile, ignoble and so forth. It is quite conceivable that the aspiring young author adhered to this tried and tested tradition in his essay in the field of drama.

It is, nevertheless, curious that Dostoyevsky should have chosen a Jewish theme at the start of his literary career. Unlike Gogol, who in his native Ukraine had observed firsthand the deep-seated hostility between the Ukrainians and the Jews, unlike Pushkin, who during his sojourns in Kishinyov and Odessa had been in contact with the large Jewish populations of those cities, Dostoyevsky did not have—nor could he have had—any direct experience of Jews, for the obvious reason that St. Petersburg counted very few Jews among its residents.

It may be assumed, therefore, that *The Jew Yankel* was based neither on living experience nor even on simple observation, but was rather the product of pure literary inspiration. It is, of course, quite natural for a beginning writer—just because he lacks the experience of life—to be influenced by the works of earlier masters. But amid the myriad themes that fill the universe of Gogol, Pushkin, Shakespeare or Balzac, one still wonders why the young Fyodor Mikhailovich decided on a Jewish theme and how he must have dealt with it. Was the action of his *Jew Yankel* laid in Europe of the Middle Ages (*Prince Kholmsky*),[7] in the Cossack *Sech* (*Taras Bulba, The Covetous Knight*) or in Russia of the 1840s, in some wretched, remote quarter of St. Petersburg?[8]

It is perhaps by trying to situate *The Jew Yankel* in both time and space that we may discover the answer to the crucial question of why Dostoyevsky was drawn to such a theme.

I am inclined to the belief that the play was most probably situated in the St. Petersburg of Dostoyevsky's day, an hypothesis that seems to be supported by a number of concordant circumstances.

In the first place, we know that Dostoyevsky was working simultaneously on *The Jew Yankel* and *Poor Folk*. It is highly conceivable that his creative imagination converged on two kindred and closely interwoven themes: on the one hand, the power of money, the role of usury, a subject he would return to again and again as the years went by; on the other, the major theme of social injustice and its victims, the insulted and the injured. The novels of Balzac, among others, had revealed to Dostoyevsky the terrible power of Mammon as incarnated by Gobseck and Nuncingen (both Jews). And the Petersburg tales of Gogol had propelled him into the world of the Akaky Akakiyeviches, all the more palpable to him as he himself had been condemned to a precarious existence in St. Petersburg, especially since 1842, and his "extreme poverty" had put him at the mercy of the moneylenders, who were charging him "barbarous interest."[9]

Mammon would make a brief apparition in *Poor Folk* in the person of Emilyan Ivanovich Markov, with his "small thievish eyes" and his "greasy dressing gown pulled together with a string" (I: 78). He wasn't a Jew; neither were the moneylenders Dostoyevsky came up against. For at that time, Jewish moneylenders were practically unknown to St. Petersburg, a fact that Dostoyevsky could not ignore. Could that have been the reason why he eventually abandoned his Yankel, who was alien to the reality of St. Petersburg?

And yet, who knows, maybe Dostoyevsky, in his wanderings

through the desolate streets of the city that was destined to play such an important role in his novels, actually stumbled on the real-life Yankel in some wretched backyard. That is, in any case, the hypothesis advanced by the young Soviet writer Dora Davydovna Bregova in her fictionalized account of Dostoyevsky's early years—up to 1849, the year of his banishment to Siberia.

In her novel *The Path of Exploration,* Bregova is the first writer to dwell at some length on the character of Yankel. Even though, as I have said, her study is a work of fiction, it is based— the preface tells us—on "the memoirs of contemporaries, letters and other documents,"[10] and it accordingly merits attention.

Bregova relates that Dostoyevsky, finding himself one day in the Haymarket, witnessed a scene that made a deep impression on him: a violent altercation between a big strapping fellow and a puny little man, the Jew Leibka, a moneylender. Though the butt of a shower of abuse and intimidation, Leibka refuses to surrender a kopek. And Dostoyevsky says to himself:

> "Ah, there's a subject for you, Leibka, Gogol's Jew Yankel, in the Haymarket! He hoards and hoards, he's probably put aside thousands already, but he haggles for a ruble! And he'll end up dying in some hole on a pillow of gold. Yes, I'll set him against the background of this tavern, of this square, amidst dirt and squalor."[11]

What led Bregova to set this scene in the Haymarket? She recalls that at one time—before the Jews had been driven out of the capital—this quarter was almost their exclusive preserve.[12] After 1826, a few families, nevertheless, stayed on even though they lived under the constant threat of expulsion and were condemned to a miserable existence. Although Bregova doesn't mention it, she must also have been reminded of the second of the four or five feuilletons (that of April 27, 1847) that Dostoyevsky had written for the *St. Petersburg Record* under the general title of *A Petersburg Chronicle.*

One damp, misty morning our dreamy and pensive chronicler is found strolling in the Haymarket in search of material for an article. In his melancholy, he gives free rein to his fantasy, transfusing his mood to the city, which quickens to life (13: 12–13; italics mine):

> Petersburg awoke sullen and angry, like a peevish young society lady fuming over last night's ball. It was flushed with rage. Had it

slept poorly, had it suffered a severe bilious attack in the night, had it had a chill and caught a cold, had it, like a boob, lost at cards the evening before to wake up the next morning completely cleaned out, was it venting its spleen against ugly and pampered wives, lazy and insolent children, against the grim, unshaven band of flunkeys, *Yid-creditors,* good-for-nothing advisers, slanderers and sundry other talebearers—it is difficult to say. . . .

For all one knows, these "Yid-creditors" could have emerged from young Fyodor's memory of his encounter with Leibka a few years back, who, in the guise of Yankel, might have been recreated, as Bregova suggests, in the manner of a Shakespeare, a Pushkin or, even more, a Gogol.

Bregova then attempts to determine why Dostoyevsky eventually lost interest in his play. In her interpretation of the facts, she goes much further than Dostoyevsky himself, who provides a convincing explanation of his disenchantment with the drama as a form of literary expression for his time. And it is this explanation and, in the absence of other evidence, this explanation alone that must stand. On March 24, 1845, Dostoyevsky wrote to his brother:

> Write dramas—come now, brother. For that you need years of hard work and tranquillity, or at least I do. It's good to be writing nowadays. The drama today has abandoned itself to melodrama. Shakespeare pales in the twilight and breaks through the fog of our dimsighted dramatists like a God. . . .

And he adds what can only be an allusion to his own essays in the drama:

> Brother, as far as Literature goes, I am *no longer the same person* I was two years ago. It was all childishness and nonsense then. Two years of reflection have brought me a great deal and cleared away a great deal.[13]

Bregova's "reconstruction" differs radically from Dostoyevsky's analysis. She suggests, in effect, that it was while he was working on the translation of *Eugénie Grandet* that Dostoyevsky perceived that his *Yankel* was not up to snuff, that his hero paled before "the monumental figure" of the old Grandet and lacked the "verisimilitude" of Balzac's portrait of that "pathological miser."[14] But Dostoyevsky, Bregova continues, was still unable to fathom the reason for his failure. It was then that he chanced to make the acquaintance, one evening, of Marya Mikhailovna, a pa-

tient of Dr. Riesenkampf.[15] It turned out that she had lived at one
time with an old schoolmate of Dostoyevsky's, a certain Vinnikov:
they had been pupils together at Drashusov's Boarding School and
later on occasionally saw each other in St. Petersburg during the
forties.[16]

Dostoyevsky continued to see Marya Mikhailovna quite often
thereafter and came to appreciate her taste and judgment in literature; and one day, he gave her the manuscript of *The Jew Yankel*
to read. She recognized at once in Dostoyevsky's hero the Jew
Leibka from the Haymarket, despite the strong Gogolian overtones of the portrait. But the portrait was false: the real Leibka in
no way resembled Gogol's Jewish stereotype. He lent money not
only at the most reasonable rates, but even at no interest at all to
the poor. Not only did he not hoard his money, he gave it all away
to those in need.

Dostoyevsky now realized that he had failed to plumb the
depths of the heart and soul of his model. It simply never occurred
to him that Leibka might not be the ridiculous, pitiful, disgusting
and greedy character true to the literary cliché of the period. "All
he had wanted to do was to show a miser shivering in the squalid
backyards of the capital. Leibka was the raw material, the means
—nothing more than that."[17]

Bregova is less convincing here than in the first part of her
reconstruction, where, like Alekseyev, she suggests the analogy between Yankel and the Jewish characters portrayed by Shakespeare, Pushkin or Gogol. And it is wholly conceivable that Dostoyevsky, in emulation of Balzac, would have placed the classical
theme of the miser in a contemporary setting. But it is harder to
accept Bregova's interpretation of the circumstances that led to
Dostoyevsky's disillusionment with his *Jew Yankel*, since it is
weakened by the introduction of elements of pure fiction (unless,
of course, she had access to documents that are otherwise unknown).

Let us, therefore, be content with the explanation given by
Dostoyevsky himself in his letter of March 24, 1845: his dissatis-
faction with the drama as a form of literary expression appropriate
to the times and with his own achievements in this field that he
qualifies as "childishness" and "nonsense."

Regardless of our inability to solve the "mystery" of *The Jew
Yankel*, the remarkable fact still remains that on the threshold of

his career Dostoyevsky was attracted by a Jewish theme, a theme that was at once anachronistic and premature in the Russian literature of the forties, a time when the Jew no longer was and had not yet become a part of the life and society that the writer would so vividly describe in his work.

Until *The House of the Dead*, the Jew was practically absent from Dostoyevsky's writings. But beginning with the years 1860 to 1862, when this book appeared, the Jew and the Jewish question would assume a place of growing importance in his thought.

In an effort to render this study as complete as possible, let us review the period prior to *The House of the Dead* and examine briefly the treatment accorded to the Jews here and there in Dostoyevsky's early works.

During this period, then, allusions to Jews were few and far between. As a rule, Dostoyevsky went no further than to place in the mouth of one of his characters the word "Jew" or, to be more precise, "Yid" (*zhid*) in association with other terms of disparagement. In *The Double*, for example, in the memorable scene where Golyadkin vents his wrath on the hapless Petrushka, who had made a mess of the mission he had been entrusted with, the former drowns him in a torrent of abuse: "scoundrel" (*merzavets*), "wretch" (*negodyai*), "loafer" (*bezdelnik*), "crook" (*moshennik*), "rogue" (*shelmets*), "knave" (*podlets*), and, to top it off, he curses him with "What a Judas you are!"—twice for good measure (I: 178–180).

In Russia of those days, this was, of course, precisely the language that a Golyadkin would have employed. But it is equally true that for Dostoyevsky such terms were synonymous with "Yid." The same Golyadkin, to demolish his rival Ivan Semyonovich, uses the term "Yid." Wondering why Ivan had taken his place at the office, he observes (I: 191):

> . . . that Ivan Semyonovich, I've known all along that he's a shady character, it hasn't escaped my notice: what a foul and disgusting old man—they say he's a moneylender and charges Yid-like rates.

Here again, Golyadkin runs true to form, but the epithets he uses —*gadkii, skvernyi*—are those Dostoyevsky customarily associates with the Jews.

Dostoyevsky is likewise faithful to the widespread belief that the Jews are past masters in the arts of craft and deceit. In his

Petersburg Chronicle of May 11, 1847, devoted to the subject of gossip, he compares the wiles of the tattler trying to whet the interest of his interlocutor—a man of principle—to the cunning of a Jewish peddler trying to make a sale (13: 17):

> You never know, you say to yourself, maybe he isn't a flatterer after all, but only a bit too naive and sincere. Why in the world put the fellow off from the start. And the fellow gets all he wanted to begin with, just like the little Yid [*zhidok*] who begs the *pan* not to buy his goods, absolutely not! What's the point? Why, the *pan* can take a look at his bundle if he likes, if only to spit on the Jew [*zhidovskii*] goods and then go on his way. And the Yid unwraps his bundle and the *pan* buys everything the little Yid wanted to sell him.

The comparison may be acceptable, but the least that can be said is that it betrays a rather strange turn of mind.

And finally in *Netochka Nezvanova* (1849), the last thing Dostoyevsky wrote before being banished to Siberia, it is the arrival in St. Petersburg of a celebrated Jewish violinist from Western Europe that leads to the catastrophe in the first part of the novel and prepares its denouement. So as to be able to attend the concert of this virtuoso, Yefimov forces his stepdaughter, Netochka, to steal the little money her sick mother still has and, in so doing, precipitates her death. Two days later, Yefimov goes out of his mind and also dies.

Yefimov, the second husband of Netochka's mother, was at one time a violinist of exceptional talent, but fame and glory escaped him. All that remains is his pride, resentment and bitter disillusionment. The arrival of the Jewish violinist, the famous S., produces a deep and painful impression on him. He wants more than anything else to attend the concert, but knowing that he could never scrape together the price of a ticket, he affects an indifference tinged with skepticism and disdain (II: 174):

> "We shall see. The grass always looks greener beyond the hills. Paris is the only place where S. ever played, and it's the French who made such a to-do about him, and I don't have to tell you what their opinion is worth!"

So much for that. But the hapless Yefimov is also looking for a scapegoat to bear the burden of his professional failure—to convince not only himself, but others as well. It was scoundrels like S., of course, who had stolen his chances of success. Here Dostoyevsky allows Netochka to speak. After learning that "you had to have at least fifteen rubles to hear this S.," she recalled that (II: 176):

> her father was unable to contain himself and, with a wave of the hand, said that he knew these geniuses coming from abroad, these incomparable talents, that he also knew S., that they were Yids, the whole lot of them, scrambling to lay their hands on Russian money, because the Russians are ready to believe any fiddle-faddle, especially when it is served up to them by the French.

Yefimov, who until then possessed nothing, at once establishes his birthright: you cannot rob a person who has nothing to be robbed of.

There is no doubt that Yefimov would have expressed himself in just that way. The words ring true both artistically and psychologically. It is, moreover, quite possible that the brother of the piano-maker Keller, who was so intimately acquainted with the music world of St. Petersburg,[18] had heard such sentiments expressed and reported them back to Dostoyevsky. Whether the grievances were well founded or not is immaterial: artists coming from abroad—particularly if they were Jews—provided a convenient target.

This leads us to the question of whether there might have been a real-life prototype for Dostoyevsky's virtuoso S. and, if so, whether Yefimov had good reason to judge him with such severity.[19] A number of concordant indices suggest that the violinist Heinrich Wilhelm Ernst (1814–1865), an Austrian Jew, served as Dostoyevsky's model. Ernst gave a series of highly successful concerts in St. Petersburg during the winter season 1846/47. On three occasions, Dostoyevsky wrote about them in his *Petersburg Chronicle*: April 13, 1847—"Then there was Ernst. All Petersburg turned out for his third concert";[20] April 27, 1847—"Sorry, I forgot the main thing. . . . Ernst is giving another concert; the receipts will be donated to the Society for Visiting the Poor and the German Philanthropic Society. Needless to say, the house will be full, there's no doubt about it" (13: 15); May 11, 1847—"The preceding remark has nothing to do with Ernst's concert, which was given for a noble philanthropic cause" (13: 19).

We have, accordingly, ascertained two facts: (1) Ernst was a celebrated violinist who made a deep impression on Dostoyevsky at the time he was writing *Netochka Nezvanova*; (2) he was a Jew coming from abroad just like the violinist S. of the novel. But the resemblance doesn't stop there. Remember Yefimov's outcry that "it's the French who made such a to-do about him." This was also true for Ernst. After completing his studies at the Vienna Conservatory, he left for Paris in 1832 and resided there for several years; he was a frequent visitor thereafter. It was first in Paris and then in London that he won recognition as a musician and composer. He was a good friend of Berlioz, who esteemed him highly.[21]

Dostoyevsky, too, admired Ernst, but this did not prevent him —like his tragic hero Yefimov—from decrying the infatuation of the Russian public with artists imported from abroad while neglecting their own, native-born talents. And this was one of the dominant themes in his feuilleton of April 13, 1847, which is strikingly reminiscent of the passage from *Netochka Nezvanova* cited above. Dostoyevsky exhorts his compatriots to take cognizance of their national values, to be less concerned by what foreigners think about what they do or say. With undisguised irony, he evokes the warm reception given to foreign artists in Russia:

> . . . we know very well that for our fifteen rubles we have had our money's worth of European entertainment, and that's enough for us. And besides, such patent celebrities come to visit our country that we have no cause to grumble. . . . There's Italy to train the artists, and Paris to launch them. Do we have the time to coddle, encourage and give a start to new talents, a singer for example? Why bother when they are sent to us ready-made, already covered with glory.[22]

Here we find those fateful "fifteen rubles" that were Yefimov's undoing and the resentment against celebrities made in France. Dostoyevsky lets it go at that, while Yefimov, not content with just taking it out on the Russians who "are ready to believe any fiddle-faddle," rails against the real culprits, the Yids who have come from afar "to lay their hands on Russian money."

No matter how false the allegation is in relation to the known facts,[23] it is, as noted earlier, perfectly plausible when proffered by a Yefimov. It may be suggested, however, that this passage in *Ne-*

tochka contains in a still embryonic form a theme that Dostoyevsky would develop in his later works and that would, in the seventies, play a major role.

By the time the last installment of *Netochka Nezvanova*
appeared in the May 1849 issue of *Notes of the Fatherland*, Dostoyevsky had already been arrested for his involvement in the Petrashevsky affair. At the end of December, following the commuta-
tion of his death sentence to penal servitude, he left for Siberia. It
would be ten years before he returned to St. Petersburg, ten years
during which this vibrant voice was reduced to silence.

2. The House of the Dead

THE FOUR YEARS spent by Dostoyevsky in penal servitude at Omsk, followed by another four years of forced military service in Semipalatinsk, were marked by intense literary activity. Even before his discharge from the army, he had published *The Little Hero* and *Uncle's Dream*; and *The Friend of the Family* (the title by which *The Village of Stepanchikovo and Its Inhabitants* is generally known) came out on the eve of his return to St. Petersburg toward the middle of December 1859. But the two works that really heralded Dostoyevsky's reentry on the literary scene of the capital were *The House of the Dead* (1860–1862), which he had begun working on in 1855, and *The Insulted and the Injured* (1861).

It is *The House of the Dead*, which Tolstoy would later describe as "the best book in all the new literature, Pushkin included,"[1] that is of particular interest within the framework of the present study. Here, for the first time, Dostoyevsky depicts a Jewish character: Isai Fomich Bumstein.[2] The fact is not remarkable in itself, the more so as Bumstein was not merely a figment of Dostoyevsky's imagination. In his memoirs, Szymon Tokarzewski, a Polish revolutionary and the writer's fellow inmate at the Omsk prison, makes brief mention of "Isaac Bumstein—the representative of Omsk Jewry."[3] And it is now known from the records of the Exile Administration that the real-life prototype of Isai Fomich Bumstein was a convict by the name of Isai *Bumstehl*, that he had been a jeweler by trade, that he had been sent up for murder, that he had received sixty-five lashes and had been branded (exactly as in the novel). The records also reveal that Bumstehl belonged to the "lower middle class" and the astonishing fact that he was a convert to the Greek Orthodox faith (IV: 283–284).[4] That is all we know about Bumstehl, but it allows us to measure the extent to which Dostoyevsky's Isai remains faithful to the original.

The narrator of *The House of the Dead*, Aleksandr Petrovich Goryanchikov, Dostoyevsky's alter ego, introduces Bumstein to the reader in the first chapter. Speaking of the various trades plied by the convicts, he notes (IV: 17):

> There were cobblers and bootmakers, tailors, carpenters, locksmiths, engravers and gilders. There was one Jew [*yevrei*], Isai Bumstein, a jeweler and moneylender to boot.

Was there anything arbitrary or malicious in Dostoyevsky's casting Bumstein in the role of moneylender, an occupation conventionally ascribed to the Jews? Probably not. It is quite conceivable that here reality coincided with convention. Moreover, Goryanchikov/Dostoyevsky speaks of the important, even positive role moneylending played in the life of the convicts—"moneylending flourished"—and Bumstein was not the only one who engaged in it (IV: 17). It also bears mentioning that the narrator employs *yevrei*, the appropriate term for Jew, in describing Bumstein, and not the derogatory appellation *zhid*; the subsequent use of the latter as well as of other unflattering terms assumes all the more significance in this regard.[5]

Dostoyevsky was undoubtedly fascinated by Isai Fomich, apparently the first Jew whom he had ever known and observed at close hand. He devotes considerable space to him in *The House of the Dead*, including a sizable part of chapter 9 (part 1), where his name figures in the title. And yet, uncharacteristically, the portrait he draws of Isai lacks depth and a human dimension. For Dostoyevsky, he is not much more than an object of curiosity.

Before proceeding to my own analysis of Dostoyevsky's portrayal of Bumstein, I shall examine briefly the views of the handful of critics who have interested themselves in Dostoyevsky's attitude toward the Jews in general, and in his characterization of Isai Fomich in particular.[6] With but one exception all Jews, they include: A. G. Gornfeld,[7] D. I. Zaslavsky,[8] L. P. Grossman,[9] A. Z. Steinberg,[10] P. A. Berlin,[11] Joshua Kunitz[12] and Robert L. Jackson.[13] Broadly speaking, they represent three tendencies: Gornfeld and Zaslavsky are situated at the diametrically opposed poles of severity and indulgence, while the others, with some variations of amplitude, fall somewhere in between.

For Gornfeld, Dostoyevsky is "one of the leading spokesmen for Russian anti-Semitism . . . an enemy of the Jews, at first deriding them and later hating them" (p. 310). Zaslavsky, though admitting that Dostoyevsky "did not conceal his aversion for the Jews" and that "Yids and Yidenehs appear occasionally in the background of his works," regards it all "as so insignificant that it's not worth bothering about" (p. 79). Grossman, like Steinberg and Berlin in his wake, sees Dostoyevsky's anti-Semitism as a complex phenomenon: "To deny flatly any anti-Semitic tendencies in Dostoyevsky would undoubtedly be a distortion of the truth," but it "is not possible to sum up his attitude toward the Jews in a simple and categorical formula" (pp. 166–167). For Kunitz, though Dostoyevsky is "one of the most original writers in the world, he was commonplace and obvious in his perception of the Jew" (p. 54). Jackson, whose perceptive study is primarily concerned with establishing an affinity between Isai Fomich and Foma Fomich (in *Stepanchikovo*), considers that the portrait of Isai was "brilliantly executed but within the bounds of both popular prejudice and standard literary convention" (p. 252).

These critics, naturally, interpret diversely Dostoyevsky's portrait of Isai:

Gornfeld (p. 310):
In his portrait of his fellow-convict . . . Isai Fomich Bumstein, D. infused nothing but the utmost contempt.

Zaslavsky (p. 7):
In his portrait, there are elements of caricature. It is neither particularly trenchant nor original, but it is free of animosity, malice or contempt.

Grossman (p. 171):
The age-old antipathy to Jewry that permeates every one of his conciliatory statements in *The Diary of a Writer* leaves its impact on several figures of his literary gallery. The distortion of the lines of a portrait to the breaking point of caricature and overcoloration to the point of pamphleteering imagery are the conventional and distinctive devices used by Dostoyevsky in his portrayal of representatives of alien nations.

In *The House of the Dead*, Dostoyevsky brushed the portrait of his fellow-convict Isai Fomich Bumstein. He did so with no particular animosity and, at times, even with a shade of good-natured humor, but all the same with an undeniable tendency toward caricature.

Steinberg (p. 96):
. . . we find ourselves face to face with a human being practically devoid of human traits, a kind of chimera incarnate, alien in body and soul to the world of men solidly anchored in life.

Berlin (pp. 80–81):
Dostoyevsky could very well have rendered this pitiful and repulsive type with disgust and left it at that. But he devotes an entire chapter to him that is tinged with benevolence and curiosity. . . . We can find no other explanation for it except that Dostoyevsky, living side by side with this pathetic Jew, hearing him pray with passion and fervor, oblivious to everyone and everything around him, discovered that the Jews were not just moneylenders . . . but also had a soul. . . . Beyond the pitiable figure of the Jew and moneylender . . . he began to perceive the Jew as the bearer of an ancient heritage, with its prophets, the long-suffering Job . . . and these biblical motifs seemed to stir to life and reverberate in Bumstein.

Kunitz (p. 53):
He saw in him what the other convicts and what most of Dostoievsky's contemporaries saw in him: a petty, filthy, despicable, greedy and comical figure.

Jackson (pp. 251–252):
Isaj Fomič, for all his entertaining vanity and posturing, was clearly the epitome of that moral and spiritual disfiguration that Dostoevskij had observed in the "insulted and injured" and to which he had devoted some of the most moving and perceptive pages in the history of literature. Yet Dostoevskij . . . did not lift even a corner of the comic curtain that concealed the *tragic* life of the Jew Isaj Fomič Bumstein.

As the story unfolds, Dostoyevsky (Goryanchikov), it will be remembered, merely notes the presence of Isai Fomich Bumstein among the prison inmates and his occupation, but it is not until chapter 4 ("First Impressions") that he really presents him to the reader. He does so in a significant way—in association with the Polish convicts whose "hatred of the Russian prisoners made them in turn hated by everyone else" (IV: 54). And Dostoyevsky continues (IV: 55):

> Of all the inmates in our barracks, the only one they [the Poles] liked was a Yid, and probably the only reason they liked him was that he amused them.[14] But then, our little Yid [*zhidok*] was liked by the other prisoners too, though everyone to a man made fun of him. He was the only one we had, and even now I can't think of him without laughing. Every time I looked at him, I was reminded of Gogol's Jew Yankel in *Taras Bulba*, who, when he got undressed at night to bed down with his Yideneh in some sort of cupboard, looked exactly like a chicken. Isai Fomich, our little Yid, was the spitting image of a plucked chicken.[15]

The caricatured quality of the portrait is patent, and the intention of the author unmistakably clear: to laugh at the little Jew and provoke laughter at his expense.[16] To render the image even more hilarious, Dostoyevsky could not resist the temptation to compare Isai with Gogol's Jew Yankel. The analogy is, however, an erroneous one, as others have pointed out, suggesting that Dostoyevsky's memory betrayed him. The witticism is not applicable to Yankel but rather to the nameless Jew, with the florid complexion, to whom Yankel conducts Bulba upon their arrival in Warsaw.

Nevertheless, in view of the importance of the scene—Dostoyevsky is introducing a new character and is undoubtedly anxious to strike the imagination of the reader—it is legitimate to ask whether the error is really attributable to a lapse of memory. All we know about Dostoyevsky's working methods makes it difficult to believe that he committed this error unintentionally. His letters, for example, show how meticulous he was about the exactitude of facts, the painstaking efforts he made to verify everything down to the last detail.[17] It would have been quite out of character for him, in drawing an analogy between Isai Fomich and Gogol's Jew Yankel, not to have checked his source. I am inclined to the view that Dostoyevsky deliberately committed this "error." But then, to what purpose?

There is nothing surprising in the fact that Dostoyevsky's portrait of Isai Fomich was so deeply influenced by Gogol (though it is surprising that so little has been written about it). At the time he was working on *The House of the Dead*, he was steeped in the atmosphere of Gogol. *The Friend of the Family (Stepanchikovo)* has strong Gogolian overtones.[18] It was published just a little more than six months before *The House of the Dead* began appearing; and it is likewise certain that Dostoyevsky had begun work on the latter before the former had been completed. The two works actually have little in common. All the more striking, therefore, is the unquestionable affinity between Isai Fomich and Foma Fomich Opiskin, the hero of *Stepanchikovo*: both grotesque, both targets of constant derision. And Dostoyevsky, probably without even realizing it, gave them both the same patronymic—Fomich—which, in the case of a Jew, is a patent absurdity.[19]

But the influence of Gogol is even more tangible elsewhere. There is, in the famous prayer scene in chapter 9 (part 1) of *The House of the Dead*, such a degree of convergence between Isai Fomich and the Jew Yankel, as portrayed by Gogol in a kindred scene in chapter 10 of *Taras Bulba*, that one cannot help but wonder where the coincidence ends and the plagiarism begins.

Here is what Taras beholds when he bursts into the house of Yankel:

> The Jew was praying, enveloped in his rather soiled shawl, and he turned around to spit for a last time, according to the rites of his faith, when he caught sight of Bulba, who had been standing in back of him.[20]

As for Dostoyevsky, he, too, comes upon Isai Fomich at the moment he was starting his prayer (IV: 95):

> He recited it in a singsong voice, wailing, sputtering, pirouetting, gesticulating wildly and absurdly. All this was, of course, prescribed by the ritual. . . .[21]

In this instance, at least, Dostoyevsky's memory did not fail him. More likely than not, he had *Taras Bulba* under his nose when he recalled the "plucked chicken," and that all but eliminates the hypothesis of an unintentional error. But what did he hope to achieve, then, in exchanging Gogol's nameless and episodic master of the house for the figure of the Jew Yankel? Obviously, greater relief and artistic intensity. Merely to have compared Isai Fomich with a hastily sketched, almost anonymous character would have blunted the sharpness of the image he was trying to project. He had to establish a direct line between Isai and the Jew Yankel to evoke, in the mind of the reader, the multitude of impressions conjured up by the image of the unscrupulous and repugnant Jew immortalized by the genius of Gogol. Furthermore, it must be remembered that the very expression "Jew Yankel"—whether in reference to Gogol's personage or not—was the stereotypic label applied to the stereotypic image of the Jew in Russian life and letters of the time and, as such, was enough to bring forth a host of associations that would reenforce the caricatured contours of Isai's portrait as the story progressed.

But Dostoyevsky has just begun to share his "first impressions" of Isai Fomich. He continues to brush his portrait, blending neutral tones with high-colored caricature, the intensity of which —though not the spirit—is attenuated by recourse to overworked elements of stereotype. They are, in fact, so conventional that one wonders whether the author achieved the effects that he sought. Bumstein, we are told, was "decidedly stupid," which he may have been for all we know. But, of course, he had to be "cunning" (*khitrenkii*), as he had to be "insolent" (*derzkii*), "truculent" (*zanoschivyi*) and "terribly cowardly" (*uzhasno truslivyi*). Dostoyevsky implies that he was an incorrigible optimist: though he was already pushing fifty, he still hoped to get married after he had served his twelve years. The narrator must have derived a malicious pleasure from the story he now tells (IV: 55):

> . . . he had hidden away on his person a prescription that his Jew [*zhidki*] friends had gotten from a doctor and gave to him when he was taken down from the scaffold. It was a prescription for an ointment that was supposed to remove all traces of branding in a few weeks. He didn't dare make use of this ointment in prison but was waiting for his twelve-year term to come to an end, after which he definitely intended to make use of it when he became a settler. "Else I vill never be able to merry," he once told me, "end I certainly vant to get married." [22]

Then, as if to soften the lines of the caricature, Dostoyevsky/ Goryanchikov insists that he and Isai were "great friends"; but in the same breath he adds (IV: 55; italics mine):

> He had an easy time of it in prison; he was a jeweler by trade, he had more orders than he could handle from the town where there was no jeweler, and, as a result, got out of doing the heavy work. *Needless to say*, he was also a moneylender and supplied the whole prison at interest and on pledge.

Dostoyevsky creates the impression that Isai Fomich was the only prisoner who engaged in moneylending, whereas he informed us previously that its practice was widespread. To claim that Isai Fomich got out of the rigors of hard labor so that he could merrily go about plying his trade leaves the reader incredulous. It is a false note, but a false note that is in tune with the conventional image of the shrewd and resourceful Jew who manages to dodge hard work and even reaps profit from adversity. (Perhaps Isai wasn't all that "stupid" after all!)

Visibly fascinated by Isai Fomich, Dostoyevsky, nevertheless, takes leave of our hero though promising that he would speak about him later. And this he does in chapter 9: "Isai Fomich. The Bathhouse. Baklushin's Story," which is, in large part, devoted to his "friend." Although the caricatured aspect of the portrait still predominates, Dostoyevsky tones it down and infuses the characterization with flashes of warmth and goodwill. Whenever the narrator speaks in his own name, he refers to Bumstein as the *yevrei* Isai Fomich, never as the *zhid* or *zhidok*. It is with sympathy, if not affection, that he evokes "the blissful countenance of my prison comrade and barracks' mate, the unforgettable Isai Fomich." He speaks good-naturedly of this "killingly funny man" that "everyone really seemed to love" (IV: 92–94). But that doesn't prevent Dostoyevsky, when reintroducing Isai Fomich, from repeating almost verbatim his earlier description of him while exaggerating and thickening the colors.[23] Thus, he reminds us that he was "a skinny, feeble, puny man of around fifty . . . with a white body like a chicken's"; that he was a "jeweler," "a moneylender," that he had it so good that "he apparently felt not the least bit regret at having ended up in prison." There follows the incredible description of his "life in clover." Is there any wonder that he was satisfied with his lot and was the envy not only of his fellow convicts but even of his fellow Jews vegetating in the ghettos? No, not at all, if you accept at face value the testimony of Dostoyevsky/Goryanchikov (IV: 93):

> He wanted for nothing, he lived even *richly*, but put by his money and lent it out at interest to the entire prison. He had his own samovar, a good mattress, cups, a whole dinner set. The Jews of the town did not refuse him their company or patronage. On Saturdays, he went under escort to the prayer house in town (which is authorized by law); he lived, in fact, in clover, though he couldn't wait

for his twelve-year term to come to an end so that he could "git married." [24]

Following this idyllic depiction of Isai Fomich's life, Dostoyevsky once again, as Grossman has remarked, "meticulously marshals a whole series of moral traits that serve to stigmatize the soul of this disgraced convict." [25] He calls attention to his "naiveté, stupidity, cunning, impudence, simplemindedness, timorousness, conceit, and insolence." No wonder that Dostoyevsky, that "connoisseur of the human heart," was astonished that a surly band of convicts could be so tolerant of Isai Fomich: "they never jeered at him, but just poked a little fun at him for their own amusement" (IV: 93).

The works of Dostoyevsky abound in scenes of incomparable pathos. One such scene—by no means the least poignant—is that of Isai Fomich's arrival in prison. While it cannot fail to arouse the sympathy and compassion of a discerning reader, it betrays, at the same time, the cold cynicism of the narrator, who sees nothing more than innocent badinage in the taunts of the convicts that greeted Isai Fomich the day he was led into the prison compound. For Dostoyevsky, the scene unfolded in a "killingly funny" way: [26]

> One early evening, after the day's work was done, word suddenly spread through the prison that a Jew [*zhidok*] had been brought in and was being shaved in the guardroom and that he would appear any minute. There was not a single Jew [*yevrei*] in the prison at that time. The convicts awaited his appearance with impatience and the moment he came through the gates they surrounded him.

Sack in hand, Isai Fomich was brought into the barracks by a noncommissioned officer who showed him his place on the bunk (IV: 93):

> He put down his sack, climbed into the bunk and sat there, his legs tucked under him, not daring to raise his eyes at anyone. Laughter broke out on all sides accompanied by prison jokes aimed at his Jewish origin.

One convict made his way through the boisterous throng and began playfully to bait the newcomer, pretending that he wanted to pawn a tattered pair of trousers for a silver ruble. Still mute and frozen with fear, Isai, at the sight of the pledge, "suddenly perked up and briskly began fingering the rags." And then, for the first time, he broke his silence (IV: 94):

> "A silver ruble, nothing doing, but seven kopeks, yes . . ."
> "Seven! Well, give me seven, then . . ."
> "With three kopeks interest, that makes ten," the Jew [*zhidok*] went on jerkily in a tremulous voice, reaching down into his pocket for the money and casting nervous glances at the convicts. He was terribly scared, but he was anxious to make the deal.
> "Three kopeks interest a year, I take it?"
> "No, not a year, a month."
> "You're quite a tightwad, Jew. . . ."

Dostoyevsky then recalls other scenes that we know he had observed firsthand.[27] Half in astonishment, half in admiration, he notes that despite everything, despite even the fact that most of the convicts were in debt to Isai Fomich, "everyone really seemed to like him," "nobody offended him." If Luchka, "who had known many Jews [*zhidki*] in his day, often teased him, it was by no means out of malice, but simply for the fun of it, just as one amuses oneself with a little dog, a parrot, trained animals, etc." (IV: 94).[28] The flood of abuse that poured out of the mouth of Luchka was as inoffensive, Dostoyevsky expressly remarks, as the humble and occasionally spirited rejoinders of the Jew (IV: 94):

> "You damned scurvy!"
> "As scurvy as you like."
> "Scurvy Yid!"
> "I couldn't care less. Scurvy maybe, but rich too; I've got money."
> "You sold Christ."
> "So be it."
> "Bravo, Isai Fomich, sublime! Don't lay a finger on him, he's the only one we've got!" the convicts roared with laughter.
> "Hey, Yid, you'll taste the whip, you're bound for Siberia."
> "Why, I am in Siberia now."
> "They'll send you further."
> "Is the Lord God there?"
> "Yes, he's there, all right."
> "What more can you ask. So long as there's the Lord God and money, life is good everywhere."

With the transition to the scene that immediately follows—Isai Fomich's observance of the Sabbath—the comical tone enters an even higher register. The notes become so strident and the distortion so excessive that it is difficult to see in Dostoyevsky's composition anything but the most extravagant caricature. As Leonid Grossman has written:

> In every word and gesture of his fellow convict, he is inclined to see buffoonery or an irrepressible occasion for laughter. Even the Sabbath ritual of the Jew provokes an ironic smile of incredulity. . . . He does not hide his amusement at a strange ritual and he persists in describing it in a mocking tone, as a burlesque. . . . In *The House of the Dead*, one of the most macabre books in world literature, this is the only page where the laughter of the author is heard.[29]

Grossman pronounced this severe judgment without drawing attention to the glaring discrepancies in Dostoyevsky's account of the ceremonial (they surely could not have escaped his notice). "The spectacle," it will be recalled, takes place on Friday evening, the eve of the Jewish Sabbath (IV: 95):

> Every Friday evening, on the eve of the Sabbath, the convicts came expressly from the others' barracks to ours to watch Isai Fomich celebrate his Sabbath. Isai Fomich was so naively vain and conceited that this general curiosity gave him pleasure, too.

Thus, it is clear that the scene that Dostoyevsky purportedly is describing was one that he and his fellow prisoners viewed with almost ritualistic regularity. And yet Dostoyevsky, whose powers of observation were exceptionally acute and who expended enormous time and effort to verify the exactitude of events he described, reports on a Sabbath ritual that is bristling with errors. Not only is Isai Fomich wrapped in a *tallith*, which is almost never worn on Friday evenings, but he is shown wearing phylacteries, which are used only on weekday mornings, *never* on the Sabbath. Moreover, there are only two phylacteries—one worn on the left arm, the other on the forehead—and not three, as Dostoyevsky describes.[30]

Dostoyevsky was, furthermore, particularly interested in Isai's religious practices, even going so far as to ply him with questions about certain aspects of the ritual, and he notes that "Isai Fomich was terribly pleased by such questions on my part" (IV: 95).

Accordingly, it seems highly unlikely that these gross errors could have been committed unintentionally.

Is it not, then, conceivable that Dostoyevsky sought, at the expense of factual truth, to heighten the comic effect to the plane of the grotesque to achieve again what he had achieved earlier by his erroneous comparison of Isai with Gogol's Jew Yankel? The Sabbath eve ritual is, indeed, richer and more resplendent than the daily morning prayers, but it lacks the ceremonial accoutrements of the latter: the *tallith* and phylacteries. It is impressive without being spectacular. But it is enough to introduce these bizarre accessories to obtain the theatrical effect desired. As to the third phylactery invented by Dostoyevsky, it can, perhaps, be attributed to a simple error of observation on his part without invalidating the assumption that the writer willfully confused and commingled the daily with the Sabbath ritual. He had, undoubtedly, frequently observed Isai at prayer in the morning and, struck more by the phylacteries themselves than by their number, could not resist the temptation to incorporate them into his account of the Sabbath eve.

Dostoyevsky does not conceal the fact that he found Isai's ritual bizarre and ridiculous, nor does he mask his intention to make it appear bizarre and ridiculous to his readers. He takes a malicious pleasure in laying bare the soul of the man at prayer. Not for a moment does he believe in—nor will he let his readers believe in—Isai's sincerity. The Jew likes nothing better than to flaunt his religious practices before the other inmates who have gathered expressly to witness the performance. And he does not disappoint his audience. With meticulous care he prepared himself for the ceremony. He opened his prayer book, lit two candles and (IV: 95):

> . . . muttering some strange mysterious words, began enveloping himself in his chasuble (*chajuble*, as he would say). . . . On both arms he fastened maniples and . . . on his forehead, a little wooden box of sorts secured by a band, so that it looked like some ridiculous horn sprouting out of Isai Fomich's forehead. Then the prayer began. He recited it in a singsong voice, wailing, sputtering, pirouetting, gesticulating wildly and absurdly. All this was, of course, prescribed by the ritual,[31] and there was nothing absurd or strange about it, but what was absurd was the way in which Isai Fomich seemed to pose before us and make a display of his ritual.

The "mysterious words" that Isai muttered were, in fact, the blessings the officiant pronounces while putting on the *tallith*, as Dostoyevsky must certainly have known since Isai—it is clear from the above—had told him about his "*chajuble*." The prayer is uttered in an undertone or, if you will, "muttered," though the word serves the writer well in demonstrating the comic talents of his character.

The demonstration continues: "sobs," "howling," "violent sobbing," a sudden "burst of laughter" and the no less sudden transition to a voice choking with "touching solemnity"—the entire gamut of human and not so human emotions. The authenticity of the scene is attested to by Dostoyevsky's reiteration that all that was "prescribed by the ritual." When, on one occasion, the camp major made an unexpected visit to the barracks while Isai was lost in prayer, the other prisoners drew stiffly to attention (IV: 96), but:

> . . . Isai Fomich began shouting and carrying on more than ever. He knew that praying was authorized . . . and that not the least bit of risk was involved. But he thoroughly enjoyed the chance of cutting a caper before the major and putting on the dog in front of us.

Some time after, Isai assured Dostoyevsky "in dead seriousness" that he had been completely oblivious to the major's presence, so carried away was he by his prayers.

Dostoyevsky's description is by no means the product of pure invention; but, at the same time, it betrays a curious propensity for treating with malicious irreverence a faith that was alien to him and toward which, at least in later life, he developed a feeling of almost pathological revulsion.[32]

While there is very little evidence[33]—aside from the text of *The House of the Dead* itself—to corroborate my interpretation of the prayer scene or to shed light on Dostoyevsky's actual intentions, there is a passage in his *Diary* for March 1877 ("The 'Jewish Question'") that merits particular attention. In a clumsy attempt to refute a correspondent's allegation that the Jews were either hated or oppressed by the Russians, Dostoyevsky, unquestionably drawing on his prison experience, wrote (11: 82):

> Admittedly, I may not be too well versed in Jewish life, but one thing I do know for sure and will stand by against one and all is this: that amongst our common people there is no preconceived, *a*

priori, narrow-minded, religious hatred of the Jew, nothing like "he's a Judas, he sold out Christ."

And yet, this was precisely the accusation leveled by Luchka at Isai the day the latter entered the prison. And Dostoyevsky continued (11: 82):

> It even fell to my lot to live with the people, side by side with them, in the same barracks, sleeping on the same bunks. There were several [*sic*] Jews there—and no one *despised* them, no one ostracized them, no one hounded them. When they prayed (and Jews scream when they pray and don a special garment), no one found it strange, interfered with them or scoffed at them . . . ; on the contrary, they would look at them and say: "That's the belief they hold, that's the way they pray," and they would go on their way quietly, almost approvingly.

It may be pure coincidence that chapter 10, which follows directly on the Jewish prayer scene, is devoted to the Christmas celebration. In his moving and poignant description, Dostoyevsky relates how the prisoners were transfigured by the solemnity of that day. And the scene of the Christmas observance offers a sharp contrast to Isai's celebration of the Sabbath eve (IV: 109):

> In the middle of the room, a little table had been set up and laid with a clean towel, and a sacred picture was placed on it with the icon-lamp burning before it. At last the priest arrived with the cross and holy water. After praying and chanting before the icon, he turned toward the convicts, and they all came forward, one by one, and kissed the cross with genuine reverence. The priest then made the rounds of the barracks rooms and sprinkled them with holy water. . . . They accompanied the cross out with the same devotion with which they had welcomed it. . . .

The Christmas repast that followed was filled with mirth and gaiety and carousing, but came to an end without incident. Most of the convicts continued to carry on with their merrymaking; the Old Believer from Starodub went on praying into the early morning, looking reprovingly on the "shamefulness," as he put it, of the prisoners' drunken revelry; the Circassians observed the festivities with curiosity, though without concealing their aversion to the drunken spectacle, which they considered ill-appropriate to the occasion. As for Isai Fomich (could it be otherwise?), "with

stubborn and haughty contempt, he lit his candle in his corner
and set to work, in an obvious effort to show that the holiday
meant absolutely nothing to him" (IV: 109).[34]

Dostoyevsky completes his portrait of Isai Fomich in two other
scenes—the bathhouse and the prison theatricals (IV: 96–104,
116–130). Chronologically, the bathhouse scene precedes the
Christmas celebration and constitutes the third and final panel of
the triptych in chapter 9, the first being Bumstein's arrival in
prison, the second—the prayer scene. Whether intentionally or
not, Dostoyevsky seems to have woven into the bathhouse scene
features borrowed from the two earlier scenes, their intrusion and
interaction underscoring the caricatured tone of the composite
portrait.

At the bathhouse: "Isai Fomich . . . crowing at the top of his
voice on the topmost tier" is somewhat reminiscent of Isai on his
arrival at the camp when, after having put down his sack, he
"climbed into the bunk and sat there, his legs tucked under him."
"He steams himself into a state of unconsciousness" just as, during
his prayers, he "fell into such a state of ecstasy that he saw nothing
or heard nothing around him." "No degree of heat seems to satisfy
him . . . and for such an occasion there's no stinting on the money
and he hires even a fifth man to wield the switch"—to the sheer
delight of his fellow convicts: "He sure knows how to steam himself, bravo, Isai Fomich!" they shouted, just as they had applauded
him during his verbal encounter with Luchka. "Isai Fomich senses
at this moment that he is superior to all of them and has got them
wrapped around his little finger; he is triumphant, and in his shrill,
frenzied voice he sings out his la-la-la-la-la, covering the general
hubbub." He experienced the same unmistakable pleasure when,
following his joust with Luchka, "he began caroling the whole
barracks with his shrill little warble: 'la-la-la-la-la' " (IV: 94–95).[35]

After a fleeting reference to Isai and how much he enjoyed
the prison theatricals, in the concluding chapter (11) of part 1,
Dostoyevsky would never again return to him throughout part 2,
except for a casual allusion in "The Grievance" (chapter 7). It would
probably not be worth mentioning were it not for the fact that it
reveals Isai in a characteristic, stereotyped attitude: the cautious,
anxiety-ridden, timorous Jew confronted by an uncertain situation
pregnant with possible danger. Seething discontent over the prison
fare led the convicts to address a petition to the camp commander.

For one reason or another, the nobles (among them Dostoyevsky), the Poles and a few scattered individuals (among them Isai) had held themselves aloof from the movement. They were all gathered in the kitchen awaiting the outcome of the affair. "Isai Fomich was there, too, looking extremely perplexed and crestfallen, listening greedily and apprehensively to our conversation. He was in great anxiety" (IV: 204).

It is with this final stroke that Dostoyevsky completes the portrait of Isai Fomich Bumstein. Winding up his analysis of that portrait, Grossman, at the risk of self-contradiction, seeks to attenuate the asperity of his earlier assessment. He concludes that

> . . . the literary genius of the author rises above his preconceived intentions and that, despite Dostoyevsky's undeniable penchant for caricature, his artistic spontaneity and humanity save his characterization from grotesqueness and reveal its profound and poignant meaning.[36]

But are his arguments in support of this position wholly convincing? Does he not exaggerate the significance of the author's seeming precision of language to explain why Isai was sent to Siberia? The latter, Dostoyevsky tells us, was sent up "on accusation of murder" (*po obvineniyu v ubiistve*) and not "for murder" (*za ubiistvo*).[37] From this Grossman infers that Dostoyevsky himself did not believe that Isai was guilty, which, in turn, would explain why the writer insisted on his "timidity," "submissiveness," "humility," "physical frailty" and so forth. He seems to forget, though, that Dostoyevsky had more insistently underscored other traits of Isai that more than outweigh these positive attributes. He was, it will be recalled, "shrewd," "cunning," "truculent," "arrogant" and "terribly cowardly." Grossman goes even further, implying that because Isai had been unjustly convicted "he earns not only the love of all the convicts, but also the friendship of an archenemy of his race—Dostoyevsky,"[38] a conclusion likewise difficult to substantiate.

Though he does not absolve Dostoyevsky of all prejudicial intent, Grossman feels that his artistry and deep sense of humanity tower above his pettiness; he writes:

> The prisoner-buffoon—though maybe the author didn't intend it that way—evokes the profound sympathy of the readers of *The House of the Dead*. We see this frail, sickly, almost-old man inno-

cently hurled into the penal hell of Siberia, amidst a pack of crimi-
nals brimming with scorn and derision for his national origins,
steadfastly and openly upholding the faith of his forefathers.[39]

Even in the highly caricatured prayer scene, "the ironical intentions of the author vanish before the majestic and moving truth
of the event described."[40]

And Grossman concludes:

> The chapters . . . dealing with Isai are an involuntary apologia for
> Jewry. The ironic tone of the narrative is relieved by notes of ten-
> der humor, and the great connoisseur of the human heart is com-
> pelled to abandon his caricature to reveal the profound traits of
> humanity in his comical subject.[41]

This conclusion is a hazardous one. If, in fact, a few human
traits do break through the thick and hard layer of caricature, they
are visible only to the most perspicacious and indulgent reader.
With the sole exception of the prison theatricals, Dostoyevsky
treated Isai as an object, an object of derision that, in the prayer
scene, bordered on sacrilege. Moreover, Dostoyevsky's portrait of
Isai is so much in harmony with the bigotry-ridden atmosphere of
Russia of the second half of the nineteenth century that one cannot
entirely dismiss the hypothesis that he drew it with an eye to the
audience he hoped to reach.

"He was the only one we had, and even now I can't think of
him without laughing" (IV: 55). "Isai Fomich, obviously, served
as a continual source of entertainment and amusement to all" (IV:
93). For Goryanchikov/Dostoyevsky, Isai was definitely a comical
figure—and the only one in *The House of the Dead.*

Although Dostoyevsky never developed in his writing what
may properly be called a theory of laughter, he has spoken of the
"terrible power of laughter" in connection with Gogol, whose
laugh he described as a "sniggering mask," a mask covering up
feelings that had nothing funny about them (13: 103). In *A Raw
Youth,* however, he has left us with a brief analysis of laughter so
penetrating that it may very well be considered as an introduction
to a Dostoyevskyan theory of laughter. What he had to say he felt
to be of such fundamental importance that he even asked the readers' forbearance for interrupting the narrative because "I consider

it to be one of the most serious conclusions I have drawn from life"
(XIII: 286), to wit (XIII: 285):

> As I see it, whenever a man laughs, in most cases it is disgust-
> ing to look at him. Ordinarily, there is something vulgar and de-
> meaning about the laughter of people, though the one who laughs
> is almost always unaware of the impression he creates. . . . There
> are some people who give themselves away when they laugh, you
> can read their thoughts like a book. . . . Laughter demands sincerity
> above all, and where do you find sincerity in people? Laughter de-
> mands goodness, and people usually laugh with malice. . . . And so,
> if you want to study a man and plumb his soul . . . take a good look
> at him when he laughs.

This we have done.

3. Time *and the "Jewish Question"*

UPON HIS RETURN from exile to St. Petersburg in December 1859, after a ten-year absence, Dostoyevsky was interested not only in reestablishing his literary reputation but also in having a tribune from which he could speak forth on the vital issues of the day. This was to be the monthly journal *Time* (*Vremya*), which began publication in in January 1861 and appeared regularly until May 1863, when it was shut down by imperial decree; it would reappear as *Epoch* (*Epokha*) in January 1864 until financial difficulties forced it to close down in March of the following year. Even though his brother Mikhail was officially editor of *Time*, it was, in fact, Fyodor Mikhailovich who assumed this role and enjoyed responsibility for the journal's literary, political and ideological orientation.

The pages of *Time* would largely reflect the profound spiritual and intellectual change that Dostoyevsky had undergone during his years in Siberia. No longer did he consider the revolutionary transformation of Russia either necessary or desirable. He now viewed Russia as a nation from which class conflict was absent, where there were no class interests as such, where the Russian spirit prevailed over what were only superficial, external divisive elements. In *Time*'s inaugural issue he wrote (13: 41):

> Our new Rus has understood that there is only one cement, one bond, one soil on which all will converge and be reconciled—this is a universal spiritual reconciliation, the beginnings of which lie in education.

Such, in essence, was the doctrine of *pochvennichestvo* or organic-rootedness-in-the-soil, the doctrine around which Dostoyevsky hoped to rally the progressive forces in Russian society that were emerging in the liberalized atmosphere of the sixties—the Era of the Great Reforms.

On February 19, 1861, exactly six years to the day after the coronation of Alexander II, the Emancipation of the Serfs was proclaimed, the most important of a series of major reforms that marked the first two decades of Alexander's reign. Among those reforms, a certain number sought to codify and liberalize the status of the Jewish population in the empire. It is these that are our main concern, for one of their immediate consequences was to focus the attention of Russian intellectual opinion on the "Jewish question."

One of Alexander's first official acts was the abolition—in the Coronation Manifesto of August 1856—of the abhorrent institution of forced Jewish juvenile conscription, which had been in force since the Ukaz of August 26, 1827. Others followed: the Law of December 2, 1857, opening up to Jewish settlement the fifty-verst zones from the Polish border; the Law of October 27, 1858, authorizing Jews to reside in the frontier zones of the border provinces in the West and Bessarabia; the Law of March 16, 1859, permitting Jewish merchants with the requisite financial qualifications to reside and trade in cities outside of the Jewish pale.[1] But particularly noteworthy—though it would have little practical effect—was the Law of November 27, 1861, which qualified Jews with university degrees for government service throughout the Russian empire. The law declared that:

> Jews possessing certificates of the learned degree of Doctor of Medicine and Surgery, or Doctor of Medicine, and likewise of Doctor, Magister, or Candidate of other university faculties, are admitted to serve in all Government offices, without their being confined to the Pale established for the residence of all Jews. They are also permitted to settle permanently in all the provinces of the Empire for the pursuit of commerce and industry.[2]

It was this law, as we shall see shortly, that gave rise to a bitter polemic between Dostoyevsky's journal, *Time*, and Ivan Aksakov's Slavophile organ, *Day* (*Den*), the former, paradoxical as it may seem, resolutely defending this law and the extension of Jewish rights against the anti-Semitic tirade of the latter. This controversy, moreover, raises the perplexing question of what prompted, *at this particular moment*, Dostoyevsky's defense of a people whom, until then, he had a tendency to ridicule and would later malign. It would be futile even to attempt to answer this question without first examining the major currents of opinion in confrontation at that time in Russia and, particularly, within the context of the Jewish question.

The attention that question received in the Russian press of the period is perhaps greater than is generally recognized. To a large extent, the press reflected the government's growing concern over this problem as well as its efforts to do something about it. As early as 1856, for example, Count Kiselyov, chairman of the Jewish Committee, reported to Alexander that "the aim of the government . . . to bring about the union of the Jewish with the general population is hampered by the temporarily established restrictions which contradict the general legislation and create confusion."[3]

Other highly placed officials went a step further, calling for the complete emancipation of the Jews. Count A. G. Stroganov, governor-general of Novorossiya and Bessarabia, addressed a long memorandum on January 22, 1858, to Count Lanskoy, minister of the interior, in which he wrote: "The existence at the present time of any legal limitations for Jews in comparison with the Christian population is out of harmony both with the spirit and the trends of the times, as well as with the aim of the government to merge the Jews with the native population."[4] Although Count Lanskoy supported this opinion, it was rejected by the Jewish Committee, then under the chairmanship of Bludov, in February 1859.

That these were more than pious aspirations is, however, attested to by the legislative reforms that followed.

The Russian press, too, began to speak out on these issues. At the end of the fifties, it was by and large favorable to the Jews; and if there were occasionally anti-Semitic outbursts, they were roundly assailed.[5] Time has now consigned to virtual oblivion one incident that was a *cause célèbre* in St. Petersburg during the second half of 1858.[6] It rallied, in an astonishing manifestation of solidarity, the literary and intellectual forces of the capital to the defense of the Jews.[7]

The prelude to this event was the publication in the *Russian Invalid* (*Russkii invalid*, no. 39, 1858), influential Petersburg daily and organ of the ministry of war, of an article urging tolerance toward the Jews. It read, in part, as follows:

> Let us be worthy of our age; let us give up the disastrous habit of holding up the Jew to shame and contumely in our literature. On

the contrary, mindful of the causes that brought them to such a state, let us not forget the innate aptitude of the Jews for knowledge, the arts and sciences. And offering them a place among us, let us take advantage of their energy, readiness of wit and resourcefulness as a new means of satisfying the ever-growing daily needs of society.[8]

Vladimir Zotov, talented journalist and editor of the St. Petersburg weekly *Illustration* (*Illyustratsiya*), blasted the *Russian Invalid* in an unsigned and virulently anti-Semitic article entitled "The Jews of the Russian West and Their Present Situation" (no. 35, 1858), claiming that the Jews were unworthy of emancipation. An accompanying piece contained a slanderous attack on the Jewish financier "N," a transparent reference to Horace (later Baron) Gintsburg, a philanthropist and civic leader particularly active in the cause of Jewish emancipation.[9]

The *Russian Herald* (*Russkii vestnik*), one of the leading if not *the* leading journal of the day, edited by the then liberal Westernizer Mikhail Katkov, joined the fray. It published in its October (no. 17) issue a riposte to Zotov from the pen of Isaak Chatskin, doctor and public figure, accompanied by a vigorous editorial note decrying the tone of Zotov's article, which, it stressed, was enough "to arouse the indignation not only of those members of the nation against whom it was directed but of any educated Christian." At the same time, *Athenaeum* (*Atenei*), a newly founded review, published another rejoinder to Zotov in an article signed by Martin Gorvits, protesting against *Illustration*'s unfounded accusations against the Jews that could have been inspired only by "religious fanaticism and national intolerance."[10]

Zotov (*Illustration*, no. 43) countered with a slanderous attack on "Reb" Chatskin and "Reb" Gorvits and the press, which he accused of being in the pay of the Jewish financier "N." The reaction was not long in coming. The intellectual élite of St. Petersburg rose to their defense, subscribing to a protest that appeared concurrently in the *Russian Herald* (no. 18), the *Petersburg Record* (*Peterburgskiye vedomosti*, no. 258), the *Moscow Record* (*Moskovskiye vedomosti*) and others. The protest bore the signatures of 147 prominent personalities—writers and journalists, historians, scientists, civic and government leaders, among them: Ivan, Konstantin and Sergei Aksakov, P. V. Annenkov, P. D. Boborykin, F. I. Buslayev, N. G. Chernyshevsky, M. N. Katkov, Ye. G. Korsh, A. A.

Krayevsky, N. I. Kostomarov, A. N. Maikov, P. I. Melnikov-Pecher-sky, N. A. Nekrasov, S. M. Solovyov, T. G. Shevchenko, I. S. Turgenev and A. M. Zhemchuzhnikov.[11]

The protest declared that "anyone who uses the printed word is responsible before society and this is all the more true when the word assumes the character of a moral act." Indicting *Illustration* for its wanton attack on the moral integrity of Gorvits and Chatskin and accusing it of libel and character assassination, it concluded:

> In the persons of Messrs. Gorvits and Chatskin, an affront has been put upon all society, upon all Russian literature. No honorable man can remain indifferent to such an ignominious act, and all Russian writers must unite in indignation to protest against it.
>
> This general protest shall be the best satisfaction to the honor of the outraged individuals and the most tangible proof of the health of that society which, by its own free will, crushes and reproves any dishonorable act.
>
> May this protest serve as an example and admonition for the future, and may it forever safeguard our literature from a repetition of such occurrences.

Although the protest avoided specific mention of the Jewish origin of the wronged individuals,[12] its intent was clear: it gave implicit recognition to the fact that Russian Jewry was an integral part of Russian society.

The *Russian Herald* went even further than just to publish the protest. In the same issue, N. F. Pavlov pointedly inquired:

> Has society the right to blame others for disregarding the ethical precepts when it itself fails to act accordingly? Should not society first trouble itself to fulfill those obligations which truth and Christian love impose upon it, and only then, if anyone so pleases, let him speak about the dirtiness and swindling of the Jews? . . . The time for making attacks on the Jews has passed, and passed forever.[13]

So much for the unequivocal stand of the *Russian Herald*. What, then, was the position of the *Contemporary (Sovremennik)*, the other leading journal of the period? Though the organ of the Revolutionary-Democrats neither published the protest nor commented on it, an imposing number of its collaborators were among the signatories.[14] Moreover, only a few months earlier, it had taken a firm stand on the Jewish question, a fact that would explain its silence on this occasion. In a long editorial in its June 1858 issue (no. 6), the *Contemporary* called for warm and sympathetic understanding of the Jewish people and renunciation of age-old prejudices, failing which "we shall always see before us only the *zhid* and not the *Izrailtyanin.*" The editorialist—like Vladimir Solovyov a quarter of a century later[15]—believes that if the Jews, isolated from Christian society, have developed undesirable traits, it is Christian society itself that bears the blame for it, and not its victims:

> How could the Jews . . . draw close to the Christians [in a land] where, in spite of the humility that lies at the core of the gospels, the Jew, in the eyes of the most God-fearing Christian, has been a creature despised and rejected and deserving death by virtue of his birth! The whole history of the Jews has been nothing but one grim picture of merciless persecutions.

Emphasizing the vital importance of the Jewish question, "since it concerns the fate of over one and one-half million people living in Russia," the author concludes with the observation that "everywhere and at all times the improvement of the lot of the Jew has been the sign of progress of European civilization."[16]

Thus, the Jewish question was very much alive among the intelligentsia when Dostoyevsky launched his journal in January 1861. On the four different occasions when *Time* tackled the problem—in December 1861, in February, May and September 1862—it allied itself with the forces of progress and reform.

In December 1861, *Time* published an unsigned article entitled "The Polemical Incident between *Foundation* and *Zion*."[17] The origin of the controversy, as reported by *Time*, lay in *Foundation*'s employment of the epithet *zhid* ("Yid" or "kike") instead of the term *yevrei* ("Jew"). This aroused the indignation of a certain P-v, who, in an outspoken letter to the editors of *Foundation* that he expressly asked not be published, requested them "in the name of present-day humanity" to desist from the use of that word forevermore.

In its July issue, in an article entitled "Misunderstanding over the Word *Zhid*," *Foundation* rejected P-v's charges as baseless, publishing his letter at the same time. It justified the use of the term *zhid* by writers of Ukrainian origin on the grounds that the only word for "Jew" in Ukrainian was *zhyd*, which derived from the Polish *zyd*, that the term was no more derogatory than the German *Jude* or the French *Juif*.[18]

At that point *Time* interjected: "You, reader, no doubt feel that the matter could have rested there . . . but not *Foundation*," which proceeded to vent its wrath against the Jews, explaining that the Ukrainians had good reason to dislike them and now accusing them of being an alien element in Ukrainian society: "For a nation nothing can be *more harmful* than the existence within its midst of other peoples who hold themselves aloof and are indifferent to its destiny or, even worse, strive to subject it to their power or influence."[19]

The "provocative" character of these "archival" elucubrations, *Time* went on, could not but incense the editors of *Zion*, which now entered the controversy (no. 10, 1861). Although dissociating itself from P-v's views but accepting *Foundation's* rationalization of the use of the term *zhid*, *Zion* took violent exception to the charges made against the Jews and assailed rather "the *harmfulness* of exclusively national aspirations." The controversy ended with a final assault against *Zion* by *Foundation's* publisher, Kulish, in his article "Progressive Jews."

Time concluded with an appeal for the reconciliation of the two organs, "both of which are inspired by equally good and similar sentiments and intentions." This rather patronizing and neutral call to brotherhood did not, however, conceal where *Time's* sympathies lay.[20]

Of far greater significance was the uncompromising stand taken by Dostoyevsky's journal in its controversy over the Jewish question with the Slavophile weekly *Day (Den)* in February 1862. From the beginning of the sixties until his death in 1886, Ivan S. Aksakov, editor and publisher of *Day*, was a vociferous spokesman for the ultra-patriotic wing of the Slavophile movement that was firmly opposed to the extension of Jewish rights and Jewish emancipation.[21] The latter he found incompatible with Slavophile doctrine—as he viewed it—of a dominant nationality and a dominant church. Distressed by the increasing liberalism of the government's Jewish policy, culminating in the Law of November 27,

1861, which, it will be recalled, opened the way for Jewish university graduates into all departments of the civil service, Aksakov launched a bitter attack on the Jews in *Day*. In its editorial of February 16, 1862 (no. 19), he wrote:

> We daresay that our defenders and zealots of Judaic interests have not understood the law as it should be understood; and, in any case, they have certainly not understood the implications of its practical application. Of course, the expression "in all departments" does not quite render a legislative concept, and obviously it cannot be construed without reservations. Thus, it is inconceivable, for example, that a Jew—a Jew not only by descent but by faith—could become Procurator of the Holy Synod!

What is the place of the Jews in a nation founded on Christian ideals and principles? Aksakov replied:

> A handful of individuals, thoroughly denying Christian teachings, Christian ideals and ethics . . . and professing an inimical and antagonistic doctrine, come into a Christian land. . . . The Jews came to the Christians, the masters of the land, as guests. The hosts can receive and even respect their guests, albeit uninvited, but they cannot install them in the masters' place and relinquish the masters' authority to those who would advocate the subversion of all proprietary order. They cannot accord them the liberty of doing as they please and running the house. . . .
>
> We have never been on bad terms with the Jews. We recognize the great talents of this people and sincerely regret they have gone astray. We are ready to wish them the guarantee of full freedom in their way of life, self-administration, development, education, trade (to the extent, naturally, that Jews are capable of respecting laws common to all citizens); we are prepared even to wish for them permission to reside anywhere in Russia. But we cannot wish for them administrative and legislative rights in Russia, a country that holds high the banner of Christianity, that was founded on and is developing according to the principles of Christian truth. . . .

Time's reaction was immediate. Already in its February issue, in an unsigned article, "The Nineteenth Issue of *Day*," variously attributed to Dostoyevsky, to his close collaborator N. N. Strakhov or, most recently, to M. I. Vladislavlyev,[22] *Time* wrote:

> *Day* makes itself a laughing stock, it alone lays itself open to shame and ridicule. In all sincerity we can say we feel sorry for it. We are

sorry to see it expose itself to the ridicule that will come its way. By discrediting itself, it compels those who are in many ways sympathetic to it to condemn it loudly and sharply.

. . . *Day* felt it important and necessary to explain that this law [of November 27, 1861] *cannot be understood without reservations.* And yet it insistently demands that it be understood with reservations. The issue is clear: *Day*'s article is directed *against* the Jews, and its intention is to restrict the rights of Jews.

After citing large excerpts from *Day*'s observations on the incompatibility of Christian and Jewish doctrine, *Time* put the question point-blank:

What, then, are the Jews after all? Are we to suppose that they are not human beings but wild beasts dangerous to the moral order and to all private, public and governmental life?

Pitiable friends who do more harm to Christianity than do its enemies! . . . Inimical! Contrary! In what way inimical? In what way contrary? Could anyone who was really interested in the question and really sensed a danger confine himself to such a hollow allegation?

. . . All of its innermost fears come down to this: "It is inconceivable," it says, "that a Jew, a Jew not only by descent but by faith, could become Procurator of the Holy Synod!"

What amazing exactitude! Who will disallow that the question is troublesome, obscure, almost intolerable? But . . . permit us this one observation: the question raised by *Day* is plainly *superfluous, unnecessary and uninteresting.* It is without the slightest significance for a believing Christian.

Day, as we have seen, thinks otherwise. If there is, within Judaism, something inherently harmful to Christianity, then the preservation of Christian society from this evil can be found only within its faith. *Day* seeks another safeguard: it would like to see it in the law; and before you know it, it will be seeking it by fire and by the sword! . . . Would *Day* have us believe that we would be acting quite logically, quite honestly and unhypocritically if we burned and hanged the Jews? For surely we would have very sound grounds for doing so. "They," we would say, "*these Jews*, crucified Him whom we recognize as God!"

It is not this spirit, it seems to us, that inspired the teachings of Him in whose name *Day* is apparently speaking. The teachings of peace, love and concord should have prompted other thoughts and other words.

In terms that cannot but surprise, *Time* then rose to the defense of the epoch impugned by Aksakov in his condemnation of Russian society of the day, which he found to be under the pernicious influence of materialism and communism:

> *Day* has a very narrow conception of the nineteenth century. . . . What distinguishes our century is not that it has engendered materialists and communists. They are, of course, manifestations of its character, but they are not the dominant traits of its personality. What is more significant and fundamental is that these materialists and these communists are at present sometimes better and more abounding in love than certain zealots of piety have sometimes been; and that society does not torture or burn communists at the stake; and that in general it regards them from another point of view than that held by *Day*.

The controversy played itself out in a minor key in the months that followed. The leading article in *Day* of March 31 (no. 35), "A Few Words about the Talmud," by an unknown author, a certain A. Aleksandrov, sought to explain the Jews' congenital inaptitude for governmental service by distorted references to the Talmud. He concluded that only when the Jews "have repudiated *en masse* the teachings of the Talmud and have returned to purely Mosaic doctrine, the spirit of which is indeed not incompatible with the Christian spirit, could they be accorded equal treatment before the law."

Time answered this new attack in its May issue.[23] It had, shortly before, received a letter from one Pyotr Lyakub requesting the editors "in the name of truth, justice and progress" to publish his article in rebuttal to Aleksandrov's attack. *Time* gave over no less than eighteen pages to Lyakub's reply.[24] An analysis of that article would be superfluous here. What is important is that *Time* once again, for the third time, came out in defense of the Jews.

What prompted Dostoyevsky's vigorous defense of the Jews at this critical moment in their history? The search for an explicit answer to this question in the extant writings and correspondence of Dostoyevsky—or of his closest collaborators or severest critics of the period—is unrewarding. The temptation is strong—but, I think, unwarranted—simply to dismiss the question and regard it as a momentary aberration or nothing more than a by-product of *poch-vennichestvo* and its doctrine of universal spiritual brotherhood. In the absence, therefore, of any unimpeachable evidence, it is suggested that some answer to this question is to be found in the ideological conflict that divided Russian intellectual thought and was particularly acute in the early sixties.

By the time of Dostoyevsky's return to St. Petersburg, not only had he undergone an intense spiritual transformation, but the political and intellectual climate of the capital had radically altered. While the old, traditional lines of opinion were drawn as before—among the conservative Slavophiles, the liberal Western-izers and the radical Westernizers or Revolutionary-Democrats [25] —the *rapport des forces* had unmistakably changed to the advantage of the latter. The Revolutionary-Democrats and their journal, the *Contemporary*, had not only assumed the ideological leadership of the growing revolutionary forces within the Russian intelligentsia, but they also had a sympathetic following within important sections of the army and even the government. Their influence among the radically minded youth of Moscow and Petersburg universities was unchallenged; and the young Jewish intelligentsia, too, were fired by the ideas of the Revolutionary-Democratic leadership—Chernyshevsky, Nekrasov, Dobrolyubov and Pisarev.[26] Such was the situation when *Time* began publishing in January 1861.

That Dostoyevsky was fully aware of the literary authority of the *Contemporary* is clearly seen in his letters to his brother Mikhail written from Tver in October 1859, a few months prior to his return to the capital. Above all else, he wanted to make his reentry into literature on the pages of the *Contemporary*, the journal that had consecrated the reputation of Tolstoy and Turgenev during his absence. And even if Nekrasov's journal would offer him less than the *Russian Herald* or *Notes of the Fatherland* (in which *The Village of Stepanchikovo and Its Inhabitants* was finally published), it was to have priority: "Look, now," he wrote to Mikhail, "it's very important that the novel be published by the *Contemporary*. That journal turned me down before but is now trying to get my text. It's very important for my literary situation."[27] Ten days later, in his letter of October 20, he was again exhorting his brother "to do what I asked you in my last letter, that is, go and see Nekrasov and Kalinovsky."[28]

If the *Contemporary* commanded Dostoyevsky's awed respect, so too did the period of which it was the foremost spokesman. No more trenchant or more faithful characterization of this period has been given than that by the *Contemporary's* literary critic M. A. Antonovich, who, in describing the first few years of the sixties, wrote:

> Literature persecuted reactionaries and conservatives with amazing unanimity and pointed them out to the public as creatures to be avoided like the plague. Conservatism and backwardness were terms of opprobrium in its lexicon. Anybody who wrote would sooner have had his hand cut off than to allow it to write anything that was unprogressive, have torn out his tongue than to utter an unliberal word.[29]

For as long as *Time* was published—and even after its break with the *Contemporary* had come out into the open—Dostoyevsky strove to avoid being identified with the forces of reaction. In his letter of November 3, 1862, to Nekrasov, in which he asked the latter for a contribution to *Time*, he posed—and forthwith answered—the question: "Is our journal really reactionary? No, not even in the eyes of our enemies. We can be accused of everything, except of being reactionary. . . . I am convinced that the public doesn't consider us as reactionary."[30]

Dostoyevsky's conviction was well grounded: *Time* succeeded in confirming itself as a liberal organ notwithstanding its advocacy of a doctrine that was heavily indebted to Slavophile thought. The doctrine of *pochvennichestvo,* or organic-rootedness-in-the-soil, held that the reforms of Peter the Great had created a chasm between the educated class of Russian society and the Russian people; that the future of Russia depended on the reconciliation and the fusion of these two classes on Russian national principles; that this unity could be achieved by peaceful means through the spread of education. And like Slavophilism, it recognized the universal mission of the Russian people, envisaging that "the Russian idea . . . will be, perhaps, the synthesis of all those ideas that . . . Europe is developing within its diverse nationalities, that, perhaps, everything that is harmful in these ideas will find its reconciliation and further development in the Russian people [*narodnost*]."[31]

Unlike Slavophilism, however, *pochvennichestvo* did not repudiate Peter's reforms entirely. It did not want to return Russia to the pre-Petrine period, it merely felt that the reform period in Russian history had run its course and that it was now time for Russia to pursue its development from within (*samobytnost*). If it advanced the Messianic idea, it was not yet the militant, mystical and fanatically religious Messianism of the later Slavophiles. For the moment, it was more akin to the Messianism of Herzen. Although rejecting socialism and revolution, it derived its ideals of harmony and universality from Utopian thought. And while Russia would "perhaps" realize Europe's mission, *pochvennichestvo* did not view those Russians who had been deeply influenced by European thought and ideas as outcasts beyond redemption.[32]

In short, Dostoyevsky conceived of *pochvennichestvo* as a synthesis of Slavophile and Westernizing thought. And *Time*, by and large, reflected this idea and aspiration: to be neither Western nor Slavophile, but Russian.[33]

To introduce into the polemical and radically oriented atmosphere of Petersburg journalism a doctrine that was vague, ill-defined and heavily obligated to Slavophile thought was, however, a hazardous venture. Dostoyevsky was fully conscious of this as well as of the limitations this situation placed on his complete freedom of action.[34] He realized that not only the success but the very survival of his program depended on his ability to avoid clashing with the prejudices of the audience he was trying to reach.[35] He perceived clearly where the danger lay—on the right, not on the left. Nothing more imperiled the independence of his program than its becoming identified with Slavophilism, which, if not yet moribund, was in a state of decline and disfavor. And nothing more imperiled the survival of his program than challenging the authority of the Revolutionary-Democrats and thereby antagonizing the very elements in Russian society that he sought to influence. *Time*, therefore, had no choice but to join battle with the forces of conservatism and reaction while scrupulously avoiding engaging—and even supporting—the forces identified with progress.

Time's first target was Katkov and his *Russian Herald*, and the ensuing polemics in which *Time* rose to the defense of the Revolutionary-Democrats served to establish from the outset its reputation as an independent and progressive organ.[36] In a series of articles (all subsequently attributed to Dostoyevsky), *Time* first ridiculed and upbraided Katkov for his abusive and vulgar attacks on the *Contemporary*;[37] then expressed bitter disappointment over his renewal of such attacks;[38] and terminated its polemics with the round condemnation of the *Russian Herald*'s aloof arrogance and abstract and abstruse sermonizing, noting that:

> these outcasts [the Revolutionary-Democrats] are, at least, doing something, are, at least, rummaging around looking for a solution. Making mistakes though they may be, they are making it possible for others to avoid such errors in the future. Consequently, what they are doing is useful even if in a negative way. And you, meanwhile, with arms melodramatically crossed, stand there chuckling.[39]

Having disposed of the *Russian Herald*, *Time* now turned its attention to the Slavophiles and their new organ, *Day*, which had begun publication on October 15, 1861. *Time*'s November issue carried a long piece by Dostoyevsky entitled "The Latest Literary Events—The Newspaper *Day*," reviewing its first five issues. In this, the first and most polemical article against the Slavophiles, he deplored their "intransigent hatred of everything that is not theirs," and inquired: "Is love for the homeland and integrity a privilege given to the Slavophiles alone?"[40] The belligerent tone of this initial engagement heightened the expectation of a still more vigorous onslaught to come.

By the time, however, that *Time* resumed its controversy with *Day* in its February 1862 issue, Antonovich had published in the *Contemporary* (December 1861) a sharp critique against Dostoyevsky's journal ridiculing its attempts to reconcile the views of the Slavophiles and the Westernizers.[41] Dostoyevsky smarted under this first attack of the Revolutionary-Democrats; in December, he made the following entry in his notebook:

> *The beginning*: You started it. We didn't want to begin although we've been vacillating for some time now. But you were dear to us, and we decided it was best to say nothing, though I can't tell you how much it distressed us to read your jibes. . . . But now you've begun, and now we'd very much like to speak out our minds fully, not just a little bit as before.[42]

Much as Dostoyevsky would have liked "to speak out our minds fully," he realized that to do so would jeopardize the progressive reputation of his journal and of himself as well. This he could not afford to do. But the fact that *Time* could not simply ignore the attacks of the *Contemporary* and would be compelled to answer them, and, by the very nature of things, adopt a policy of greater moderation toward the Slavophiles, placed Dostoyevsky before a dilemma: how to pursue, in effect, a conservative course and still preserve *Time*'s progressive reputation. Although the attempt to conciliate such divergent ends was doomed to failure—and that failure would be confirmed and consummated by *Time*'s successor, the journal *Epoch*[43]—*Time* strove throughout the year 1862 to reconcile the irreconcilable.

It is to be noted, first, that Dostoyevsky avoided any direct, identifiable connection with the more vehement and vituperative articles directed against the *Contemporary*. All of them, without exception, came from the pen of his intimate collaborator N. N. Strakhov.[44] Moreover, on the two occasions (in 1862) that Dostoyevsky entered the controversy, he combined the cautious reserve of anonymity with the prudence of moderation.

His February article "Two Camps of Theorists—Concerning *Day* and Something Else" now reflected an ambivalent attitude toward both the Revolutionary-Democrats and the Slavophiles, with perhaps a measure of greater toleration toward the latter.[45] By September, when his second article, "The Slavophiles, the Montenegrins and the Westernizers—The Latest Skirmish," appeared and the breach with the *Contemporary* was wide open, Dostoyevsky still carefully avoided a separate confrontation with the Revolutionary-Democrats for fear of being unequivocally identified with the Slavophile camp. If he now manifested even more indulgence toward the Slavophiles than he had in February, he nonetheless condemned the fanatical doctrines of both: the future of Russia lay with the new and young emergent forces in which neither of the two extremes believed.[46]

Lest, however, Strakhov's intemperate attacks against the *Contemporary* coupled with Dostoyevsky's measured criticism of the Revolutionary-Democrats still be construed as a defection from the progressive camp, the editor of *Time* sought—or, at least, found and adroitly employed—an additional safeguard against such an eventuality: the Jewish question.

At all times the attitude toward the Jewish question has been the acid test of liberalism. At this juncture in Russian history this was, as we have seen, particularly true. To argue that Dostoyevsky could have remained silent on the question and the fact that he did not is proof of a genuine feeling of solidarity with the Jewish people (no matter what his attitude had been in the past or would be in the future) is to misunderstand both Dostoyevsky and the times. If he were to be counted among the progressive elements of society and not be considered reactionary, he would have to speak out in their favor. It is not surprising, then, that *Time* took a stand on this question. What is surprising and, accordingly, revealing was the extraordinary rapidity of *Time's* reaction, as noted earlier in passing. The reply to Aksakov's anti-Semitic editorial of February 16 appeared in *Time's* February issue, which came out on February 27![47] Noteworthy, too, was the position of this article in the layout of the February issue: it was the last of three consecutive polemical articles. The first was Strakhov's "Microscopic Observations," violently attacking Chernyshevsky; the second, Dostoyevsky's unsigned article "Two Camps of Theorists," critical of both the Revolutionary-Democrats and the Slavophiles; and the third, "The Nineteenth Issue of *Day*," relentless in its criticism of the Slavophiles.[48] Though the evidence is not conclusive, in the light of everything we do know there is good reason to believe that this article was hastily prepared to constitute the triad and strike a balance between criticism of the right and criticism of the left. And the fact that this article went beyond the defense of the Jews to refute Aksakov's allegations against the communists and materialists—was this not unassailable proof of *Time's* objectivity, should there be any doubt about it?

Similarly, the decision to publish Lyakub's "Reply to Mr. A. Aleksandrov" in the May issue of *Time* may have been motivated by Dostoyevsky's desire to provide some sort of counterweight to Strakhov's hostile article against the *Contemporary*, "Something about a Discredited Journal," by keeping alive the polemics with *Day* over the Jewish question. It is likewise curious to note that Dostoyevsky returned, if only briefly, to the Jewish question in September. His piece on "The Slavophiles, the Montenegrins and the Westernizers" contained only a fleeting allusion to the famous February article, but it served to underscore a point of contention with the Slavophiles, thereby attenuating the brunt of the criticism unmistakably directed against the Revolutionary-Democrats.[49]

The only collateral evidence that can be adduced in support

of this skeptical if not cynical interpretation of *Time*'s utilization of the Jewish question to its own ends is to be found in an article by the other protagonist of the controversy, Aksakov himself. It was not until May 26, 1862, that he answered the critics of his February editorial in an article entitled "Why Should the Jews in Russia Enjoy the Equality of Rights Denied to Our Schismatics?" Neither mentioning *Time* by name nor, understandably enough, its controversy with the *Contemporary*, Aksakov called into question the sincerity behind "the outburst of indignation among many, primarily Petersburg, journals of progressive and liberal orientation." Taking a malicious pleasure in recognizing that, by their action, they had "given the public new evidence of their nobility, their liberalism, their magnanimity, their sympathy toward their smaller brother *in general* and the oppressed *in particular*," he went on:

> We have often asked ourselves the question: This compassion for humanity, is it a sincere movement of public opinion; in a word, is it a phenomenon engendered by the positive moral demands of society, or is it merely the expression of a protest . . . an ill-defined, abstract sympathy . . . based not on love of what is good, but on the denial of evil? The first, i.e., love, is incomparably more difficult because it demands of man positive acts and sacrifices and, in general, genuine manifestations. The second is much more facile and can, at small expense, place man in an attractive public posture. . . .[50]

To what extent Aksakov's caustic observation applies to Dostoyevsky it is difficult to say, but the fact remains that the Jewish question provided *Time* with a precious polemical instrument that allowed it to maintain its liberal reputation at a difficult moment in the short-lived history of that journal.

4. Svidrigailov's Suicide—Shatov's Credo— The "Rothschild Idea"

IN THE SUMMER of 1862, Dostoyevsky made his first of many subsequent trips abroad, including a long period—1867 to 1871—of forced expatriation from Russia to escape imprisonment for debts. He has described his first encounter with Europe in *Winter Notes on Summer Impressions* (1863), while in *The Gambler* (1866) he has left us some unforgettable and highly flavorful characterizations of the French, German and English in the persons of Mlle. Blanche and Des Grieux, the *Vater*, Mr. Astley. The French would remain for Dostoyevsky throughout his lifetime an object of systematic denigration. His original sympathy and respect for the English weathered Whitehall's or, more precisely, Disraeli's "perfidious" role during the Russo-Turkish War. As for the Germans, who had come in for their share of derision and ridicule, by 1873, the year Dostoyevsky became the editor of the *Citizen* (*Grazhdanin*), they had won his admiration as an effective ally against the Catholic church and socialism, opening the way for the triumph of the Slav idea.

The decade of the sixties was rich in achievement, the most prolific period in Dostoyevsky's literary career: his journals *Time* and *Epoch*, four major works (*The Insulted and the Injured, The House of the Dead, Crime and Punishment, The Idiot*) and a number of important but less ambitious ones (*Winter Notes on Summer Impressions, Notes from the Underground, The Gambler*, etc.). Nothing could stem Dostoyevsky's creative élan. And yet, those ten years were marked by a series of personal tragedies and unrelieved material hardship: a passionate and unrequited love affair with Apollinariya Suslova; the death of his first wife, Mariya Dmitriyevna, followed shortly by that of his brother Mikhail; the closure and bankruptcy of *Epoch* and hounding by creditors; financial obligations toward his brother's family and toward his stepson, Pasha; victimization by a rapacious publisher (Stellovsky); and then more than four years' exile to Europe (accompanied by his second wife, Anna Grigoryevna née Snitkina), epilepsy, roulette, moneylenders, pawnbrokers, deadlines . . .

But it was, undoubtedly, the period of his prolonged and involuntary European exile—April 1867 to July 1871—that exerted a telling influence on the formation (or deformation) of Dostoyevsky's thought and writing during the last fifteen years of his life. In the solitude and loathsome isolation of Europe, Dostoyevsky's belief in the uniqueness of Russia, his conviction that it was predestined to resurrect all of mankind, grew into a veritable obsession. His letters of the period—particularly those to Maikov—affirm and reaffirm his passionate belief that "Russian thought is paving the way for the great spiritual regeneration of the whole world,"[1] that Orthodoxy, the Russian idea and the Russian Christ would emerge triumphant over the moribund civilization of Western Europe. This belief in the election of Russia, nation-Messiah, in the Russian people as the sole God-bearing people, determined Dostoyevsky's implacable hostility toward anyone or anything—individuals, peoples, nations and the ideas they embodied—that represented a challenge to this belief. Hence his repudiation of "the Turgenevs, the Herzens, the Utins, the Chernyshevskys"[2] and his condemnation of revolution and nihilism; hence his abjuration of Belinsky; hence his diatribes against Poland (and the Poles), against Turkey and England (for supporting the Turks), against the Vatican and Roman Catholicism, against France and socialism (culmination of the Catholic idea); hence his growing indulgence, tinged with occasional admiration, toward Germany (though not toward the Germans as such) and Protestantism, an opportune bulwark against the spread of socialism, atheism and materialism pending the triumph of the Slav idea.

And Dostoyevsky's denigration of the Jews? Is not this the deep source from which it springs? Now that it fell to the Great Russian nation to fulfill the Messianic idea, it was essential to disqualify that people who had given the idea to the world. Thus, in this new period and to the end of his life, Dostoyevsky's attitude toward the Jews would take on a new dimension: Jews are no longer just an object of derision and contempt, they represent a dark and sinister force detrimental to the accomplishment of Russia's historical mission. This will be seen most particularly in *The Diary of a Writer*, the subject of the concluding chapters of this study. And even though Dostoyevsky's Jews, now and hencefor-ward, rarely rise above the nineteenth-century stereotype in which he imprisoned them, the explanation may lie in the writer's sub-conscious desire to undermine their claim to a birthright of which he adjudged them no longer worthy.

Until the appearance of the innocuous Jewish "revolutionary" Lyamshin in *The Possessed* (published at the beginning of 1871, some six months prior to Fyodor Mikhailovich's return to St. Pe-tersburg), Jewish characters played only a minor and episodic role in the works of Dostoyevsky. Nameless, phantom-like and incon-spicuous as they may be, they are not, however, devoid of interest. I shall, accordingly, devote some attention to them before pro-ceeding to a more detailed examination of the hapless Lyamshin in the chapter that follows.

Within the context of this study, the interest of *Crime and Punishment* (1866) would be negligible, were it not for the appari-tion, in a scene of extraordinary dramatic intensity, of an anony-mous Jewish character—the fireman who is the sole and helpless witness to the suicide of Svidrigailov.[3] The symbolism of the scene is unquestionable but well-nigh inscrutable.

It will be recalled that Svidrigailov, waking up from a night-mare just at the moment he was about to violate a five-year-old girl, dressed hastily and went out in the deserted, wet, fog-laden streets of early-morning Petersburg. While he was making his way to Petrovsky Island, the site that he had chosen for his suicide, his attention was suddenly arrested by the sight of a high watchtower that loomed up on his left (VI: 394–395):

> "Bah!" he thought, "here's a place, why go on to Petrovsky Island? Here, at least, I'll have an official witness." He almost smiled at this new thought and turned into [Sezhin]skaya Street. A large build-ing stood at this spot with a watchtower. With a shoulder leaning against the massive closed gates of the building, a little man was standing, wrapped in a grey soldier's coat and wearing a copper Achilles helmet on his head. He cast a drowsy, cold, sidelong glance in the direction of the approaching Svidrigailov. His face wore that look of eternal peevish dolor that is so sourly imprinted

on all the faces of the Jewish tribe without exception. Both of them, Svidrigailov and Achilles, scrutinized each other in silence for some time. At last, it struck Achilles as odd for a man not drunk to be standing three steps from him, staring and not saying a word.

"Vat is it, vat is it, now, you vant here?" he muttered, without stirring or changing his position.

"Why nothing, brother, good morning," Svidrigailov answered.

"Dzis is not dze place."

"I'm going to foreign parts, brother."

"To foreign parts?"

"To America."

"America?"

Svidrigailov took out his revolver and cocked it. Achilles raised his eyebrows.

"Vat, vat you're doing, dzis is no place for such prenks (pranks)!"

"And why, tell me, is it not the place?"

"Vai, because dzis is not dze place."

"Well, brother, it's all the same. It's a good place; if anybody asks you, just say he said he was on his way to America."

He pressed the revolver to his right temple.

"No, not here, dzis is not dze place here!" cried Achilles, rousing himself, the pupils of his eyes growing wider and wider.

Svidrigailov pulled the trigger.

Could any more bizarre witness to Svidrigailov's end have been imagined by Dostoyevsky than a Jewish fireman in St. Petersburg of the 1860s! It is almost as if Isai Fomich had doffed his phylactery and donned a fireman's helmet: the voice, the intonation is the same. But one loses oneself in conjectures about the *significance* to be attributed to this pathetic figure. That he held *some* significance for Dostoyevsky is borne out by one brief but direct reference to him in the "Notebooks" for *Crime and Punishment* (VII: 197):

N.B. Vat is it, vat is it, now, you vant here? Dzis is not dze place!
... I'm going to foreign parts, brother.
—To foreign parts?

But nothing more.

For the usually perceptive critic Viktor Shklovsky, "the whole scene ... is intentionally toned down by the rejoinders of the Jewish fireman," and he tries, without much success, to find a parallel in Goethe's treatment of the suicide of Werther.[4] Gus, for his part, remarks that the shot was fired "in an intentionally underscored vaudevillesque situation."[5] But as to what lay behind the author's *intention*, neither Shklovsky nor Gus provides any insight.

A more ambitious effort to interpret the symbolism of this scene was made earlier by the émigré critic A. Z. Steinberg. No other scene in *Crime and Punishment*, in his opinion, is imbued with such profound allegorical significance as Svidrigailov's "sinister farewell to life." Its meaning, which, at first glance, seems inscrutable, is "readily" perceived in "the comparison between Svidrigailov's 'idea' and Dostoyevsky's own view of the essence of the Jewish people."[6] And Steinberg continues:

Svidrigailov is thoroughly revolted by the idea of eternity or immortality as being an infinity devoid of sense; he rebels against the perpetual marking of time, the coming back again, again and again. And what could more graphically illustrate the utter inanity of existence merely for the sake of existence than his meeting with the Jew who for centuries has been leading a shadow-like existence, the Wandering Jew! Like a tamed "parrot," he repeats over and over again his pitiful "this is not the place"—this is not the place to die, to rebel against "the law" of life and its immutability. Let the phantoms grieve and resign themselves to such a negative affirmation of life: a person who is really alive prefers complete self-annihilation to the curse of self-preservation. It is not he who is dragged up before his God like a meek sacrificial victim who has the duty and the right to live, but he—and he alone—who opens up the way to Him and to the Savior anointed by Him.[7]

Whatever reservations one may have about Steinberg's interpretation, he is the only critic (to my knowledge) to have attributed any symbolic significance to the circumstances surrounding Svidrigailov's adieu to life.[8] He has lifted—at least in part—the shroud of mystery in which this uncanny scene is wrapped. But let us carry our investigation further.

To begin with, the sheer incongruity of the situation: the presence in St. Petersburg in the 1860s of a Jewish fireman! The phenomenon is so incredible, so inconceivable as to be utterly absurd. Therein lies the key to the enigma. The scene cannot but have a symbolic meaning, and its action is marked by the presence of this extraordinary witness. Was Svidrigailov's final interlocutor this helmeted Jew or was he not rather a figment of his—or Dostoyevsky's—imagination, a pure phantom? Was not Svidrigailov, in short, the victim of an artistically inspired hallucination? Did not Dostoyevsky set up a confrontation between Svidrigailov and the phantom that was pursuing and haunting him, Dostoyevsky?

The interpretation suggested by these questions is based on another entry in the "Notebooks" for *Crime and Punishment* in which Dostoyevsky queries Svidrigailov about *"His opinion on the apparition of phantoms."* Svidrigailov holds that "phantoms appear only when a person is in a morbid state" and that the notion that they exist is "consequently an absurdity." Though agreeing that "we come into contact with them only when our organism begins to be destroyed" and that "the apparition of phantoms is the sign of a sick organism," Dostoyevsky insists that "it is by no means possible to conclude from this that phantoms do not exist." Svidrigailov's "Opinion" is accompanied by the cryptic marginal notation: "He was, therefore, already thinking about it," a veiled reference, perhaps, to the suicidal act (VII: 165).[9]

No matter how grotesque the form in which this phantom appears, he is omnipresent. Even in the bitingly ironic guise of Achilles—radiant incarnation of virile beauty, strength and valor—the timorous Jew emerges as a bitter reminder to Dostoyevsky that he still may be something more than just the feeble shadow of his former greatness. His brow remains marked by the stamp of the eternal and his ghostlike presence represents an eerie challenge to the Messianic role of the Russian people that Dostoyevsky would like to preempt for them. Until this phantom could be exorcised for all times and ground into ethnographical dust, Dostoyevsky would be assailed by tormenting doubts as to the legitimacy of the exclusive God-bearing vocation and mission of the Russian people.

The Russian Messianic idea found its most virulent and perverse expression in *The Possessed*, where, in the famous conversation between Stavrogin and Shatov, Dostoyevsky placed these words in the mouth of his irresolute hero (X: 199–200):

> I reduce God to the attribute of nationality? . . . On the contrary, I raise the people to God. . . . The people—the people is the body of God. A people is only a people so long as it has its own god

and excludes all other gods in the world irreconcilably; so long as it believes that by its god it will conquer and drive out of the world all other gods. Such, from the beginning of time, has been the belief of all great peoples, all who were in any way remarkable, who were in the vanguard of humanity. . . . The Jews lived only to await the coming of the true God and left the world the true God. . . . If a great people does not believe that it is the sole (the one and only) repository of the truth, if it does not believe that it alone is qualified and destined to raise up and save all mankind by its truth, it ceases then and there to be a great people and turns into ethnographical material, not into a great nation. A truly great people can never reconcile itself to a secondary role in humanity or even to a primary role, it must occupy the first, the exclusive role. A people that loses that faith is no longer a people. But the truth is one and, therefore, there can be only one people from among all the peoples that possesses the true God, even though the other peoples have their own gods and great ones at that. The sole "God-bearing" people is the Russian people. . . .[10]

There is, perhaps, no other passage in Dostoyevsky that more eloquently acknowledges the debt of the Russian Messianic idea to Judaic thought. But with no less eloquence does Dostoyevsky (again through Shatov) proclaim that the torch has now passed to the Russian people, "the sole 'God-bearing' people on earth" who are "destined to renew and save the world in the name of a new God and who have been vouchsafed the keys of life and of the new word" (X: 196). He refuses to admit that there is no other Messianism but the Hebraic or, as Berdyayev would say, that "the messianism within Christendom is always a rejudaization of Christianity."[11]

In other words, Dostoyevsky sees "the Russians as the God-chosen people, the reincarnation of Israel."[12] He thus replaces true Messianism, which is universalist, by its antithesis—a nationalistic, even chauvinistic Messianism. To step over the thin line that separates a national from a nationalistic Messianic consciousness is to vitiate the true sense of a national vocation for leading mankind to salvation; it is, in its exclusiveness, the very negation of that vocation. It is precisely this pseudo-Messianic doctrine that is espoused by Dostoyevsky-Shatov, the selfsame belief that Dostoyevsky, in *The Diary of a Writer*, would impute to the Jews, seeing it as the source of their national exclusiveness, to wit "the belief that there exists in the world but one national personality—the Jew—and though others may exist, it makes no difference, it is to be presumed that they don't exist at all" (12: 83–84).

Dostoyevsky cannot legitimize the role he claimed for Russia without eliminating, in a manner of speaking, that other people whose existence invalidated his claim. The only way out of the dilemma was to contend that the Jews no longer existed. There's no denying they had existed, that they *had been* the chosen people who brought the Messianic idea to the world, but, after having "left the world the true God," they ceased to exist and became nothing more than "ethnographical material." The mere assertion that the Jews no longer existed was not enough, however, for Dostoyevsky; his mind was still tormented by grave doubts on that score. In his subconscious desire to dispel them, he conjured up the Jew with the conscious design of maligning and repudiating him. And the Jew that emerges from the torn and despondent mind of Dostoyevsky is not the venerated biblical sage and prophet. He has even lost title to his name—*yevrei*; he is the "Yid" —the *zhid, zhidok, zhidishka, zhidyonok.* He is the moneylender par excellence, the speculator, the thief, the informer, the spy, the buffoon, the lickspittle and even . . . the ritual murderer. He is the phantom come from the netherworld to accompany Svidrigailov on his final journey, a specter to whom Dostoyevsky would have willfully refused the breath of life—for he was unworthy of it—had he been able to conclude that "phantoms do not exist." And he could not even bring himself to conclude, once and for all, that the Jew existed only as a phantom.

Through the thick morning mist hanging over the Little Neva, a shapeless form came into view. A pale glimmer of light, like a flickering candle, revealed a melancholic face, its drawn features marked by centuries of suffering and affliction. Dostoyevsky recognized it at once and recoiled in horror.[13]

The philosophical ramifications of Dostoyevsky's anti-Semitism should not be allowed to obscure the lowly origins from which it sprang. It is clear that his fundamental politico-metaphysical attitude toward the Jews grew up out of—or even was predetermined by—an innate, almost organic aversion, a phenomenon customarily described as *natsionalnoye ottalkivaniye.* For all of his brilliant psychological probings into the darker recesses of others' minds, Dostoyevsky failed or refused to recognize within himself—when the question was put to him—any *a priori* feelings of repugnance toward the Jews.

Are we to infer, then, that he judged them *a posteriori*? But, then, it may be recalled that prior to his departure abroad in 1867, Dostoyevsky had been in contact with only *two* Jews for any length of time: Isaac Bumstehl (Bumstein) and N. F. Katz, a conscript with whom Dostoyevsky served in the same line battalion in Semipalatinsk following his release from the prison camp in Omsk.[14] This can hardly be described as a great deal in the way of firsthand experience. No, what counted for Dostoyevsky was his notion of what a Jew was, an instinctive feeling indistinguishable from that found in the conventional anti-Semite. For Dostoyevsky, "Jew" and "usurer" were synonymous, an established fact that required no substantiation. Never mind if not a single Jew was among the army of creditors who dogged him from the time *Epoch* was founded until his flight abroad to escape them.[15]

It is against this background that the evolution or, more precisely, the aggravation of Dostoyevsky's concern over the Jewish question during the four years of his European exile is best apprehended. The early period—April 14 to August 24, 1867—has been chronicled by his bride of a few months, Anna Grigoryevna.[16] In the opening pages of her *Diary*, describing their journey from St. Petersburg to Berlin, she noted down a number of incidents that other travelers, less sensitive to the Jewish question than the Dostoyevskys, might have considered not worth recording. Their first stopover was Vilno, a city with a large Jewish population, where they arrived early in the afternoon of April 15. It was Holy Saturday and the streets were bustling with activity: "The Yids with their Yidenehs, wearing yellow and red shawls and kerchiefs on their heads, were especially numerous."[17] Rising early the following morning to catch their train, the Dostoyevskys were just about to leave the hotel room when "some Yid came in asking if we would like to buy something from him." Anna Grigoryevna continues:

> We had forgotten to bring along soap and so I bought a cake from him for fifteen kopeks. A friend of his offered to sell us a Polish

icon that, he said, had cost him fifteen rubles but which he would sell us cheaper; we said no, however. Before long, our room was filled with Yids who had come to see us off; each one of them said good-bye to us, they all grabbed hold of our baggage and, in the end, they all asked for tips. We had already taken our seats in the carriage and had gone quite a distance when suddenly a Yid came running alongside; he wanted to sell us two amber cigarette holders; we sent him packing.[18]

And their traveling companion in the smoker from Eydtkuhnen to Berlin was "some Yid or other."[19] Decidedly, an inauspicious beginning.

In the months that followed, Dostoyevsky lost heavily at the gaming tables in Baden, a situation that placed him at the mercy of the moneylenders and pawnbrokers, in particular, two Jews—Weismann and Josel. Whole pages of Anna Grigoryevna's *Diary* are filled with pathetic scenes of petty haggling between the Dostoyevskys and these individuals.[20] Notwithstanding the fact that neither Weismann nor Josel appears to have been particularly unscrupulous in his dealings, there can be no doubt that Dostoyevsky keenly felt the humiliation of having to resort to their services at all. The following fragment from his wife's *Diary* will serve as an illustration:

> I got back home and did some ironing. It was two o'clock already, but no sign of Fedya. The frightening thought entered my mind that my poor Fedya must be loitering around Weismann's house waiting for him to show up. . . . Finally, at two o'clock Fedya returned and explained that he had not found Weismann at home and that his sister had asked him to sit down and wait while she was eating. . . . Fedya waited for over an hour. (Poor, poor Fedya! He who is so good, so talented, so noble, has to sit around with some Yids or other, because Weismann is almost certainly a Yid.)[21]

How could Dostoyevsky have forgotten such affronts? There is undoubtedly a connection between the indignities he suffered at the hands of a Josel or a Weismann and his stigmatization of the usurious practices of the Jews in their exploitation of the Russian masses, a dominant theme in his journalistic writings of the seventies. But during the same period a distinctly new and, in many respects, more fundamental theme also emerged from Dostoyevsky's pen—the "Rothschild" theme. Though it may be temerarious to suggest a connection between the genesis of this theme and the indignities he swallowed at Baden, the coincidence is, nevertheless, an interesting one.

Before becoming the major theme of part 1 of *A Raw Youth* (1875), the Rothschild theme found its first expression in the "Notebooks" for *The Idiot*, although in the final version of the novel (1868) it received only limited development. The theme reappeared in the "Notebooks" for *The Brothers Karamazov* only to be suppressed in the definitive text (1879–1880).

Dostoyevsky first encountered the "Rothschild idea" at the end of the forties, when he was a member of the Petrashevsky Circle. Mikhail Petrashevsky, when speaking of James de Rothschild, the youngest and most influential member of the family, would refer to him as "King of the Jews," while attributing the persecution of the socialists in the West to the coalition of the liberals and the bankers. He accused Rothschild and other capitalists of turning the credit mechanism and manipulating the stock market to their own nefarious ends. "There is not a single national disturbance," he claimed, "that some clever banker like Rothschild, after apparently sustaining initial losses, has not capitalized on." [22]

But what was the spark that rekindled Dostoyevsky's interest in the personality of Rothschild twenty years after—in the late sixties and throughout the seventies? More likely than not, it was the publication in Geneva, in 1867, of part 5 of Alexander Herzen's memoirs, *My Past and Thoughts*, which contained a chapter (39) entitled "Money and Police—The Emperor James Rothschild and the Banker Nicholas Romanov—Police and Money." The episode that Herzen relates—the details of which may be omitted here—revealed the extent of the political power of the Baron James ("His Majesty," the "King of the Jews," as he also describes him), a power so immense that it obliged the tsar of all Russia to submit to his will. And Herzen recalls these words of Rothschild: "You'll see how they'll come round, I'll show them what it means to play with me." [23]

In the "Notebooks" for *The Idiot* (IX: 140–288), both the general theme of usury and the King-of-the-Jews leitmotiv are broadly developed. The "uncle" who was to have been the main character of the novel and was the natural father of Myshkin is a usurer (IX: 142). With his natural son he speaks "frankly about the role of usurer" (IX: 175); Myshkin and the uncle's other natural son "speak about usurers" (IX: 175); under the heading "About Uncle and Usury" there appears the first allusion to the Rothschild theme: "About the King of the Jews" (IX: 176), followed shortly thereafter by this thought of the Idiot (who in the "Notebooks" bears scant resemblance to Myshkin of the novel): "Design for the future: I shall be a banker, King of the Jews, and I'll keep them all in chains at my feet. 'Either to dominate them all like a tyrant or die for them all on the cross . . .'" (IX: 180).²⁴ To the question of why the heroine (i.e., Aglaya) should not love and marry him, the Idiot answers: "'Me? A monster . . . the son of a usurer, despised and hated by everyone?'" (IX: 181); Umetskaya (who was to have been the heroine of the novel) delivered a "terrible tirade to the Uncle about *the King of the Jews*," then "became engrossed in reading the Gospels" and "disconcerted the Uncle" (juxtaposition again of the two themes) (IX: 183); further on, in a very obscure context, an emphatic notation "*Tirade about the King of the Jews*," with explicit reference to Umetskaya: "Fits of Jewish [*zhidovskaya*] stinginess" (IX: 212–213); Varya (the general's daughter) talks about "the King of the Jews" (IX: 214); Ganya has a "conversation with Ptitsyn about the King of the Jews" (IX: 246); on several pages devoted primarily to Ganya, the "King of the Jews" is mentioned five times (IX: 261–262); and, finally, Velmonchek (perhaps Radomsky of the novel) "wanted to dupe Aglaya, but he got incensed over the Yids and had it out with Aglaya. (Death of Uncle, and *the Yids were hounding* [him])" (IX: 270).

As noted earlier, in the final version of *The Idiot* the Rothschild theme found only the most limited expression—on just two occasions. In part 1, we find Ganya describing his financial ambitions to Myshkin: "In our country, though everyone is a usurer at heart, few have the courage of their convictions, but with me it will be a different story . . . in fifteen years people will say: 'Why there's Ivolgin, the King of the Jews'" (VIII: 105).²⁵ Ganya does not return to this theme until the beginning of part 4, where, in a conversation with his brother-in-law Ptitsyn, on whom he and his parents were dependent for support, he berates him for his indifference to the idea of "becoming a Rothschild": "Since you are a usurer," he exclaims, "go all the way, squeeze people, make them cough up money, be somebody, become the King of the Jews!"

Without losing his composure, Ptitsyn argues "that he was not doing anything dishonest and that Ganya had no reason to call him a Yid" (VIII: 387). Dostoyevsky thus explicitly equates "King of the Jews" with "Yid."

As to the more general theme of usury, which figured so largely in the "Notebooks," it, too, found only pale reflection in the novel, and in a scene that was absent from the original plan. In a comical interlude reminiscent of Gogol, Lebedev, one of Rogozhin's cronies, is put upon by his nephew for his duplicity in a scandalous affair. Implored by an old woman to represent her in a trial against "a scurvy moneylender who had bilked her of five hundred rubles, all that she possessed," Lebedev had, instead, acted for the usurer "some Yid or other by the name of Seidler" (VIII: 161). The artistic motivation for this episode is obscure, but the inspiration for it is readily traceable to Dostoyevsky's ordeals with the Baden moneylenders: the Weismanns, the Josels, the Meiers, the Benders and so forth. A name like Seidler bears too close a resemblance to the others to have been chosen accidentally.

Amid the glittering multiplicity of thematic strands that are woven into the literary fabric of *A Raw Youth* (1875), the warp and woof of the novel is the Rothschild idea. By July 1874, Dostoyevsky had decided that the hero of his novel would be "an adolescent" infatuated with "the idea of getting rich," of "becoming a Rothschild" (XVI: 24). The story of *A Raw Youth* is that of Arkady Dologoruky's frenetic search—amid the seething cauldron of ideas of his time—for the answer to the question of how man must live; and it is also the story of the answer he found to that question. And he could not have found it, Dostoyevsky assures us through the intermediary of Arkady's spiritual mentor and protector, Nikolai Semyonovich, had he not been originally inspired by the Rothschild idea. "Your 'idea,'" writes Nikolai in a letter cited by the narrator, Arkady, at the end of the novel, "preserved you from those of Messrs. Dergachov & Co." (XIII: 452). This is, as it were, the coda that concludes and defines the symphonic structure of the novel that opens with the Rothschild theme, which, after reaching a crescendo halfway through part 1 (chapter 5), fades into the background.

The setting in which Dostoyevsky introduces the "idea" still

hidden beneath the level of Arkady's consciousness is an auction
at the St. Petersburg apartment of one Mrs. Lebrecht. The hero
is bent on putting a still inchoate idea to the test. This is how Arkady remembers the scene, the crowds of people milling around
the first room off the hallway: "half of them were dealers, the others, by the looks of them, were either spectators or amateurs, or
people operating for the Lebrechts; there were also merchants,
and Yids eyeing the objects in gold, and a few people who were
'trimly' dressed" (XIII: 37).[26]

In the grips of a violent emotion, Arkady vacillates like a
gambler unable to decide where to place his bet, and his agitation
grows as one object after another—far beyond his means—is
knocked down. His choice finally settles on a thoroughly useless
object, an album bound in red leather. There are no other bidders,
and he carries it away for two rubles five kopeks. Feverishly examining his acquisition, he decides that "it was a piece of junk."
Just as he is about to reconcile himself to his loss, he is approached
by a well-dressed gentleman who, having arrived too late to put
in a bid for the object, now offers to buy it from him. Unabashed-
ly, Arkady asks ten rubles for it. Ten rubles?! "He looked at me
wide-eyed; I was well dressed, I didn't look one bit like a Yid or a
dealer" (XIII: 37). His entreaties are in vain; Arkady remains adamant (XIII: 39):

> "Come, now, you know that's dishonest! Two rubles and you're
> asking ten?"
> "Dishonest, why? It's the market!"
> "A market here, what are you talking about? . . ."
> "Wherever there's a demand, there's a market. . . . Look here,
> when the late James Rothschild. . . ."

And the "idea" was born.

Arkady's reflections on how he intended to realize the "idea"
are decidedly elementary. It takes no more, he assures us, than
strength of character, a spirit of sacrifice, caution and ruse. Thievery was, of course, out of the question for an Arkady. Moreover,
he had long ago made up his mind that he would never be "either
a pawnbroker or a moneylender: for that, there are the Yids and
the Russians who have neither intelligence nor character. Loans
and usury are the business of mediocrities" (XIII: 69).

But is money an ideal worthy of man? Do not the problems of society, of justice and humanity impose other obligations on him? Arkady replies: "But do you know how I would use my wealth? Is there anything immoral or base about these millions falling out of the dirty and harmful clutches of a multitude of Yids into the hands of a clearheaded and strong-minded recluse directing his penetrating gaze on the world" (XIII: 76)?

The voice is Arkady's, but the thought is Dostoyevsky's. For a Dostoyevsky, such a consideration would certainly be the moral justification of money, though it bears no relevance to the "Rothschild idea." Arkady's justification is the power to do good that his future millions will make possible. He desires money only because it will allow him to achieve the ultimate expression of his will: to distribute his wealth among mankind and to fall into nothingness —to become a simple beggar. And, thus, "in my poverty, I would at once become twice as rich as a Rothschild" (XIII: 76)!

This is as far as Arkady goes in the elaboration of his "idea." But he soon becomes aware of the irreconcilability between the ideal he aspires to and the means required to attain it. As the plot develops and reveals with cold clarity the terrible and ignominious power of money, the hero becomes increasingly disillusioned with the Rothschild myth, and he sets out in quest of an alternative path for mankind's salvation. In his fervent search, he turns to his natural father Versilov and plies him with questions: "How will the states as we know them and the world come to an end and how will social harmony be restored?" Versilov, at first, parries the questions, but finally consents to speak (XIII: 172):

> "I think it will all come to pass in a quite ordinary way. . . . To put it quite simply, all states, despite their balanced budgets and 'absence of deficits,' *un beau matin* will find themselves in utter confusion and refuse, each and everyone of them, to honor their obligations so as to pave the way for a general recovery in a whole-sale bankruptcy. Meanwhile, all the conservative elements in the world will try to thwart their design because as shareholders and creditors they'll be left holding the bag and bankruptcy won't be to their liking. Then, not surprisingly, a sort of general oxidation will get under way; *a lot of Yids* [*mnogo zhida*] *will come along and the reign of the Yids* [*zhidovskoye tsarstvo*] *will begin*; and then all those who never had any shares or anything else for that

matter, that is, all the paupers, will naturally have no intention of participating in the oxidation . . . A struggle will ensue and after seventy-seven defeats the paupers will annihilate the shareholders, confiscate their shares and take their places. . . ."[27]

"What, then, is to be done?" Arkady persists. To which Versilov replies: "the best thing to do is to do nothing." But the adolescent will not be put off: "How must I live?" he cries. "Be honest, never tell a lie, covet not your neighbor's house, in a word, reread the ten commandments" (XIII: 172).

This was still not the answer he was seeking, and his quest would be a long one. Ultimately he found the answer in his talks with Makar Ivanovich (the precursor of the *starets* Zosima), and it was summed up by one word: *blagoobraziye* or beauty. It was to be attained by heeding the words of Christ: "Go and distribute your riches and become the servant of all." If you remain true to this precept "you will acquire not a small fortune . . . but the whole universe" (XIII: 311).

To be sure, when Arkady was still under the spell of the "idea" (Rothschild), he had dreamt of returning all those millions to society, but then—as he recognized now—this was but the arrogant expression of a "depraved will," a thirst for power and splendid isolation, wholly alien to any idea of humility, charity or communion with and service to the people.

Fired by Makar Ivanovich's evangelism, Arkady blurts out: "but that's communism, absolute communism, you're preaching there," though he hastens to admit his incompetence in the matter (XIII: 311).

The adolescent, then, ends by embracing the idea of a Christian socialism: truth is in Christ and there is no other truth. And apprehending this truth, he perceives the emptiness of the Rothschild idea.

As remarkable as the novel is in its description of Arkady's spiritual itinerary, it betrays, nonetheless, a fundamental weakness, the lack of conviction that marks its treatment of the "Rothschild idea." Dostoyevsky himself realized it. Early on in the narrative, he confesses to his inability to grapple with the theme, placing these words in the mouth of his hero: "I have finished with my 'idea.' If I have described it insipidly, superficially, it is I who am to blame, not the 'idea' " (XIII: 77). Never does Arkady's "idea" achieve the intensity it was originally meant to have, that fixity of purpose, that, for example, characterized another idea, the "idea" that drove Raskolnikov to his crime; it is never anything more than the dream and fancy of an adolescent's mind.[28] And when Dostoyevsky attempts to persuade us that it was this idea that "preserved" Arkady from the revolutionary contagion of his time, that it was this idea that enabled him to find the truth in Christ, one cannot but feel that he was guided more by considerations of artistic unity than those of artistic truth.

The "Notebooks" for *The Brothers Karamazov* (1878–1879) provide further evidence of Dostoyevsky's attachment to the Rothschild theme. And the fact that it was not incorporated in the novel itself reflects, perhaps, once again the writer's inability to give it artistic expression. The "Notebooks" reveal clearly, moreover, the symbolic value that Dostoyevsky attributed to the Rothschild theme.

It is already significant that the references to Rothschild are found in the pages of the "Notebooks" concerned with "the confession of the *starets*," pages 49–63 of the manuscript (XV: 243–254), which relate to book 6 ("The Russian Monk") of the novel. Thus, on page 50 (XV: 243): "*Vide* 'The Russian solution of the question! . . . the dream that all are brothers and not 1/10 over 9/10. . . . (1) Rothschild. . . . IN THE WORDS OF THE STARETS. . . . (36) It's not possible that the world should exist for 1/10 of mankind. . . ."; page 52 (XV: 244): "(55) Be ye brothers and there shall be brotherhood, or else—the Tower of Babel"; pages 52–53 (XV: 245): "(67). . . .—1/10. Without brothers, there will be no brotherhood. . . . I began my wanderings—great confusion, solution of the 1/10 problem"; pages 55–56 (XV: 247): "And then give everything away. Rothschild. Christ. Just as God gives freedom to all. . . .—It's not possible that 1/10. —And that's what we (in Russia) are heading for"; and finally, on page 57 (XV: 248): "—1/10, that cannot be. Why such grumbling and discontent? Just because of that. . . . I walked over Russia, 1/10" and so on and so forth.

A. S. Dolinin, who published the first edition of the "Notebooks" for *The Brothers Karamazov*, was the first to call attention to the significance of the "1/10–9/10" motif. This curious formula represented, in his view—and it is wholly warranted—Dostoyevsky's conception of the state of the world after the French Revolution, a world in which three-quarters of mankind were enslaved and exploited by the other one-quarter. For Dolinin, "Rothschild" symbolizes the domination of the bourgeoisie; and "Jesus," placed in immediate juxtaposition, evokes the reign of Christ. Together they symbolize the two diametrically opposed paths of human history.[29] It was between these two paths that Arkady had made his choice, and it was Dostoyevsky's innermost conviction that, despite the obstacles along the way, the Russian people, the God-bearing people, would make the same choice as Arkady. And he vigorously affirmed this belief in this entry on page 60 of the manuscript (XV: 251–252): "Well, there's no denying it, things are foul in Russia . . . The kulaks, the middlemen, but it's not all black, the precious diamond has been overlooked. —The God-bearing people, how polished it is."

We can, therefore, conclude with Dolinin that the Rothschild theme in Dostoyevsky's mind is inextricably joined with the Christ motif. But can we at the same time conclude that Dostoyevsky associates the idea of domination by the bourgeoisie, implicit in the Rothschild theme, with the explicit idea of domination by a *Jewish* bourgeoisie? All told, probably not, even though Dostoyevsky now and then allows some doubt to subsist on this score, as seen, for example, in Versilov's vision of the establishment—ephemeral, to be sure—of a *zhidovskoye tsarstvo*. Somewhat equivocal, too, are the frequent allusions to the "King of the Jews," which rumble like an ominous refrain through the "Notebooks" for *The Idiot* but become decidedly less foreboding when the thundering epithet is identified by the name it only personified in *A Raw Youth* and the "Notebooks" for *The Brothers Karamazov*. This is not to say, however, that the "Rothschild idea" is formulated with any particular clarity: in Ganya's unimaginative mind, it is the ultimate expression of usury as practiced by the Jews, but Arkady completely divorces it from such a vulgar association by leaving usury up to "the Yids and the Russians who have neither intelligence nor character." On the other hand, as we shall see, time and again in *The Diary of a Writer* Dostoyevsky gives free rein to sentiments worthy of the frothy ravings of the Black Hundreds. But if he takes a malevolent pleasure in exaggerating the perfidious role of the Jews, it is not to be forgotten that he points an accusing finger at those elements in Russian society—the kulaks, the money grubbers and even priests who would sell the words of Christ for money—who are bringing the people to their ruin. And when he jotted down the following entry in the "Notebooks" for *The Brothers Karamazov* on page 60 (XV: 250): "Here the 1/10. The Yid's gold, that's not the issue," he had finally grasped and given expression to a fundamental truth. The doubts that may have assailed him—and are they not implicit in his affirmation?—seem to have vanished, at least toward the end of his life.

5. The Possessed

HAVING DEPARTED from the strict chronology of our narrative in an effort to trace the origins and the development of the "Rothschild theme" in Dostoyevsky's works, let us turn the clock back some ten years to examine—from the particular standpoint of our study—the novel that heralded the writer's return to St. Petersburg from European exile in 1871: *The Possessed*.[1] In this virulent satire of the revolutionary idea, Dostoyevsky artfully introduced the unprepossessing figure of a Jewish revolutionary in the person of Lyamshin. Dwarfed by the towering characters of Nikolai Stavrogin and Pyotr Verkhovensky and his father, Stepan, relegated to a minor role in the secret revolutionary society of five of which he was a member, Lyamshin has failed to arouse the interest of literary critics almost to the point of being completely ignored.[2]

And yet, the denouement of the novel—the denunciation of the conspiracy to the authorities following the murder of Shatov —hinges on the confession of Lyamshin. This fact alone suggests that Dostoyevsky attributed much greater importance to the "Yidel" (*zhidok*)—as Lyamshin is first introduced to the reader (X: 30)—than the critics have allowed us to believe. Moreover, as a careful reading of the novel makes clear, Dostoyevsky, with a few masterful strokes, brushed a portrait of Lyamshin that, though verging on flat, conventional caricature, is sufficiently fleshed out to justify artistically the role of Judas he reserved for him from the outset. Nor is it sheer coincidence that Dostoyevsky's traitor is a Jew—an emancipated Jew as only a revolutionary could be— and, in all probability, a convert.[3] But convert or not, his speech uncontaminated by even the slightest trace of a Yiddish intonation, his surname irreproachably Russian, Lyamshin—Dostoyevsky makes sure—possesses the entire panoply of unattractive characteristics that brand him unmistakably as the Yid incarnate.

Authenticity and objectivity were not, of course, the first of Dostoyevsky's concerns in drawing the portraits of the revolutionaries in *The Possessed*; no one is spared. And yet, his portrayal of Lyamshin is much more heavily caricatured than that of the Russian revolutionary. It is not a caricature of a Jewish revolutionary that Dostoyevsky has drawn, but rather that of a feckless, cowardly, occasionally buffoonish little Jew, a "*zhid* Yankel," whose participation in a revolutionary plot is, moreover, utterly inconceivable.

So much is known of the actual events and real-life personalities underlying the conception of *The Possessed* that it is impossible to dismiss Lyamshin as simply a fortuitous character, a pure figment of the author's imagination. It is almost superfluous to recall that the central theme of the novel was largely inspired by the Nechayev affair—the arrest in St. Petersburg, in November 1869, of Sergei Nechayev and the members of the secret revolutionary society *Narodnaya rasprava* (The People's Vengeance) for the murder of the student Ivanov, a dissident member of the circle. Apart from Nechayev, who was the leader of the group, P. Uspensky, A. Kuznetsov, I. Pryzhov and N. Nikolayev were charged with the crime. Dostoyevsky, we know, used them (and other contemporary figures, too) as prototypes for some of his characters in the novel. Thus, solely with regard to the revolutionary quintet in *The Possessed*, the following parallels have been established: *Pyotr Verkhovensky* (the leader) = Nechayev; *Liputin* = A. P. Milyukov; *Virginsky* = Uspensky (and Kuznetsov); *Shigalyov* = V. A. Zaitsev; *Tolkachenko* = Pryzhov; and *Lyamshin* = ?.[4]

Lyamshin alone remains unaccounted for. Who, then, is the original model on whom he was patterned?[5]

It is reasonable to assume that Lyamshin's prototype is to be found among the Jewish revolutionaries of the period; and the pursuit of our investigation in this direction cannot, by the nature of things, take us too far afield. For, with but a single exception, no Jew played any appreciable role in the Russian revolutionary movement until the early seventies.[6] Not a single Jew was involved either in the Nechayev affair or in the no less celebrated (though unsuccessful) plot of the Ishutin-Karakozov group against the life of Alexander II in 1866. The one and only exception was Nikolai Isaakovich Utin, the son of a converted Jew, who, in the early sixties, was a leading figure in the secret organization *Zemlya i volya* (Land and Liberty) and an active participant in the student movement at the University of St. Petersburg. A police report in 1862 went so far as to describe him as "the right hand of Chernyshevsky," which may have been a slight exaggeration even though the two men are known to have been very close to one another. Tracked by the authorities, Utin fled to London in the summer of 1863, where his arrival was announced by Herzen in *Kolokol* (no. 169, August 15, 1863). At the end of 1864 and the beginning of 1865, he participated in the Congress of Russian Emigrés in Geneva. From 1868 to 1870, he was a close collaborator of *Narodnoye delo* (The People's Cause), becoming editor-in-chief when Bakunin, the founder of the journal, withdrew over policy differences. A vigorous opponent of the anarchical doctrines of Bakunin and Nechayev, Utin played an instrumental role in the organization of the Russian Section of the Internationale and supported Marx in his struggle against Bakunin. After the Hague Conference and the dissolution of the Russian Section of the Internationale, Utin took up residence in Brussels, where he studied engineering, and gradually withdrew from the revolutionary movement.[7]

Is there reason to believe that Dostoyevsky knew Utin personally? According to Dolinin, it was quite possible that Dostoyevsky, who, it will be recalled, lived in Geneva from August 1867 to May 1868, had met him at Ogaryov's, where both were frequent visitors.[8] At the very least, he knew *of* Utin and, moreover, held him in low esteem. For in a letter to Maikov, sent just a few days after his arrival in Geneva, Dostoyevsky wrote: "And what, tell me, have they brought us, the Turgenevs, the Herzens, the Utins, the Chernyshevskys, to replace the supreme divine beauty that they spit upon? They are all so obscenely vain, so shamelessly petulant, so frivolously haughty that for the life of me I can't understand what they want and who will support them."[9] Though this was the only time Dostoyevsky ever referred to Utin in his letters, the fact that he mentions him in such illustrious company is evidence that he considered him an influential political personality and somebody who was also known to Maikov.

The plausibility of the Utin-Lyamshin affiliation is also suggested by another circumstance. For Dostoyevsky, the name Utin evoked not only the image of Nikolai the revolutionary, but that of his elder brother Yevgeny, who had gone abroad with him. Now the Utin brothers were close acquaintances of Apollinariya Suslova; Yevgeny was, in fact, a frequent visitor to her Paris apartment in 1864–1865, and her lover to boot.[10] Dostoyevsky, still infatuated by Suslova at the time, could not but have been aware of their liaison, which must have caused him deep chagrin. If our theory about an Utin-Lyamshin link is correct, it goes a long way toward explaining the virulence of Dostoyevsky's characterization of Lyamshin in *The Possessed*. For Dostoyevsky did not suffer rivals gladly; he would not have missed the opportunity to avenge the real or imagined affronts to his amour propre suffered at the hands of the Utins at a delicate phase of his relationship with Suslova. The hypothesis is not as audacious as it might seem at first glance, particularly when one remembers that Dostoyevsky used *The Possessed* to square a number of personal accounts and that the dramatis personae include, besides Nechayev and his acolytes, Granovsky, Turgenev, Nekrasov, Herzen, Belinsky, Chernyshevsky, Ogaryov, Pisarev and Saltykov-Shchedrin. In some instances, the disguise is so transparent that the identity of the model is easily established; in others, it is more impenetrable. At any rate, the device is so extensively employed in *The Possessed* that it is reasonable to assume that further prototypical study of the characters of the novel would reveal associations that have not yet been fully determined. Viewing, then, the hypothesis of an Utin-Lyamshin parallel with all the circumspection that the absence of conclusive evidence demands, let us now examine Dostoyevsky's portrayal of Lyamshin.

As noted earlier, Lyamshin is a decidedly episodic figure whose two fleeting appearances in part 1 of the novel would hardly seem to predestine him for the capital role Dostoyevsky assigns to him in the denouement of the plot. It would almost seem that at the end of part 1—one-third through the novel—the author did not quite realize himself the role our hero would play in succeeding installments, but Dostoyevsky is quick to dispel this erroneous impression early in part 2, showing that he knows only too well where he is heading.

It is shortly after the novel opens that the reader makes the acquaintance of the *zhidok* Lyamshin, an occasional visitor to the home of Stepan Trofimovich Verkhovensky, where a small circle of liberal intellectuals gathered regularly. But it was not for his intellectual accomplishments that he was welcomed into the group: "When things got really boring, the Yidel Lyamshin (a minor postal employee), an excellent pianist, sat down to play, and between pieces he would imitate [the sounds of] a pig, a thunderstorm, a childbirth with the first cry of the baby and so forth and so on; this was, in fact, the only reason why he was invited" (X: 30–31). With that, Lyamshin vanishes and nothing more is heard of him until Shatov—in that memorable scene where he proclaims his faith in the God-bearing mission of the Russian people—discloses to Stavrogin that, fearing for his life, he has spent his "last deniers on buying a revolver from that good-for-nothing Lyamshin" (X: 190). A detail of little importance at the time—or so it seemed—it, in fact, paves the way long in advance for the decisive confrontation between Shatov and Lyamshin just a few hours before the former is murdered (X: 445–447) and proves that Dostoyevsky had determined from the outset the role that Lyamshin would play.

In the interval between these two events in which the revolver serves as the unifying element, Dostoyevsky gets down to the task of filling in Lyamshin's portrait. With a deft hand, he applies a stroke here, a stroke there, introducing episodes or seemingly trivial details the significance of which is not immediately apparent. The story of a young couple on their wedding night is one such episode. Discovering that his wife's virtue is not intact, the husband, to avenge "the stain on his honor," roughs up his bride. News of the scandal leaks out thanks to Lyamshin, who has witnessed the incident and who "as soon as day dawned, made the rounds spreading the amusing tale" (X: 250). Clearly a parallel, if not a direct line, is to be drawn between Lyamshin's conduct at this time and his later denunciation of the revolutionary conspirators.

While everyone in the novel finds this incident rather entertaining, the same cannot be said for another one "of a very special character" that Dostoyevsky, in his role of narrator, relates directly thereafter and qualifies as "intolerable." It concerns the first of two acts of sacrilege that are all the more reprehensible when it is remembered that they were perpetrated by a Jew.[11] The story is told of an itinerant bookseller, a respectable lady, who arrived in town selling gospels. The next thing you learn is that "that culprit Lyamshin"—abetted, it is true, by a young divinity student—"managed to slip into the bookseller's bag . . . a whole package of lascivious obscene photographs" (X: 251). Only thanks to the timely intervention of the police is she saved from the wrath of the outraged public and subsequently released when her innocence is established.

Under normal circumstances, this incident would have been reason enough to bar Lyamshin from the salon held by Yuliya Mikhailovna, the wife of von Lembke, governor-general of the province. But, as it happens, preparations are in full swing for a large reception she is giving, and Lyamshin has composed a musical interlude for the occasion. His friends implore Yuliya Mikhailovna to give him another chance and persuade her to audition his satirical musical fantasy entitled "The Franco-Prussian War." That very same evening (right after the bookseller affair), they bring him around to the house. Lyamshin sits down at the piano and begins to play. As the piece opens, the air fills with the vibrant strains of the *Marseillaise* and then, scarcely audible at first, a countertheme—*Mein Lieber Augustin*—insinuates itself, gaining vigor, fading out, then returning with ever greater authority. The *Marseillaise* counterattacks and succeeds, momentarily, in drowning out *Augustin*, but to no avail. By the time the final chord is struck, the *Marseillaise* has surrendered ignominiously to the arrogantly triumphant and impudent strains of *Augustin*.[12]

Lyamshin's performance is wildly applauded, and Yuliya Mikhailovna has to admit that she is incapable of sending him packing. "The scoundrel really did have talent," the narrator also has to admit, but lest this begrudging admission be misconstrued by the reader, Dostoyevsky injects a note of caution: "Stepan Trofimovich assured me on one occasion that the greatest artists could be the worst scoundrels and that there was nothing incompatible between the two." But, as if that were not enough, he adds: "The word got around later that Lyamshin had stolen the piece from a gifted and modest young man he had run into and about whom nothing further had been heard; but I mention this in passing" (X: 252). If the reader, meanwhile, may have forgotten another of Lyamshin's talents—that of impersonator—Dostoyevsky now expands the repertoire of "that good-for-nothing" to include the mimicry of "all sorts of Yids"[13] and even the caricature of Stepan Trofimovich himself (X: 252). And for good measure he repeats that Lyamshin enjoyed such success that "in the end there was no question of turning him out: he had made himself too indispensable" (X: 252). What's more, he has managed to worm his way into the good graces of the younger Verkhovensky, Pyotr Stepanovich.

Plut, shut, merzavets, negodyai, bezdelnik, thief, sycophant, blasphemer—Dostoyevsky gives Lyamshin no quarter; anything goes so long as it serves to blacken or ridicule. But even this is not enough. Resorting to a rhetorical artifice of the most primitive quality, Dostoyevsky pauses to solicit the reader's indulgence for having dwelled at such length on such a reprehensible character, but it is only a ploy to cast further discredit upon him: "I should not have wasted my time in talking so much about this scoundrel and, as a matter of fact, he wouldn't be worth dwelling on, were it not for one other revolting incident in which, people say, he also had a hand, and this incident is something I simply cannot pass over in silence" (X: 252).

With this, Dostoyevsky introduces the story of an "abominable sacrilege"—the profanation of a large icon of the Virgin in one of the most ancient churches of the city. It is discovered one morning that the glass encasing the icon has been shattered and that several precious stones have been removed from the crown. But far more despicable than the theft itself is the desecration of the icon: "behind the broken glass . . . a live mouse was found. It now has been thoroughly established . . . that the crime was perpetrated by Fedka the convict, but for some reason or other it is also said that Lyamshin was involved in it, too. At the time, no one mentioned Lyamshin or even suspected him of anything, but now everyone maintains that it was he who planted the mouse there" (X: 253).

It is not difficult to imagine the effect this story was calculated to have on the reader: is there anything more revolting than an act of sacrilege, especially when it is committed by a Jew?[14]

There is no need to dwell on two other episodes that are recounted in the pages that follow and in which Lyamshin is relegated to his role of simple buffoon—the scene in the hotel room where a young man has just committed suicide (X: 255–256) and the audience given by the Holy Man Semyon Yakovlevich (X:

256–261). They do permit Dostoyevsky, however, to sustain interest in an apparently minor character and to prepare Lyamshin as well as the reader for the role the former will ultimately be called on to play.

It is only halfway through the novel that the author provides the first intimation of Lyamshin's duplicity. The province in which the action of the book is laid has for some time been the scene of a series of disorders (fires, epidemics, thefts) that the authorities suspect are being fomented by revolutionary groups, a suspicion reinforced by the discovery of subversive tracts. Sensing the danger of being exposed, Pyotr Stepanovich Verkhovensky, in a conversation with his friend Governor-General von Lembke, succeeds in allaying his suspicions that he is in any way involved, putting the finger upon Shatov. But Blum, the governor's secretary and right-hand man, is not at all convinced of Verkhovensky's innocence. He suggests to von Lembke that a search be made of Verkhovensky's quarters and tells him that "Lyamshin and Telyatnikov [secretary of the former governor] affirm that we will find everything we're looking for" (X: 283). From this it is clear that Lyamshin has already been in touch with the authorities and is playing a double role.

When Lyamshin next appears—at the meeting of the revolutionaries in the home of Madame Virginskaya (in the famous chapter "Birds of a Feather," X: 300–319)—it is in the role of buffoon-revolutionary par excellence. The humiliation he suffers and, more than that, his awareness of the abjection to which he has sunk are pathetically underscored. Even when professing his revolutionary credo—the only time he is permitted to express any kind of opinion—he is exposed to ridicule. (No matter how extravagant the caricature of Lyamshin, it is an essential ingredient in the artistic effect that the author sought to obtain in a chapter that is a striking revelation of Dostoyevsky's virtuosity in the realm of humor and satire.)

The chapter, it will be remembered, opens with a description of the participants in this clandestine meeting. Apart from Stavrogin, Pyotr Stepanovich, Shatov and the five members of the secret society (Liputin, Virginsky, Shigalyov, Tolkachenko, Lyamshin), a number of outsiders, apparently sympathetic onlookers, are present. One of the least significant among them is the young divinity student "who had helped Lyamshin slip the vile photographs into the bookseller's bag" (X: 304), the sole reason for his presence being to remind the reader once again of what Lyamshin is capable. The meeting is a boisterous and chaotic affair until Madame Virginskaya proposes that a vote should be taken on whether the gathering is to be considered an informal get-together or an official meeting. Since the utmost precaution is deemed necessary even for so simple a formality, the hostess requests Lyamshin to take his place at the piano (X: 308–309):

> "Again!" cried Lyamshin. "I've pounded enough for you."
>
> "I beg you earnestly, sit down and play; don't you want to be useful to the cause?"
>
> "But I can assure you, Arina Prokhorovna, that no one is eavesdropping. It's all in your imagination. And besides, the windows are high, and even if someone were listening in, he wouldn't understand what's going on."
>
> "We don't even understand ourselves what's up," someone muttered.
>
> "But I tell you that you can never be too careful. I mean in the event there should be spies," she explained to Verkhovensky, "anyone passing by and hearing the music will think we're having a party."
>
> "Goddam!" Lyamshin swore, and sitting down to the piano, he began banging out a waltz, blindly thumping the keys practically with his fists. . . .
>
> "Mr. Lyamshin, do us a favor, you're pounding so hard we can't hear ourselves talk," the lame teacher observed.
>
> "Believe me, Arina Prokhorovna, nobody is listening in," Lyamshin cried, leaping up. "I just won't play! I came here as a guest, not as a drummer."

The meeting now opens, offering Shigalyov the opportunity to expound his famous theory: to establish paradise on earth, you start from unlimited freedom and end up with unlimited despotism. This is Lyamshin's cue. Perhaps to prove to himself even more than to the others that he is not just a piano thumper, he exclaims (X: 312–313):

> "If I had my way, instead of paradise . . . I'd take the nine-tenths of mankind, if I didn't know what to do with them, and blow them to smithereens, and leave only a handful of educated people who could live happily ever after on scientific principles."

"Only a buffoon can talk like that!" the young girl student blurted out.

"He's a buffoon, but a useful one at that," Madame Virginskaya whispered to her.

Or, perhaps, Lyamshin's outburst is for the benefit of Pyotr Stepanovich—the occasion to prove to him his trustworthiness should the latter suspect him of having been in contact with the authorities (as the author has hinted that he was). Despite this tenuous psychological motivation that provides artistic justification for Lyamshin's espousal of such a ruthless doctrine (which is, as Shigalyov readily admits, the logical extension of his own theory), there's no escaping the fact that these words in the mouth of Lyamshin not only are without precedent but are controverted by his final act of denunciation. It will be recalled that in a conversation with Stavrogin shortly after the meeting at Madame Virginskaya's, Pyotr Verkhovensky is manifestly unconcerned about the loyalty and discretion of his entourage and can cynically declare: "There's not a scoundrel who doesn't have his weak point. Lyamshin is the only one who doesn't, but still I have him in my clutches" (X: 322). But what makes him so sure? The question must remain unanswered.

By the time Lyamshin appears at the fête of Yuliya Mikhailovna, which opens the third and final part of *The Possessed*, he has become a familiar figure to the reader. In the two chapters devoted to the fête, Dostoyevsky, with consummate artistry, composed a devastating satire of the liberal intelligentsia and their confederates in the bureaucracy, they, too, contaminated by progressive ideas, linking the one and the other to the revolutionary underground in the celebrated "Literary Quadrille." But he adds little that is significantly new to the portrait of Lyamshin, merely providing him with another opportunity to parade his talents of a clown in his burlesque of a Moscow daily as his contribution to the literary divertissement. The spectacle of Lyamshin walking upside down, symbolizing the muddle-headedness of this newspaper, provokes a ripple of laughter and a wave of consternation; von Lembke, beside himself with rage, orders the rogue and scoundrel to put an end to his antics (X: 391).

The rogue and scoundrel, abetted by Liputin, we learn on

good authority, has also managed to get some of the town's "riff-raff" into the fête (X: 358), including some "wretched little Jews [*zhidishki*] with a sorrowful but arrogant smile" (X: 354). Could there be a more appropriate moment than this one for Dostoyevsky to introduce into the narrative a casual allusion to the influx of the Jews into the province, plying their familiar practice of money-lending? There is the price of admission to the fête that had to be paid, and one has to be properly dressed for the occasion. Thus, "many people from the middle class, as it turned out, had pawned all they possessed for that day, even the family linen, even the bedsheets if not the mattresses, to the local Yids, who, as if on purpose, over the last two years, had settled in droves in our town and who, as time goes by, will be moving in in ever greater numbers" (X: 358).

That same evening, incendiaries are at work in the outskirts of the town—Yuliya Mikhailovna's fête ends, bathed in the sinister glow of distant flames. The monstrous conflagration will precipitate the rapid unfolding of a series of tragic events: the discovery of the bodies of Captain Lebyadkin and his sister Marya Timofeyevna, the lynching of Liza, Stavrogin's departure for St. Petersburg and the condemnation and execution of Shatov by the conspirators. Our analysis resumes at the moment when the quintet seals the fate of Shatov.

The day after the fires and the discovery of the heinous crimes mentioned above, the Group of Five gathers at the lodgings of Erkel (a young ensign who was present at the meeting at Madame Virginskaya's). They have been called together by Pyotr Stepanovich and are waiting for him to show up. Meanwhile, disturbed by the turn of events, they decide to call him to account and, should he fail to justify his conduct, to proceed with the reorganization of the group along more democratic lines. This is, at least, the majority position, Liputin, Shigalyov and Tolkachenko resolutely endorsing it. Virginsky, however, insists on first hearing what Verkhovensky has to say. Lyamshin alone says nothing, "though he seemed to go along with [the majority]" (X: 416). In short, he is waiting to see which way the wind is blowing. Moreover, in the stormy discussion that follows the appearance of Pyotr Stepanovich, Lyamshin does not break out of his reserve. Verkhovensky skillfully quells the rebellion, evoking the danger to which all of them are exposed: all of them risk arrest as arsonists since Shatov is about to turn them in. Ergo, Shatov has to be eliminated.

An icy silence ensues, broken at last by the booming voice of Tolkachenko: "Right, send him off to kingdom-come!" Lyamshin, mute until then, finally decides that the moment has come for him to be heard: " 'And it ought to have been done long ago!' Lyamshin put in angrily, striking the table with his fist" (X: 419).

Pyotr Stepanovich thereupon exposes his plan of action. The quintet will be absolved of any suspicion thanks to the timely suicide of Kirillov, who has agreed to kill himself when instructed to do so and take the blame for Shatov's murder. Failure to acquiesce in this plan would mean certain arrest for all of the conspirators save Pyotr Stepanovich. This time Lyamshin is the first to signify his accord: "Yes, we are ready to act" (X: 421). Only Virginsky remains recalcitrant, but he, too, finally yields.

The stage has now been set for Shatov's murder, appointed for the following day.

The approaching tragedy is heightened by the sudden return of Shatov's wife, Marya Ignatyevna, already in the throes of childbirth. It is past midnight when a distraught and anguish-ridden Shatov knocks at the door of the Virginskys to summon the aid of Madame Virginskaya, who is a midwife. To Shatov's astonishment, the latter agrees without hesitation to come to his assistance, unconcerned whether she will be paid or not.

" 'Why, even in these people, there's something generous!' Shatov thought, as he set off to Lyamshin's" (X: 445–446). And had not Kirillov, a moment earlier, offered him tea and given him almost his last ruble? But now Shatov, desperately in need of money, heads for Lyamshin's, hoping to buy back the revolver he sold him some time before.

Dostoyevsky prepared the reader long in advance for this ultimate confrontation. And the tragedy of Shatov, who has but a few hours to live, is made even more poignant by the abject humiliation he is seen to suffer at the hands of Lyamshin. The hearts of readers will swell with still greater compassion for Shatov and seethe with horror, rage and revulsion toward Lyamshin.

Toward Lyamshin-the-Jew, that is. The reader need no longer be misled by the purity of his speech. Lyamshin has been unmasked: he is a direct descendant of Gogol's *zhid* Yankel (*Taras Bulba*), of Pushkin's *zhid* Solomon (*The Covetous Knight*) and, perhaps, even more unsavory to the extent that (the analogy is admittedly farfetched) Shatov is incomparably more noble than either Bulba or Albert. The situation is no longer ambiguous, we are back on sure ground, the stereotype emerges: the Christian, bound hand and foot, delivered up to the wily and unscrupulous Jew. Lyamshin, whom Dostoyevsky heretofore spared from these particular traits, now appears in an all too familiar light.

Cast now in the role of pawnbroker *malgré lui*, Lyamshin suddenly acquires at this juncture all of the traits that Russian literature—particularly that of the first half of the nineteenth century—was wont to ascribe to the Jew: an exaggerated preoccupation with his health, cowardice, skepticism, cunning, feigned indigence, subterfuge, sham indignation, double-dealing.

The scene opens in a highly burlesqued, slapstick manner, in the best Gogolian tradition. Shatov knocks at Lyamshin's door, Lyamshin jumps out of bed and, barefoot and clad only in his nightclothes, rushes to open the casement. Shatov is astonished because it is not like Lyamshin to risk catching a cold because "he was terribly anxious about his health and constantly concerned about it" (cf. Isai Fomich). There is, however, a special reason for his precipitation: "Lyamshin had been shaking all evening and the jumpiness he felt after the meeting of the group had prevented him all this time from getting to sleep; he had visions of uninvited and thoroughly undesirable visitors coming by. More than anything else, the news of Shatov's denunciation tormented him . . . And suddenly, as luck would have it, there was this terribly loud rapping at the window" (X: 446).

At the sight of Shatov, Lyamshin slams the casement and scurries back to bed. In the course of the scene, the window keeps clicking open and shut, accentuating the outbursts of the antagonists, the torments and vacillations of Lyamshin and the desperation and fury of his suppliant.

An almost hysterical Shatov beseeches Lyamshin to buy back the revolver for fifteen rubles, ten rubles less than he had paid him for it. There follows a scene of petty haggling, reminiscent of the marketplace. Were it not for the tragedy of the situation, the staccato, spirited quality of the dialogue, punctuated by the opening and closing of the casement, the inherent comedy of the episode might be appreciated. But on the contrary: the deep personal tragedy, the deep spiritual tragedy of Shatov—of Shatov who fervently believes in Holy Russia, in the God-bearing mission of the Russian people—is felt even more acutely.[15]

Lyamshin remains adamant, but Shatov pleads with him to take back the revolver, explaining why he needs the money so badly. But Lyamshin is distrustful (X: 446):

> "You're lying, your wife hasn't come back to you. It's . . . it's simply because you're planning to run away."
>
> "Fool, what would I be running away for? It's for your Pyotr Verkhovensky to run away, not me. . . . Ask anybody. My wife is in labor. I need money; come across!"

At this point, the narrator interposes himself, remarking enigmatically: "A whole fireworks of ideas flared up in Lyamshin's wily mind. All of a sudden, everything took on a different coloration, but fear still prevented him from thinking clearly" (X: 446). What, then, would he have done had he been calm and collected? Is Dostoyevsky perhaps suggesting that Lyamshin was on the verge of warning Shatov of the danger threatening him?

Be that as it may, Lyamshin refuses to acquiesce, claiming that he has nothing like fifteen rubles to his name. By this time, Shatov is at his wit's end. Shifting brusquely to the familiar form of address, he cries out: "You always have money; I took off ten rubles for you, but everyone knows you're a notorious Yid [*ty izvestnyi zhidyonok*]" (X: 447). That Shatov, driven to the breaking point, would blurt out this invective is not inconceivable. But it is also the occasion for the author—at a crucial point in the narrative—to remind the reader of Lyamshin's origins.

In the face of Shatov's wild rage and mounting abuse, Lyamshin finally gives some ground. He hands him a five-ruble note through the now broken window, grudgingly adding another two, anything to get rid of him. As Shatov leaves, he yells (X: 447):

> "To hell with you, then, I'll come by tomorrow. I'll beat you to a pulp, Lyamshin, if those eight rubles aren't ready."
>
> "You won't find me at home, you fool!" the thought flashed through Lyamshin's mind.

But then, inexplicably, Lyamshin cries out to Shatov, as he departs, asking him if it was true that his wife has returned. Shatov takes no notice.[16]

The plot now unwinds to its inexorable end. The evening after the scene just described, Shatov leads Erkel to the spot where he has buried the printing press (it was on the pretext that the quintet wanted to recover the press that Erkel lured him into the trap). There he is immediately set upon by Erkel, joined by Tolkachenko and Liputin, who have been lurking in the shadows; Pyotr Stepanovich finishes him off with a bullet through his head. Virginsky had rushed Shatov along with the others but did not lay a hand on him. Shigalyov is not there. As for Lyamshin, he joins the group only after the shot has been fired. And until he appears there is even some doubt whether he will show up at all: that afternoon Virginsky visited Lyamshin who told him that "it was none of his business, he knew nothing, and [asked] that he be left alone" (X: 455).

Shatov's corpse now has to be disposed of. The air quivers with the taut silence of nervous tension—as the conspirators set about their macabre task—until it is rent by the bitter cry of Virginsky, who shouts: "No, no, it's not right, it's just not right!" But, almost at the same instant, his voice is drowned out by the piercing, inhuman wail of Lyamshin as he succumbs to a fit of convulsive hysteria (X: 461):

> There are moments of intense fear, for example, when a man sud-
> denly lets out a cry in a voice not his own, unlike anything one
> could have ever imagined him capable of, and this can be even
> terrifying at times. Lyamshin screamed in a voice that was more
> bestial than human. . . . He went on wailing, without letup, his eyes
> popping out of his head, his mouth wide open, his legs tapping
> the ground as if beating a drum. . . . Stumbling against the corpse,
> he fell over it onto Pyotr Stepanovich and, pressing his head to the
> latter's chest, he held him so tightly in his grip that neither Pyotr
> Stepanovich, Tolkachenko nor Liputin could momentarily do any-
> thing about it. Pyotr Stepanovich yelled, swore, pummeled his head
> with his fists; at last, somehow managing to wrench himself free,
> he grabbed hold of his revolver and thrust it straight into the open
> mouth of Lyamshin, who was still howling. . . . But, in spite of the
> revolver, Lyamshin went on wailing.

It is not until Erkel has succeeded in introducing a gag into his mouth that Lyamshin is brought under control.

The scene in its truth and intensity is overwhelming. For

once, Dostoyevsky reveals—perhaps in spite of himself—Lyam-shin's profound humanity. For nothing is more human than his voice "more bestial than human." As he flails about like a rabid beast, deaf to the exhortations of creatures that once were men, whose language is no longer intelligible to him, he reaffirms his right—so long denied him—to human dignity and honor. Dosto-yevsky here renders homage—albeit unconsciously—to the feeling of compassion that is the eternal hallmark "of the Jewish tribe without exception." This is not the first time we have heard the cry of Lyamshin. It is the same cry as uttered by "Achilles" to Svidrigailov in *Crime and Punishment*: "Dzis is not dze place"; but it is a voice crying in the wilderness.[17]

Pyotr Stepanovich is not unduly perturbed by Lyamshin's frenzied outburst. Blinded by his egocentricity, by his unshakable conviction that man is governed only by fear, he is more than ever persuaded that Lyamshin "will come to his senses and realize that he will be the first to go to Siberia if he squeals." He is sure not only of Lyamshin but of everyone else: "No one will squeal now" (X: 463).

Verkhovensky is sadly mistaken: the betrayal is inevitable, just as inevitable as it is that the informer will be Lyamshin. All that Dostoyevsky has told us of his persona has earmarked him for this infamous role. Any other solution would have undermined the internal cohesion of the story and its artistic truth.[18]

And yet, Dostoyevsky himself betrayed the artistic truth of the plot he had so carefully elaborated by imputing to Lyamshin the basest of motives that *now* could not be justified either psy-chologically or artistically. They lost their justification the moment that the author elevated Lyamshin from the role of lifeless, un-feeling buffoon to the status of human being at the scene of Sha-tov's murder. The question arises, then, whether Dostoyevsky might not have been carried away by his subject. The hypothesis implicit in the question seems to be borne out by a puzzling entry in the "Notebooks" for *The Possessed*: "THE MURDER OF SHA-TOV. Lyamshin was not there" (XI: 298).[19] Thus, as originally conceived, Lyamshin was not present at the scene of the crime. And only if the novelist had stuck to this initial version would the motives he ascribes to the informer be plausible and valid. But Lyamshin, finally, was there, and this shift allows us to perceive even more clearly Dostoyevsky's own motivation in casting him in the role of traitor. For he now will be forced into a willful misrepresentation of Lyamshin's act of betrayal in order to remain true to his original intent: to show that Lyamshin's basic motivation is fear and, particularly, the desire for self-preservation or, to put it more crudely, the desire to save his own skin.

This is just no longer true. There is, to be sure, nothing heroic in Lyamshin's act. Nor is it an act of civic courage or contrition. It is neither noble nor virtuous, but it is, nonetheless, a profoundly human act, arising out of an organic, human revulsion to an act of cold-blooded murder. As such, it arouses our sympathy. But Dostoyevsky—that champion of the insulted and the injured—will have no part of it; and he has no qualms about turning a purely human act into one of calculated betrayal. He is willing to forget his hatred of the Russian nihilists just long enough to cast Lyamshin in the role of a Judas.[20]

Let us take up the novel again at the crucial moment of Lyamshin's confession.

Lyamshin, in a state of nervous prostration following the execution of Shatov, is placed in the custody of Tolkachenko and Erkel and taken back to his room. He lies abed there the whole next day, oblivious to the fact that Shatov's corpse has been discovered and the police are investigating the crime. Toward evening, Tolkachenko (Erkel has left earlier), aware of and frightened by these new developments, takes flight, abandoning his charge. After sizing up the situation, Lyamshin decides to flee as well; he wanders a few blocks from home, but then reconsiders his action, sensing that it is fraught with danger. Returning to his room, he locks himself in; he makes an unsuccessful suicide attempt. At noon the next day, he hurriedly leaves his quarters, rushes over to the police and turns himself in. Dostoyevsky offers us the spectacle of a cringing, crawling, craven creature, groveling before the authorities (X: 510):

> It is reported that he crawled on his knees, whimpered and wailed, kissed the floor, shouting that he was not even worthy of kissing the boots of the officials standing before him. . . . He confessed everything, absolutely everything, he divulged everything, everything he knew down to the last detail; he ran ahead of the questions, he couldn't wait to make a clean breast of it, he even volunteered unnecessary information.

To drive the nail even deeper by demonstrating that Lyamshin is motivated by considerations of base self-interest, the narrator cites verbatim a passage from his deposition in which he expressed the hope that the officials "would not fail to remember and bear fully in mind how frankly and forthrightly he had exposed the affair and that, consequently, he could very well render useful services to the authorities in the future" (X: 510).

But Dostoyevsky goes even further than this. With almost malign pleasure, he reveals that Lyamshin places the entire blame on Pyotr Stepanovich while shielding Stavrogin: "Interestingly enough, though, he completely exonerated Nikolai Stavrogin from any involvement in the secret society or from any collusion with Pyotr Stepanovich" (X: 511). And then, in a characteristic aside, the narrator hastens to explain to the reader the reason for Lyamshin's surprising generosity toward Stavrogin (X: 511):

> *Nota bene.* Two months later, Lyamshin admitted that he had deliberately shielded Stavrogin at that time, hoping that he would use his influence and wangle for him, in Petersburg, a mitigation . . . of his sentence, and that he would provide him with money and letters of recommendation while he was in Siberia.

Exit Lyamshin. But the ignominy of his behavior is seen with even more clarity when compared with the comportment of the other conspirators. Thus, Virginsky, sick and feverish when they came to arrest him, "is giving evidence frankly, but with a certain dignity" (X: 511); Erkel, though "wholly unrepentant," evokes the sympathy of his judges because of his exemplary conduct toward his mother, and "a lot of people feel sorry for Erkel" (X: 511–512); Liputin, arrested in a brothel in St. Petersburg, "is preparing for his trial with a certain solemnity" and "is even planning to make a speech" there (X: 512); and, finally, Tolkachenko is conducting himself with civility, "is not lying, is not being evasive, is telling all he knows, and is not trying to justify himself" (X: 512).

One can readily understand the note of sympathy that is struck for Virginsky. But Erkel and Tolkachenko, those two hatchetmen of Pyotr Stepanovich who murdered Shatov with their own hands! Can the author's magnanimity toward them be understood in any other way but as a subconscious desire to deal a final blow to the hapless Lyamshin?

POSTSCRIPT

"The Stock Market Side of Socialism"—this new, enigmatic theme is given embryonic expression in the "Notebooks" for *The Possessed* (no. 3, p. 40, XI: 189). Although this idea is absent from the final version of the novel and is never given extensive development in his subsequent writings, it is, nonetheless, of fundamental importance to an understanding of Dostoyevsky—the man and his works—in the last ten years of his life.

It is, moreover, not at all clear why Dostoyevsky, in the "Notebooks," should have chosen Stepan Trofimovich Verkhovensky—the man of the forties and spokesman *par excellence* of the liberal nobility—as the exponent of an idea that is unmistakably Dostoyevsky's own, to wit: for the Jew, socialism is the means whereby he will come to power and establish his hegemony. Thus, Stepan Trofimovich, nettling his son, declares: "Socialism (St Tr-ch), I daresay even if it be out of sentimentality (and how many houses, the Yids are rubbing their hands, etc.)" (XI: 189).

Then, somewhat further on, in a passage devoted to Nechayev and his methods of action, it is again Stepan Trofimovich (still uncharacteristically) who, in reply to Virginsky's expression of admiration for the dedication of Nechayev's followers, exclaims: "But how many Yids are involved?"—a remark that Virginsky brushes off with the cryptic statement "Yids, there always have been" (no. 3, p. 51, XI: 107).

Finally, in a section of the "Notebooks" entitled "WHAT NECHAYEV WANTED" (XI: 276–280), Dostoyevsky, writing this time "in the name of the author," suggests that the Jews could be used in the revolutionary cause, a fact that Nechayev had, apparently, taken into account in his program of action. Point 7 of his program, as outlined by Dostoyevsky, calls for the preparation of acts of arson and sacrilege and the mobilization of the Jews: "It would be a good thing to stir up the *Jews* [*yevreyev*]" (XI: 278).[21]

It was in *The Raw Youth* (1875)—as will be recalled from the preceding chapter—that Dostoyevsky, through Versilov, first gave artistic expression to his apocalyptic vision of the *zhidovskoye tsarstvo* coming in the wake of the universal bankruptcy of nations. While Dostoyevsky-Versilov does not say in so many words that the Jews would use the arm of revolution to establish their dominion, the implication is there. And that idea, lacking both clarity and originality, would continue to prey upon Dostoyevsky's mind for the rest of his life and, in the process, grow into the conviction that the Jews were behind the nihilist and socialist movement, the aim of which was not only Jewish financial hegemony but the destruction of all Christian civilization.

In this new form, the thesis of the advent of the Antichrist would find vigorous expression in Dostoyevsky's letter of August 29, 1878, to V. F. Putsykovich, who had succeeded him as editor of the *Citizen (Grazhdanin)* in 1874, and it would be reaffirmed with even greater force and precision in a notebook entry at the end of 1880, just a few months before the writer's death. We shall consider both of these documents in chapter 8.

Dostoyevsky had his first vision of the Antichrist in 1871, shortly before his return to St. Petersburg. And he would believe in it almost to the end of his days, relentlessly denouncing the mortal danger that imperiled Holy Russia.

6. *Dostoyevsky as Journalist:* The Citizen, The Diary of a Writer—*Correspondence with A. G. Kovner*

IN MANY RESPECTS, Dostoyevsky's return to St. Petersburg from European exile in July 1871 is reminiscent of his return from Siberia some twelve years before. Then as now, Fyodor Mikhailovich's first concern was to reestablish his literary reputation. A decade earlier, *The House of the Dead* had marked his reentry on the literary scene, and now it was *The Possessed* that heralded his homecoming. So, too, Dostoyevsky felt—perhaps even more keenly now than before—the imperious need to make his voice heard on the burning issues of the day. This is not to say, however, that his vocation as tribune would dampen his creativity as artist, for in this, the final decade of his life, he would reach new heights with *The Brothers Karamazov*. But it will all the same be remembered as a period of intense journalistic activity. *The Diary of a Writer*, with its hundreds upon hundreds of pages, is a monument in itself;[1] but not to be forgotten either are the numerous unsigned articles that appeared in Prince Meshchersky's journal the *Citizen* (*Grazhdanin*), of which Dostoyevsky was editor-in-chief in 1873–1874. The authorship of many of these articles was long ago definitively attributed to Dostoyevsky, but more recent research has brought to light a number of new attributions.[2]

The fact that Dostoyevsky's journalistic activity was more extensive than had been previously supposed, the fact that he devoted so much of his time to this genre, can only strengthen the conviction of those who, like the late Soviet scholar V. A. Desnitsky, believe that the writer's literary legacy is one and indivisible, that his "journalistic writings cannot be divorced from his art since they spread through his novels, too, determining their 'personalities,' their layout, becoming an integral part of them, even intruding on the dialogue of the characters, shaping their content and form" (11: xiii).[3] And just as political, social, economic and religious ideas developed in his articles and correspondence were often incorporated in his novels, so, too, views espoused in his novels were now and again echoed in his journalism.[4]

What light does this interaction, this convergence, throw on the evolution of Dostoyevsky's ideas on the Jewish question during the last ten years of his life? In March 1877, we know, Dostoyevsky felt compelled to tackle this question head-on in his *Diary of a Writer*, devoting no less than two-thirds of the entire issue to it. If any doubts could still have persisted about the importance he attached to the Jewish question, they were now dispelled for all times. But, as the preceding chapters have shown, this belated "profession of faith" was by no means the beginning of his concern, nor would it lay it to rest. Before proceeding to an examination of this key text in the chapter that follows, I shall first consider Dostoyevsky's views on the Jewish question as they developed within the context of his personal evolution in the seventies, as expressed in *The Diary of a Writer* as a whole, as set forth in his letters of the period to Jews and non-Jews alike and as recorded on the pages of his notebooks. *The Brothers Karamazov* will likewise be considered from this particular standpoint in chapter 8.[5] And, finally, I shall take a look at the various political, social and economic factors that exerted an influence on Dostoyevsky's overall treatment of the Jewish question and intensified his preoccupation with the problem.

An indisputable fact in the biography of Dostoyevsky in the last decade of his life is that he chose to identify himself more and more closely with the most conservative elements in the highest spheres of government—with those who saw but one answer to the growing political, social and economic unrest: the return to fundamentals, the reaffirmation and reapplication in Russian life of the principles of autocracy and Orthodoxy, the appeal to the traditional virtues of the Russian people, their patriotism and self-abnegation.[6] These views Dostoyevsky ardently shared, and he became a vehement advocate of them.

It would be disingenuous to regard as purely fortuitous Dostoyevsky's meeting with Prince V. P. Meshchersky in the autumn of 1871, that is, just a few months after his return to St. Petersburg.[7] There is good reason to believe that this meeting was ar-

ranged by an intimate of the prince, Tertius Filippov, whom Dostoyevsky had consulted, through the intermediary of his old friend
Apollon Maikov, on a point of church history.[8] However that may
be, Dostoyevsky's meeting with Prince Meshchersky marked his
entry into the world of Petersburg's high society. It was through
Meshchersky that Dostoyevsky, early in 1872, made the acquaintance of K. P. Pobedonostsev, the eminent jurist and tutor of the
tsarevich, the future Alexander III, marking the beginning of a
long and close friendship and collaboration. On Pobedonostsev's
recommendation, Dostoyevsky, early in 1878, would gain admission into the imperial family as tutor to the two younger sons of
Alexander II, the grand dukes Sergei and Pavel. Similarly, it was
Dostoyevsky to whom the younger brother of the tsar, Grand
Duke Konstantin, would entrust the spiritual guidance of his sons
Konstantin Konstantinovich and Dmitry. As for the tsarevich himself, though Dostoyevsky would not meet him personally until
sometime in 1880 at the invitation of Konstantin Konstantinovich,[9]
the relations of the two dated back to 1873 when Dostoyevsky, at
Pobedonostsev's behest, sent the future Alexander III a copy of
The Possessed.[10]

Indeed, so successful was Dostoyevsky in gaining acceptance
into the aristocratic society of the capital that by the end of the
seventies he was frequenting this milieu almost exclusively; his
contacts with literary circles dwindled accordingly.[11] No other
writer in nineteenth-century Russia was on such intimate terms
with the ruling aristocracy.

How is Dostoyevsky's sudden predilection for such a milieu
to be explained? There is little room for doubt that he was drawn
to the aristocracy both psychologically and ideologically. While he
could claim membership in the hereditary nobility, he realized
only too well the modesty of his credentials (and there were some
who even called them into question). The result was a feeling of
insecurity that manifested itself, for example, in the form of hostility toward Turgenev and diffidence toward Tolstoy, both of
whom he viewed with envy if not disdain.[12] Thus, to be received
in the salons of St. Petersburg was, for Dostoyevsky, a kind of personal triumph that validated no less in his own mind than in the
minds of others his claim to nobility.[13] But above all else, Dostoyevsky was drawn to that class whose aims and ideas he now in-

creasingly supported and whose anxieties over the present and future of Russia he fully shared.

The cement that sealed this new union was Slavophilism, the first symptoms of which, as noted earlier, were discernible in Dostoyevsky as far back as 1856. We saw, too, how this ideology became more pronounced in the sixties and found expression in Dostoyevsky's doctrine of *pochvennichestvo*, extolling the virtues of attachment to the native soil, the return to the wellsprings of Russian reality. By the time of his return from Europe, Dostoyevsky's Slavophilism had evolved still further under the readily traceable influence of Yury Samarin and Nikolai Danilevsky. But it would achieve its ultimate form and most extreme expression in the seventies under the pressure of events inside and outside Russia and under the influence of Dostoyevsky's new entourage.

So strong was the influence exercised by Slavophile doctrine on Dostoyevskyan thought that the latter can be fully understood only within the context of that doctrine and, especially, the writer's own concept of it. As originally conceived, Slavophilism was based on two fundamental principles: on the one hand, the rejection of Western ideas and practices and their importation into Russia; on the other, the affirmation of Russia's originality, its specificity (*samobytnost*). The early Slavophile thinkers—Kireyevsky, Khomyakov, Apollon Grigoryev, Samarin and Ivan Aksakov (of the period prior to 1870)—though advocating a program for the endogenous development of Russia, were not inspired by narrow nationalistic considerations; in addition, the religious element occupied an important place in their system of thought. But toward the close of the sixties and, particularly, in the decade that followed, Slavophilism would assume—among a certain segment of its supporters—a more militant and chauvinistic character; it would discover and proclaim the brotherhood of all the Slav peoples and their aspirations for unity and thus become endowed with a third principle: Panslavism, "the ugly step-child of the philosophic Slavophiles," as one writer has described it.[14] As for *samobytnost*, it would evolve into a doctrine of national exclusiveness, affirming the superiority of the Great Russians not only over the other nations of the world but even over the other Slav peoples. At the same time, Orthodoxy would become the sole repository of Christian truth, Catholicism and Protestantism having become spiritually bankrupt, Islam and, of course, Judaism—anathemas.

Despite the obvious hazards of such a schematic and cursory presentation of such an extraordinarily complex system of thought, I shall leave it at that since the main thing that interests us here is to determine what Dostoyevsky owes to Slavophile doctrine and the particular current he allied himself with. It will become clear that he unquestionably identified himself with the militant wing of the Slavophile movement that gained ascendancy in the seventies.

It would be erroneous, however, to regard Dostoyevsky as a theoretician; his Slavophilism is highly derivative. He owed a great deal to Apollon Maikov, who as far back as 1856 had proclaimed the supremacy of the Great Russians over the other Slav peoples.[15] He was also influenced by Samarin in his later period and by his works such as *The Russian Borderlands* (*Okrainy Rossii*, 1868–1876) and *The Jesuits and Their Attitude toward Russia* (*Iyezuity i ikh otnosheniye k Rossii*, 1868), in which the author gave free rein to his nationalistic feelings and prejudice against Roman Catholicism.[16] Samarin did not particularly care for the Jews either, but whether he had any palpable influence on Dostoyevsky in this regard remains an open question, even though they shared kindred points of view on certain matters related thereto.[17]

On the other hand, the influence of Ivan Aksakov on Dostoyevsky was lasting and profound. Under the impact of the troubles in the Balkans (the "Eastern question" as it is called in the litera· ture of the period) in the 1870s, Aksakov's Slavophilism degenerated into the most aggressive, bellicose strain of Panslavism and chauvinistic drumbeating. Dostoyevsky's impassioned pleas for the liberation of the Slavs and their union under the Great Russian banner that fill page after page of his *Diary* for 1876–1877 bear a striking similarity to the themes developed by Aksakov during this crucial period in his speeches before the Moscow branch of the Slav Committee.[18] On the Jewish question, about which Aksakov wrote extensively—much more, in fact, than Dostoyevsky —their views are so concordant that the least that can be said is that they exercised an influence on each other. There is, moreover, a direct correlation between Panslavism and anti-Semitism: the more extreme the former, the more virulent the latter. And there is certainly a relationship between Dostoyevsky's enthusiastic rallying to Panslavic ideals and his sharpening antipathy toward the Jews.

Dostoyevskyan thought was also indebted to N. Ya. Danilevsky, the author of *Russia and Europe*; Dostoyevsky became acquainted with this major work from the moment it began serial publication in the magazine *Dawn (Zarya)* in 1869. Unlike his predecessors, Danilevsky denied the traditional Slavophile belief that the Russian people had a universal historical vocation, but he vigorously affirmed the idea of Russia's particularity, a specificity that, for that matter, was endemic in any "cultural-historical" entity; hence, he concluded, Russia had to discover and pursue its own path of development distinct from that of the West. Dolinin has thrown light on the place occupied by Danilevsky in the formation of Dostoyevsky's *Weltanschauung* in the seventies and on the impact he had on the latter's treatment of the "Eastern question" in his *Diary of a Writer*.[19]

These, then, were some of the Slavophile thinkers from whom Dostoyevsky drew inspiration. The influence they exercised was mainly through their writings, for Dostoyevsky had little or no personal or epistolary contact with any of the personalities we have mentioned except for Aksakov and his old friend Maikov. But Dostoyevsky's thinking was, furthermore, influenced by the persons he began cultivating in 1871, and this has been, in fact, the subject of a long essay.[20] I shall explore one particular aspect of the question in an effort to determine to what extent and in what manner Dostoyevsky's treatment of the Jewish problem was affected by his new entourage.

In assuming the editorship of the *Citizen* toward the end of 1872, Dostoyevsky openly allied himself with the most conservative elements of Russian society and officialdom, men who were dedicated to the defense of Orthodoxy and autocracy and committed to the struggle against liberal thought. According to Prince Meshchersky, publisher of the journal, it was Dostoyevsky himself who volunteered his services as editor and who did so "out of sympathy with the aims of the publication."[21] The latter counted among its most ardent supporters the tsarevich, the future Alexander III, Pobedonostsev, Apollon Maikov, Tyutchev, Strakhov and B. M. Markevich.

This new venture in many ways proved to be a turning point in Dostoyevsky's life. It marked the beginning of his lasting friendship with Pobedonostsev, a member of the influential Council of State, an intimate of the imperial family, future Procurator of the Holy Synod and adviser to Alexander III throughout his reign. Through the good graces of Pobedonostsev and Meshchersky, Dostoyevsky not only gained entrée into the imperial household but also widened his circle of acquaintances in public life and the administration, Tertius Filippov and Ivan Kornilov among them. (The latter, it will be seen, played the role of a catalyst in the hardening of Dostoyevsky's position on the Jewish question.)

The image of the gaunt figure of Pobedonostsev towering over Russian history of the last quarter of the nineteenth century has become almost legendary. His name has practically become synonymous with all that is sinister and maleficent. He has served as the prototype of Bely's Senator Ableukhov, and it was again he who, in Blok's unfinished poem "Retaliation," "spread his owlish wings" over Russia.

There is abundant and conclusive evidence attesting to the close ties that bound Dostoyevsky and the Councillor of State. It can, perhaps, even be said that Pobedonostsev became the writer's closest friend in the closing decade of his life. This has led some (Grossman, among others) to the not wholly justifiable conclusion that Dostoyevsky succumbed to the malevolent influence of this evil genius, which would, as it were, explain his drift toward reaction. But another scholar has argued—more convincingly—that it is virtually impossible to determine "to what degree one man has influenced another" and reaches the general conclusion that "both men had worked out the fundamentals of their philosophical positions before they met and that their general agreement during the months they each wrote for *Grazhdanin* demonstrates that neither influenced the other appreciably."[22]

This judgment would appear to hold true for their positions on the Jewish question. Indeed, there was such a convergence of views between the two men that neither felt the need to discourse at great length on this problem, at least in their correspondence.[23] Among the rather important letters they wrote one another, there is but a single exchange of letters on this particular issue, and it is interesting to note that it was Dostoyevsky who initiated the discussion. In his letter of August 9/21, 1879, from Ems, he wrote:

This present visit is the worst ever: the riffraff from all Europe is here in the thousands (not many Russians, and they're all the unfamiliar sort from the Russian borderlands). . . . <And mark you: literally half of them are Yids. During my stopover in Berlin, I mentioned to Putsykovich that, in my view, Germany—Berlin, at any rate—was becoming Judaized. And now here I read in *Moscow Record* an extract from a pamphlet that has just appeared in Germany: "Come Now, Where Is the Jew Here?" It is one Yid's answer to a German who dared to write that Germany was becoming terribly Judaized in all respects. "There is no Jew," and the German is everywhere, but if there is no Jew, there is a Jewish influence everywhere, for, it says, the Jewish spirit and nationality are superior to the German, and they have indeed infused into Germany *"the spirit of speculative realism,"* etc., etc. Thus my view turned out to be right: the Germans and the Yids testify to it. But apart from the speculative realism that is rushing toward us, too,> you wouldn't believe how dishonest everything is here, i.e., in business at least, etc.[24]

Pobedonostsev answered on August 19/31:

And what you write about the Yids is fully justified. They have taken everything over, they have undermined everything, but the *spirit of the century* is with them. They are at the root of the revolutionary-social movement and regicide, they control the periodical press, they have the money market in their hands, they are enslaving the popular masses financially, they are even guiding the principles of present-day science that is seeking to place itself *outside of* Christianity. And in addition to all that, the moment anyone says a word about them, a chorus of voices goes up in defense of the Jews supposedly in the name of civilization and tolerance, i.e., indifference to faith. Just as in Romania and Serbia, no one here dares so much as to mention that the Jews have taken everything over. Why even our press is already becoming Jewish. *Russian Truth, Moscow,* why even the *Voice*—they are all Jewish organs, and what is more, there are special journals that have got started like the *Jew,* the *Jewish Herald* and the *Jewish Library.*[25]

Pobedonostsev's catalogue of the classic grievances and accusations of the ultraconservatives and anti-Semites against the Jews—financial hegemony, enslavement and exploitation of the masses, fomenting social unrest and revolutionary activity, control of the press and so forth—contained, of course, nothing new for Dostoyevsky. From 1873 onward, he made the same (and even worse) allegations over and over again in his literary works, journalistic writings and correspondence. He alone among Russian writers of the first rank donned the robe of public prosecutor. Without attempting to exonerate Pobedonostsev—the baneful consequences of his anti-Semitism on governmental policy especially after the assassination of Alexander II are only too evident—it is fair to say that during the period of his friendship with Dostoyevsky he exercised considerably more restraint and circumspection in the public espousal of anti-Jewish sentiment than did the author of *The Diary of a Writer*. Thus, no trace of anti-Semitism is to be found in his *Historical Studies and Articles (Istoricheskiye issledovaniya i stati*, 1876) or in the series of twenty-two articles he contributed to the *Citizen* in 1873. And in his long treatise on conservatism entitled *The Moscow Collection (Moskovskii sbornik*, 1896), there is but one anti-Semitic allusion.[26]

It is, therefore, highly unlikely that Pobedonostsev exerted any appreciable influence on Dostoyevsky's thinking on the Jewish question during the period under review. Moreover, the anti-Semitism of the former was "traditional," quite in line with that of official and conservative circles, whereas Dostoyevsky's, especially after 1876, assumed a much more virulent character. The explanation of this phenomenon must, accordingly, lie elsewhere.

Like any other anti-Semite, Dostoyevsky was completely indifferent to the justice of the accusations he made against the People of the Book. This did not deter him, however, from keeping on the alert for material that served to support his thesis and fortify his indictment: new evidence, contemporary documents. He found more than he could even have wished for in a book that enjoyed wide notoriety at the time, *The Book of the Kahal (Kniga Kagala)*, the work of the Jewish apostate and convert Yakov Brafman, which gave new impetus to the anti-Semitic movement in Russia during the second half of the reign of Alexander II.[27] Could there be more eloquent testimony to the importance Dostoyevsky attached to the book than the fact that he possessed no fewer than three editions of it in his personal library: the first edition (Vilno, 1869), the second edition (Vilno, 1870)[28] and part 2 of the second enlarged edition (St. Petersburg, 1875)? The last mentioned, moreover, was inscribed with the following dedication in the author's hand: "To Fyodor Mikhailovich Dostoyevsky as a token of the profound esteem of the author, April 6, 1877."[29] There is no evidence that Dostoyevsky acknowledged the gift, which may have been Brafman's way of expressing the satisfaction he must have felt on reading the March issue of *The Diary of a Writer*.[30] For the theme of *status in statu* runs like a leitmotiv through the chapter Dostoyevsky devotes to the Jewish question—it is even the title of the third section—tangible evidence that he retained the essential lesson of *The Book of the Kahal* where a phrase, attributed to Schiller, is placed in an epigraph: "Die Juden bilden ein Staat im Staate." This citation (moreover, inaccurate) for a long time thereafter became the watchword of the anti-Semitic movement in Russia.[31]

In all likelihood, Dostoyevsky learned of Brafman's book from Ivan P. Kornilov, member of the Council of the Ministry of Education and chairman of the Slav Philanthropic Society, whom he met in 1872 and remained on very friendly terms with until the end of his life.[32] It was thanks to Kornilov, who in the sixties was in charge of the Vilno school district, that Brafman received a subsidy of 2,500 rubles to cover the cost of the first edition of the work.[33] Subsequently republished at state expense and distributed to local administrations throughout the empire, *The Book of the Kahal* soon acquired the authority of a quasi-official document. It was invoked in the highest governmental spheres and specifically used against those who, in the newly established (1872) Special Committee for the Reorganization of Jewish Life (in the Ministry of the Interior), recommended some liberalization of the status of the Jews. V. V. Grigoryev, influential member of that committee and spokesman for the majority, declared that "so long as the Jews remain what they are, the government cannot treat them on a footing of equality with the other nationalities of the Empire."[34] Now when it is remembered that Dostoyevsky was on close terms with Grigoryev, a prominent Orientalist and right-wing Slavophile, and "took particular pleasure in his conversations" with him, it is fair to assume that they discussed the Jewish question, among others.[35]

The first oblique indication of Dostoyevsky's familiarity with *The Book of the Kahal* is found in a letter to his wife, written from Ems on June 21, 1875: "My neighbor is a Russian Yid and a lot of the local Yids come by to see him, and it's all *Geschäft* and one big *kahal*—that's the kind of neighbor God visited on me."[36]

The theme of the Jews as constituting a law unto themselves or *status in statu* was exploited by Dostoyevsky for the first time in the June 1876 issue of *The Diary of a Writer*. He has no hesitation in endorsing and crediting with his full authority the most extravagant calumnies of Brafman and other exponents of rabid anti-Semitism of the time (11: 320):

> And now we see the Yids becoming landowners—and people everywhere are shouting and writing that they are exhausting the soil of Russia, that the Yid, once he has laid out the money for the purchase of an estate, in order to recoup his capital plus interest, promptly sets about draining dry the land he has purchased of all its productive resources. But just try to say anything against that and a hue and cry goes up about infringing the principle of economic freedom and civic equality. But what has civic equality got to do with it when what you have here is, first and foremost, flagrant and Talmudic *status in statu*, not only the exhaustion of the soil, but also the impending exhaustion of our peasant, who, emancipated from the landlords, will now for sure in no time, by entire communes, fall into much worse slavery and under much worse landlords—under those new landlords, the same ones who have already sapped the vitality of the peasants in Western Russia, the same ones who now are not only buying up estates and peasants, but also have already begun buying liberal opinion and are continuing to do so quite successfully. Why is all this happening with us? Why such wavering and disagreement over every decision . . . ? As I see it, it is by no means due to our inaptitude or our incapacity for action, but rather to our continuing ignorance of Russia, of her essence and individuality, of her meaning and spirit. . . .

If this passage were not dated June 1876, the temptation would be strong to link it not only to *The Book of the Kahal* but also to another, much less well known contribution to the anti-Semitic literature of the day. Three months later (on September 11, to be precise) a pamphlet was published in St. Petersberg under the limpid title of *On the Pernicious Influence of the Jews on the Life of Russia and the System of Jewish Exploitation*. There is only one thing remarkable about it: it, too, was in Dostoyevsky's private library.[37] The author, one Marcellus Grinevich, trots out Brafman's favorite themes, applying them to the situation in the Russian southwest: acting under the orders of the omnipresent *kahal* and in accordance with Talmudic prescription, the Jews were bringing the country to ruin; the "Yid"—a parasite and exploiter, "a worm eating away at the fruit, bleeding white the population of the southwest districts" (p. iv); a speculator, driven only by the passion for lucre, riding high in place after place, especially Odessa (p. 8); intoxicator of the peasantry (pp. 56, 59) and so on *ad nauseam*. And yet, Dostoyevsky apparently gave credence to these and other allegations of this third-rate pamphleteer. For, as we shall see, more than one passage of Dostoyevsky's essay on the Jewish question in the March 1877 issue of *The Diary* bears a striking similarity, both in spirit and form, to Grinevich's text.[38]

A major preoccupation of Dostoyevsky from the moment he assumed the editorship of the *Citizen* was the economic situation in Russia, and quite understandably so. The expansion of capitalism and the industrial development that followed in the wake of the Emancipation of the Serfs placed a tremendous strain on the country's traditional structures. The situation in the countryside was particularly alarming: the period 1869 to 1875 was marked by four years of crop failures, and 1873 was a year of famine.[39] As the muzhiks became more and more impoverished, they sought solace in drink; drunkenness assumed almost epidemic proportions. Profiteers—kulaks and others—took advantage of the situation to enrich themselves at the peasants' expense.

With the growth of industry in the towns and cities, a middle class began to appear, with its merchants and financiers; speculation flourished, dishonesty spread. And it is a fact that despite the severe disabilities the Jews labored under, a few of them did make their way into the world of high finance, men like Polyakov and Varshavsky, a handful, to be sure, but all the more conspicuous because they were Jews. For Dostoyevsky—but by no means for him alone—"it was the emergence of the Jewish financier in the capitals that was the most significant and abhorrent phenomenon in Jewish life."[40]

These two figures—the Jew-tavernkeeper and the Jew-financier—would coalesce, in Dostoyevsky's mind—into an apocalyptic vision: the Jew, undisputed master of the Russian land, reigning supreme over the prostrate body of the Russian people. Nothing could avert this catastrophe except a great upsurge of national feeling, uniting the educated classes of Russian society with the popular masses under the banner of Christ and the tsar. Already in the third issue of the *Citizen* (January 15, 1873), Dostoyevsky was sounding the alarm over the misery of the people, "the decline of morality, cut-rate vodka, the Yid-tavernkeepers [*zhidy-kabatchiki*]" (11: 30). And an anonymous article in the same issue decried the spread of alcoholism among the working class and the menacing proportions it had assumed, especially in Odessa, "and all that is the work of Jewish tavernkeepers."[41]

In May (issue no. 21), Dostoyevsky returned to the attack, this time linking the question to the broader problem of the state budget. (In the seventies, he devoted a great deal of attention to the matter of public finances.) He observed with distress that "nearly one-half of our current budget is covered by vodka," again pointing an accusing finger at the "Yid" with his "cut-rate vodka," who, no longer able to subsist on the sale of alcohol alone, makes ends meet by resorting to "debauchery of the people, thievery, receiving stolen goods, usury" and so forth. Only work and industry could sustain the budget and provide it with "genuine, sound capital . . . failing which the only capital that can be generated will be that of the kulaks and the Yids." The people must take care (11: 96–97):

> If they don't come to their senses, in no time they'll all fall into the clutches of Yids of every stripe, and no communal organization is going to save them: their community will be nothing else but a brotherhood of paupers, mortgaged and enslaved by entire communes, and it will be the Yids and the kulaks who will be defraying the cost of the budget instead of them. A petty, vile, thoroughly depraved bourgeoisie will come on the scene along with an infinite multitude of paupers enslaved by them—that's the picture! The Yids will be drinking the people's blood and feeding on their debauchery and abjection, but since it will be they who are footing the budget, they are the ones who will have to be supported. A bad, a horrible dream—and, thank God, it's only a dream![42]

But Dostoyevsky concluded on a note of optimism. The nightmare would be dispelled because the people would "find within themselves the principles of preservation and salvation" that would bring them to opt for work, order and honesty and not the pot-house (11: 97).

So strong was Dostoyevsky's faith in the innate wisdom of the Russian people that he was, apparently, ready to believe that the renovation of the nation could come about even if the educated classes of society failed to go to the people and unite with them. Although he would never, in fact, abandon the hope that ultimately all strata of Russian society would fuse into a single, harmonious entity under tsar and God, he cautioned against the self-delusionment of those who believed that this union was near at hand, when just the opposite was true; there was "almost no moral consensus about anything; everything has fragmentized and continues to fragment. . . ." To those who were intoxicated with the idea that unity was in the air because "banks, companies and associations are sprouting up" everywhere, Dostoyevsky replied in March 1876: "But surely, now, you can't be alluding to that mob of triumphant Yids and Yehudis [*zhidishki*] who have swooped down upon Russia. Triumphant and exalted, because now even exalted Yids of Judaic and Orthodox persuasion have made their apparition" (11: 222–223).[43]

It was in this curious way that Dostoyevsky reopened the discussion of the Jewish question in the pages of his *Diary*.[44] Two months later (May 1876), the Russian General Chernyayev assumed command of the Serbian armed forces and, shortly thereafter, his troops, strengthened by large contingents of Russian volunteers, launched their attack on the Turks; and in April 1877, Russia formally entered the war against the Ottoman empire. However, Dostoyevsky did not wait for the official opening of hostilities to become a vociferous spokesman for the war party. In April 1876, he was already extolling the regenerative virtues of the battlefield on the lifeblood of the nation, even going so far as to reconcile the clash of arms with Christian principles. As the war fever of the country mounted, Dostoyevsky added fuel to the flames. In a time of national crisis, if there was one weapon that could not be allowed to be blunted, it was that constituted by the traditional animosity of the people against the traditional internal enemy—the Jews.

Let no one err or dare forget: "The Russian land belongs to the Russians, to the Russians *alone* . . . and so it shall ever be" (11:

405–406). In these solemn terms, Dostoyevsky, in September, called to order those who attributed the unrest in the Caucasus in that summer of 1876 to the harassment of the Tatars by the tsarist authorities. But this lofty proclamation also provided the context of and the sanction for one of Dostoyevsky's favorite themes: the usurpation by the Jews of the Russian lands to ensure their domination over the country and its hapless population. This was, as we saw earlier, the reckless charge he made in the June 1876 issue of *The Diary*. In the following issue (July–August) he returned to the attack, taking as his point of departure an article in the *Moscow Record* on the depopulation of the Crimea resulting from the mass exodus of the Tatar population. While agreeing with the author that there was no cause for undue concern since the void could be filled by the introduction of Russian colonists, Dostoyevsky, nevertheless, injected a note of pessimism: "should the Russians fail to settle there, the Yids will surely swoop down on the Crimea and exhaust the soil of the region" (11: 334). Perhaps, indeed, Dostoyevsky conceived of this as a real danger if one is to judge from his growing concern over the incapacity of the Russians to manage their affairs, with the result that "practice was, perforce, falling into the hands of the Israelites [*iudei*] alone" (11: 224). The failure of the Russians to solve the land problem after the Emancipation was a case in point: it had opened the way for all kinds of speculation, particularly in railroad stocks. And who was behind it all? The "Yids," of course (11: 377).

The pernicious influence of Zion was not, however, limited to Russia alone. It was enough to look at the events taking place outside of the empire to be convinced of this. The "Bulgarian atrocities" perpetrated by the Turks in May 1876 as they marched northward to engage the Serbian armies inflamed Russian opinion. And they made a deep impression on Dostoyevsky. He expressed his indignation not only in the pages of his *Diary* but also, a few years later, in *The Brothers Karamazov* (XIV: 217–218). That Europe, that England, in particular, could condone the massacre of "hundreds of thousands" of their Christian brethren by the Turkish infidel and proffer sympathy and support to the Turks in order to protect their vulgar mercantile interests, allegedly imperiled by Russian expansionist ambitions in that part of the world, was proof of their complete moral bankruptcy (11: 339–342). If Europe could so turn its back on the loftiest traditions of civilization and trample underfoot the most sacred principles of morality and humanity, it meant that it was no longer master of its own destinies. And what was the cause of this moral and spiritual decline? Dostoyevsky provided the answer in the form of a rhetorical question: "Can it really be true that the Yid has once again enthroned himself everywhere, and not only 'has enthroned himself' again but never ceased to reign" (11: 342)? This was a transparent allusion to European finance, personified by the Rothschilds, and to Benjamin Disraeli, the earl of Beaconsfield. After the outbreak of the Russo-Turkish War and especially during and after the Congress of Berlin (June–July 1877), the ruling circles in St. Petersburg held the Rothschilds and the British prime minister responsible for the anti-Russian policy of the Western powers.

Dostoyevsky now zeroed in on the earl of Beaconsfield, devoting the whole first chapter of the September 1876 issue of his *Diary* (11: 385–389) to this illustrious personage.[45] In this brilliant but mordant piece of political satire, he sought to inflame the Panslav ardor of his readers even if it meant appealing to their baser instincts. An amusing little incident that had occurred some years back while Dostoyevsky was staying in Florence—the commotion caused by the discovery of a *piccola bestia*, a tarantula, in his hotel room—serves as the point of departure for his thoughts on the Eastern question. It soon becomes clear that were it not for the *piccola bestia* that was crawling over Europe, that question would long ago have been resolved. The metaphor is, for the moment, obscure, but not for long. The tarantula is none other than "Viscount Beaconsfield, born Israel (*né d'Israeli*)" (11: 387), though, for rhetorical effect, Dostoyevsky hastens to add that he has in mind "only an idea, and not a person, and besides it would be giving Mr. Beaconsfield too much credit, although it must be admitted that he does very much resemble a *piccola bestia*" (11: 388). Lest his racial origins have escaped the notice of the inattentive reader, misled by the "family-album name" of Beaconsfield that he assuredly invented for himself "when he was trying to get his peerage from the queen," Dostoyevsky reestablishes his identity: "that Israel, that new judge of honor in England." And he turns again to that sinister metaphor: "Spider, spider, *piccola bestia*; he really does resemble it enormously; in truth, a small, hairy *bestia*! And, wow, does he travel fast! And that massacre of the Bulgarians, why he's the one who permitted it, nay, more, he's the one who thought it up; he's a novelist, you know, and that's his *chef d'oeuvre"* (11: 388).

But the best is yet to come. The image of the tarantula, with all that it inspires of revulsion, perfidy, cruelty, craftiness, and guile, fades into the background. The time has come to excoriate Disraeli for his cynicism and profound amorality in the face of the torturing and crucifixion of two Orthodox priests by the sultan's bashi-bazouks (11: 389):

> "Well, now," Beaconsfield muses, "those black-clad corpses on those crosses . . . hum . . . of course it's . . . But then 'the state is not a private person, it cannot sacrifice its interests out of sentimentality, the more so since in political affairs magnanimity is never itself disinterested.' It's amazing the beautiful maxims that are thought up," Beaconsfield reflects, "they're even refreshing and, the main thing, so well turned. When you come to think of it, the state . . . But, on the other hand, I'd better turn in . . . Hm. Well, why all the to-do about those two priests? Those popes? Popes, they call them, *les popes.* It's their own business if they happened to be around there; well, they could have hid themselves somewhere . . . under a couch . . . *Mais, avec votre permission, messieurs les deux crucifiés,* you have bored me stiff with your stupid adventure, *et je vous souhaite la bonne nuit à tous les deux."* [46]

For Dostoyevsky, the reign of the Jews was now synonymous with the ascendancy of materialism, the vampire [47] that had sucked European civilization dry of its spiritual substance and life-giving forces and was now casting its shadow over Russia. Unless the demon was impaled on the fiery cross of true Christianity, Russia, too, would be ravaged by it. The monster of materialism was already at work, the "kulak" and the "bloodsucker" (read "Yid") were thriving; corruption and depravity were rife. Under the pernicious influence of the Jews, the Russian merchant had succumbed to the temptation of the "gold bag"; so venal had he become that he was ready "to join up with the first Yid who came along to betray everybody and everything if his profit depended on it; patriotism, civic spirit is practically nonexistent in these hearts" (11: 439). And yet, all hope was not lost—there were still the people. Although they had been exposed to the contagion of materialism, they had not forsaken their ancestral beliefs, they were the valiant torch-bearers of Christendom, lighting the way out of darkness to ensure the salvation of Russia and of all mankind. For Dostoyevsky, the Russo-Turkish War was the crucible in which their faith was being tested and the battleground of their martyrdom for Christ.

As for those who questioned or would deny the justice of the Slav cause, they were the disciples of the Antichrist. With seemingly cool detachment, Dostoyevsky divided them into two categories (11: 503):

> The first category is what may be called *the Judaizers*. They keep harping on the damaging effects of the war on the economy, they conjure up the specter of bank failures, falling exchange rates, the stagnation in trade, and even our military weakness. . . . Now what are they really griping about, the Judaizers? The answer is clear: first and foremost, the discomfort that they are occasioned; but, without dwelling on the moral side of the issue, let us note, secondly, their abysmal lack of understanding of the historical and national significance of the task lying ahead. They regard the affair as some sort of momentary little caprice that can be terminated at will: "you have had your fling, so to say, enough is enough, and now let's get down to business again"—stock-exchange business, of course.
>
> The second category is *the Europeanizers*, that old penchant we have for Europeanizing. From this quarter, the most "radical" questions are still heard: "The Slavs, what are they to us, and why should we love them? Why should we fight for them . . . ?"

In all fairness it must be said that Dostoyevsky's tone here is surprising in its moderation. In assailing the Judaizers, he is, by all evidence, singling out not only the Jews as such, but also all the moneyed elements of Russian society who were unscrupulous in the pursuit of their own selfish interests. It was on this note of disenchantment that Dostoyevsky brought to a close his *Diary of a Writer* for 1876.

The anti-Jewish tone of *The Diary* did not leave Dostoyevsky's Jewish readers indifferent. Of the nearly two hundred known letters the author received from his readers in 1876 and 1877, around thirty were from Jewish correspondents, one-half of which concerned the Jewish question. About some of these letters, we possess only the barest information: name of correspondent (if the letter was not anonymous), date, place of origin, length, size of paper, text (if any) of Dostoyevsky's annotation—always laconic, sometimes acrimonious, highly revealing.[48] About others, we have much more extensive knowledge: the full or partial texts of the letters and biographical information about the authors. This is notably true in the case of the two most important of Dostoyevsky's Jewish correspondents, Arkady Grigoryevich (Avraam-Uriya) Kovner and Sofya Yefimovna Lurye, the only ones, as far as is known, with whom he engaged in a dialogue, which spread, moreover, to the pages of his *Diary*.

An anonymous two-page letter dispatched from Moscow on May 12, 1876, is noteworthy for being the first known manifestation of readers' concern over Dostoyevsky's treatment of the Jewish question in *The Diary*. Since the text of this letter has never been published, we are reduced to pure conjecture as to its substance. But given the date of the letter, it may be supposed that its author or authors commented on the few anti-Semitic innuendos contained in the March and April issues of *The Diary*.[49] Could the content and the tone of this letter have been such as to precipitate Dostoyevsky's intemperate and full-blown attack against the Jews in the June issue, where, as related earlier, he fully endorsed the Brafmanian thesis of *status in statu*? The link is not inconceivable when one recalls how violently Dostoyevsky reacted to adverse criticism.[50] There was no further negative reaction from readers to Dostoyevsky's handling of the Jewish question in the extant letters for the year 1876.

At the end of January 1877, Dostoyevsky received a twenty-four–page letter from Arkady G. Kovner, erstwhile radical journalist and now convicted embezzler, awaiting transfer to Siberia from his Moscow prison.[51] Born into a poor Jewish family in Vilno in 1842, Kovner at an early age rebelled against his traditional Talmudic upbringing and, abandoning his young wife and small children, he settled in Kiev where he plunged into the study of Russian, foreign languages and the natural and social sciences. In the radical atmosphere of the sixties, he soon came under the influence of Chernyshevsky and Pisarev and became a fervent disciple of the latter. Writing in the militant style of his intellectual mentor, he came to be known, in time, as the Jewish Pisarev.

With his fiery pen, Kovner battled against his fellow Jews on two fronts: against Talmudic traditionalism and against the reformism of the Haskalah or enlightenment movement. The former he dismissed as obscurantist; and the program of the latter, he contended, was ill-suited to the demands of the times. Kovner denied the existence of a Jewish literature and scored the attempts of the Enlighteners to revive Hebrew as a living language as opposed to Yiddish. For Yiddish was the only language understood by the Jewish masses and, until such time as it was replaced by the Russian language—as it surely would be—Yiddish remained the sole vehicle for the propagation of scientific knowledge. (A true Pisarevian, Kovner insisted at the time that the only valid purpose of literature was utilitarian.)

In the two (and only) books he wrote in Hebrew—*Heker Dabar* (*A Critique*, 1865) and *Zeror Perahim* (*A Bouquet of Flowers*, 1868)—Kovner assailed traditionalist Judaism, lashing out against the secluded life of the ghetto, Talmudic doctrine and religious and national fanaticism. Only by completely breaking with the past could the mass of Russian Jewry accede to the benefits of universal knowledge and culture. Both of these books were met with a storm of criticism by Orthodox Jewish leaders who branded Kovner a renegade and nihilist.

At the time his second book was published, Kovner had already been living in Odessa for two years and writing for various organs of the Yiddish-language press. But following the campaign of denunciation, all doors were closed to him and he was compelled to abandon his career in Jewish journalism. In 1871, after spending one year as a private tutor in the city of Kungur, in the Middle Urals region, Kovner arrived in St. Petersburg to begin his career as a Russian journalist. He collaborated with a number of radical journals, among them the *Cause* (*Delo*) and *Universal Labor* (*Vsemirnyi trud*), and in 1872 he became the feuilletonist of Krayevsky's liberal newspaper, the *Voice* (*Golos*). It was on the pages of this journal that Kovner, in 1873, first joined battle with Dostoyevsky, accusing him of having betrayed his former ideals and having abandoned the defense of "the insulted and the injured" by defecting to the reactionary camp of the *Citizen*.[52]

In that same year, however, personal circumstances forced Kovner to quit the field of journalism for more lucrative employment. On his arrival in Petersburg, he had taken a furnished room in the apartment of a poor Jewish widow by the name of Kangisser, the mother of four. In the course of the next few years, Kovner not only became the family's sole source of support but also developed an attachment to the eldest daughter, Sofya, who suffered from tuberculosis. Seeking a way out of his financial predicament, he ended up by taking a job in the St. Petersburg Discount and Loan Bank, which was run by the well-known financier Abram Zak. With each passing month, with each passing year, the futility of his action, the hopelessness of his situation, became more and more apparent; the fifty rubles he earned per month were sorely inadequate; his repeated requests for an increase were turned down; he sank deeper and deeper into debt. It was then that Kovner made his fateful decision, the details of which he related to Dostoyevsky in his first letter to him of January 26, 1877: [53]

> My observations of the bank's operations over a two-year period convinced me that all banks are based on fraud and deceit. Seeing people making millions, I let myself be tempted and decided to embezzle a sum equal to three percent of the annual *net profits* received by the stockholders of the richest bank in Russia. Those three percent amounted to 168,000 rubles.

Explaining further the personal motives that led him to commit his act and that he felt no remorse whatever, he continued:

> In the light of all that, is it not excusable that I should have appropriated those three percent? They would have enabled me to ensure the support of my old and infirm parents, my large poor family, my young children from a first marriage, a beloved and loving young girl, her family and, besides, many other "insulted and injured" souls, without causing any *serious harm* to anybody.

It was this disciple of Raskolnikov,[54] this son of Israel who had been repudiated by his own people, this felon who, from the depths of his prison cell, now called the great writer to account for his hatred of the Jews. And yet, it is somewhat surprising that Kovner, who himself shared or seems to have shared some of the same prejudices that Dostoyevsky had against the Jews, should now come out as their staunch defender. How is this to be explained?

It would seem that Kovner no longer saw things quite in the

same light as in the sixties. Though his main concern remained what it always had been—the emancipation of the mass of Russian Jewry—he now discovered that there were other more serious, more fundamental obstacles to the achievement of that goal than those erected by and within the Jewish community itself. The "marvelous decade" of the sixties held out the promise of the progressive extension of the rights of Jews, of the enjoyment of full civic equality, of access to the vast world that lay outside. But the Jewish leaders would have none of it: the liberals of the Haskalah no less than the Talmudic conservatives were determined to perpetuate the ghetto or, at least, the spirit of separatism. For the young Kovner, the problem was to combat and overcome the enemy from within.

But hope was followed by disillusionment in the wake of the intensification and spread of anti-Semitism, favored if not fanned by a governmental policy that, from the early seventies onward, was becoming more and more reactionary. Kovner's ideas, too, about Judaism and the Jews had also perceptibly changed.[55] The young rebel of yesterday had been fired by the youthful ardor and wrath of the apostate, but, at the same time, his breadth of vision and experience of life were narrow and limited. He had fled the Vilno ghetto but had not escaped from it: in Kiev first and then in Odessa, he again found himself in an exclusively Jewish milieu. It was only after his arrival in Petersburg that this Jew, who saw himself as fully emancipated, discovered how isolated he was, how much the Jew, wherever he was, remained a prisoner of the ghetto. And little by little, Kovner came to realize that this isolation, this withdrawal into oneself, stemmed from other causes than the attitude of the Jews themselves. Alarmed by the new danger imperiling the cause of Jewish emancipation, the upsurge of anti-Semitism now backed by the authoritative voice of a writer of Dostoyevsky's stature, Kovner could not keep silent.

The first half of his letter of January 26 to Dostoyevsky is largely autobiographical, and from the outset he announces its main intent: "First of all, I am a Jew and you don't like Jews very much (I'll have something to say about this later on)." Before coming to the heart of the matter, Kovner notes his disagreement with Dostoyevsky's views "on patriotism, on national character in general, on the spirit of the Russian people in particular, on the Slavs, and even on Christianity," while adding that he had no intention of elaborating on such questions. And he continues:

> But I do intend to deal with one matter that completely escapes my understanding. That is your hatred of the "Yid," which manifests itself in practically every issue of your *Diary*.
>
> I would like to know why you inveigh against the "Yid" and not against the exploiter in general. I cannot stand any more than you the prejudices of my people—I have suffered quite a bit from them myself—but I will never concede that shameless exploitation is imbued in the blood of that people.
>
> Can it be that you are unable to bring yourself to acknowledge that fundamental law of all social life by virtue of which all citizens of one state without exception, so long as they assume all the obligations necessary for the existence of the state, ought to enjoy all the rights and privileges conveyed by it, and by virtue of which those who violate the law, harmful members of society, are subject to one and the same measure of punishment, common to all? Why, then, must all Jews be circumscribed in their rights, and why, then, must they be governed by special penal laws? In what way is exploitation by foreigners (the Jews are, after all, Russian subjects) —Germans, Englishmen, Greeks, and there are a helluva lot of them in Russia—better than exploitation by Yids? In what way is the Russian Orthodox kulak, parasite, seller of spirits, bloodsucker, who have spread in such profusion all over Russia, better than the Yids of that ilk, who, for all that, operate in a limited sphere? In what way is *Gubonin* better than *Polyakov, Ovsyannikov* better than *Malkiel, Lamansky* better than *Gintsburg*?[56] I could ask you questions like that by the thousands.
>
> However, when speaking about the "Yid," you include in that term the whole destitute mass of the three-million Jewish population of Russia, at least 2,900,000 of whom are waging a desperate struggle for a miserable existence, while being morally cleaner not only than other nationalities but also than the Russian people whom you deify. You also include under that designation a respectable number of Jews with a higher education who are distinguishing themselves in all spheres of state life—take, for example, *Portugalov, Kaufman, Shapiro, Orshansky, Goldstein* (who died a hero's death in Serbia, fighting for the Slav cause), *Vyvodtsev* and hundreds of others who are working for the welfare of society and mankind.[57] Your hatred of the "Yid" even extends to Disraeli, who probably doesn't even know himself that his ancestors were, at one

time, Spanish Jews and who, obviously, is not directing the policy of the Conservatives from the viewpoint of a "Yid." A propos, in one issue of your *Diary* you said something to the effect that Disraeli *wheedled* his lordship out of the queen, whereas it is common knowledge that when the queen *offered* him a lordship in 1867, he declined it because he wanted to continue serving in the House of Commons.

No, unfortunately, you know nothing about the Jewish people, its life, its spirit or, for that matter, its forty-century–old history. I say unfortunately because you are, in any case, a sincere and absolutely honest man, but you are causing unintentional harm to a huge mass of destitute people, while the influential "Yids" who are receiving in their salons ministers, "members of the Council of State," have, of course, no fear of the press or even of the impotent wrath of the exploited. But enough on that subject. There is little chance of convincing you of my way of thinking, but I would be extremely pleased if you convinced me. . . .

Perhaps you may wish to say something in your *Diary* about some of the matters I have touched on; feel free to do so, but without mentioning my name, of course.

Dostoyevsky would accede to Kovner's wishes, devoting the major part of the March 1877 issue of *The Diary* to "The 'Jewish Question.'" Furthermore, except for a few minor deletions and stylistic modifications, he faithfully reproduced the incriminatory passages of Kovner's letter, which even served as the introduction to his essay.

Prior to the publication of the March issue, Dostoyevsky showed Kovner the courtesy of a personal reply on February 14, which, as will be seen, was also an answer to a second letter from Kovner, that of January 28. In that letter, much briefer than the first—six pages in all—Kovner expressed some regret over having sent his first letter, so moved was he by the profound feelings of compassion that infused Dostoyevsky's article on the Kornilova affair in the December 1876 issue of *The Diary* (11: 475–482). But his main reason for writing this time was to dispute the view expressed by Dostoyevsky in the article entitled "Unsubstantiated Statements" in that same issue (11: 485–488), namely, that "there is *only one* supreme idea in this world and that is the idea of the immortality of the human soul." But, Kovner maintained, the existence of the soul and, *a fortiori*, its immortality presuppose the existence of God; and that God does not exist has been cogently demonstrated by the discoveries of science, Darwinism, our knowledge of the solar system and so forth.[58] "In view of all this," Kovner asks, "of what importance to me (and everybody else) are Judaism, the cradle of the newest religions, Christianity, all those legends about miracles, the apparition of God, Christ and his resurrection, the Holy Ghost . . . all those ringing and hollow phrases like immortality of the soul, humanity, progress, civilization, national spirit, etc., etc.?" One might just as well, opined Kovner, speak not only of the immortality of the human soul but also of the immortality of the soul of a pig, dog, groundhog and even bacteria.

Anticipating that Dostoyevsky might counter with the argument that "man carries within him the spark of God" and stands, therefore, above all other living creatures, Kovner concludes with a provocative brutality:

> But how many men are there like that? Literally, a drop in the ocean. You will have to admit that of the eighty-million strong Russian people, on whom you have set your heart and in whom you think you have found a panacea . . . a good sixty million of them live literally like animals and don't have the slightest rational understanding either of God or Christ or of the soul or its immortality.[59]

Dostoyevsky replied to Kovner's two letters on February 14. Before broaching the Jewish question, he complimented his correspondent on his first letter—"I have rarely read anything more intelligent"—and touched briefly on other points raised by Kovner. He then proceeded to the subject that was close to both their hearts and occupied fully one-half of his four-page letter:

> Now about the Jews. As I mentioned earlier, it is impossible to enlarge on a theme like that in a letter, *especially with you.* You are so intelligent that, even in a hundred letters, we wouldn't resolve an issue as controversial as that, we would only tear each other apart. I can tell you that I have received similar observations from other Jews also. In particular, I recently received a letter of sublime nobility from a Jewish girl, and signed by her, that also contained bitter reproaches.[60] I shall, I think, write a few lines about the grievances expressed by Jews in my February *Diary* (which I haven't begun writing yet for I still haven't fully recovered from a recent attack of epilepsy). And now let me tell you that I am

not at all an enemy of the Jews nor have I ever been. But their forty-century–old existence, as you put it, proves the exceptional vitality of that people that, throughout its entire history, could not help but manifest itself in various forms of *status in statu.* The most pronounced form of *status in statu* is, undoubtedly, that possessed by our Russian Jews. And that being so, how could they fail to come into conflict, at least *partially,* with the autochthonous nation, the Russian people? You mention the Jewish intelligentsia, but you, after all, are part of that intelligentsia, and just look how you hate the Russians, and precisely *just because you are a Jew,* even though a cultivated one at that. Your second letter contains a few lines about the moral and religious consciousness of sixty million of the Russian people. Those are words of terrible hate, yes, hate, because you as an intelligent man ought surely to understand that you have no competence whatsoever to pass judgment in that sphere (i.e., in the question of to what extent and on what scale the ordinary Russian is a Christian). I would never speak about the Jews as you speak about the Russians. Throughout my fifty years of life, I have seen Jews, both good and bad, refuse even to sit down at the same table with Russians, while the Russian would feel no qualms about sitting down with them. Who, then, hates whom? Who is intolerant of whom? And what's this idea about the Jews being an insulted and injured nation? On the contrary, it is the Russians who are insulted in every way as compared with the Jews, for the Jews, besides enjoying almost full equality of rights (they even become officers and in Russia that's everything),[61] also have their own code, their own law and their *status quo,* which is under the protection of *Russian* laws.[62]

But let us leave it at that; the subject is a vast one. An enemy of the Jews, that I have never been. I have Jewish acquaintances. There are Jewish girls who even now come to see me for advice on different matters; they read *The Diary of a Writer,* and although they are touchy, as all Jews are, about the Jews, they are not unfriendly toward me; on the contrary, they come to see me. . . .[63] Your (first) letter is delightful. I would like to believe with all my heart that you are sincere. But even if you are not sincere, it makes no difference: for in the given instance, insincerity is, in its way, a very complex and profound matter. Believe in my complete sincerity in shaking the hand that you have extended to me. . . .[64]

Dostoyevsky thus ended his letter by calling into doubt Kovner's "sincerity," a singular reaction that gives rise to a number of questions. In what way might he have been insincere? In his hypersensitivity to the "Jewish question," as Dostoyevsky suggested? In exaggerating the anti-Jewish prejudices of the author of *The Diary*? One becomes lost in conjecture unless it is assumed that Dostoyevsky was seeking here implicitly to establish justification for his own lack of sincerity. Is he not, then, pleading his own cause in this dialectic of the good faith that lies and the bad faith that speaks the truth? The line that separates the one from the other is so thin, the border, so blurred. Ambiguity is an unassailable stronghold, and Dostoyevsky finds comfort and safety inside it. Who, then, would dare accuse him of bad faith when he claimed that the Jews enjoyed virtually full equality under the laws of the Russian empire and, more than that, special privileges?

In reality, to speak here of a lack of sincerity would be inappropriate. Anyone who knowingly disregards incontrovertible facts is guilty of much more than that. The lie is more than equivocation and brings its full weight to bear even on the pages of a private letter. But what is to be said of the lie that is adroitly fabricated and intentionally disseminated in the thousands of copies of a *Diary* intended for thousands of readers who are, perhaps, eagerly waiting to hear the great writer confirm their own lies and prejudices?

It would be futile to plead extenuating circumstances for Dostoyevsky, alleging his ignorance of the facts. For he himself furnishes the proof that he was perfectly aware of the arsenal of special laws that placed the Jews of Russia under the severest disabilities, constraints and restrictions of every order.[65] Not only was he aware of these laws, but he considered them legitimate and indispensable, Russia's only safeguard against a cancerous growth that, if allowed to spread any further, would destroy the organism of the state. They had already been circumvented by too many Jews; the vital forces of the nation were being sapped; and unless the state was vigilant . . . Such is, as we shall see, the dominant theme of "*Pro* and *Contra*," a major section of Dostoyevsky's essay on the Jewish question in the March issue of *The Diary*. It took as its point of departure a passage from Kovner's third letter of February 22, his reply to Dostoyevsky's of February 14. This third letter merits particular attention not only because it (together with the first two) throws light on chapter 2 of the March *Diary*,[66] but also because Kovner makes a serious attempt to clear up the misunderstandings caused by some of his earlier remarks that Dostoyevsky had found offensive. But Kovner was wasting his time; Dostoyevsky would take no account of these clarifications in his March article.

Kovner wrote Dostoyevsky the following on February 22:

> As far as the Jewish question is concerned, it is really too vast a topic and I shall not elaborate on it. I stand by my conviction, however, that it is above all necessary to give them [the Jews], as well as all other foreign peoples in Russia, all civic rights. Just think that Jews even today are deprived of the most fundamental right, the right to choose freely their place of residence, which is the source of multiple and severe constraints on the bulk of the entire Jewish population;[67] and then they are asked to fulfill their obligations to the state and the native-born population.[68] I will add that you grossly exaggerate [the importance of] the Jewish *status in statu*. It hardly exists any longer today, and if traces of it are still found in some places, the only reason is that they [the Jews] are forcibly crammed together in one spot and are condemned to a relentless struggle for a miserable existence.
>
> Moreover, I cannot imagine where you ever got the idea that I "hate" the Russians and, the more so, "precisely just because I am a Jew." My God, how wrong you are! How could you have drawn such a conclusion from my letter? Do you know that I love the whip-lashed and downtrodden masses of the Russian people incomparably more than I do the Jewish people? When I speak of sixty million Russian people as being idolators, these are not "words of terrible hate, yes, hate," as you claim, but quite the contrary; they are words of the deepest sympathy because, as you know only too well, the immense majority are kept in such a state of ignorance and mortal fear that they don't have the vaguest idea of the teachings of Christ or of true Christianity.

Kovner goes on to tell of a personal incident. While traveling by stagecoach from Kiev to Odessa in 1866, he made the acquaintance of a retired Russian general, who got on near Yalta. The general, a large landholder, complained bitterly of the situation in Russia since the Emancipation Act. "I did not have many peasants," he said, "maybe two hundred souls in all, but I was their uncontested master, I had the power of life and death over them, their wives served my pleasure, their daughters were my silent slaves. And now? Now these same animals not only are no longer in my power; they all but laugh at me, jeer at me; they insult my wife, my family, they don't take off their hats to us."

But Kovner had always been a fervent advocate of the Emancipation: "a poor Jew who has nothing in common with the Russian people, who is tolerated in Russia only as an unavoidable evil, who is without rights, powerless, rejected by all," and who, whatever Dostoyevsky might think, "rejoices from the bottom of his heart that a people who are alien and hostile to him have been called to a new life and are protected from the knout and the stick of a 'master.'" And he continues:

> And now, judge for yourself whether I nourish that "terrible hate" toward the Russians just because I am a Jew! I swear to you . . . that I ardently love the honest and industrious Russian people; yes, I feel myself much more a Russian than a Jew. Nonetheless (or rather for that very reason), I daresay that sixty million of them continue to live without any idea of Christianity (I am not, of course, referring to the ritualistic side) and are no way different from pagans.

And finally, disputing Dostoyevsky's view that he, as a Jew, was not competent to judge the religious feelings of the ordinary Russian, Kovner wrote: "I have a good knowledge of the history of Christianity, I daresay I know its spirit, I know Russian history, and finally I know the life of the Russian people infinitely well. Why, then, am I incompetent?" [69]

These, then, are the three letters that, Kovner hoped, would lead to a genuine and fruitful dialogue with the great writer. But Dostoyevsky saw them only as a defiant challenge; he would lose no time in taking it up.

7. The "Jewish Question"

THE MARCH 1877 issue of *The Diary of a Writer* is comprised of three chapters; it is only the last two that will be of concern to us here. The key chapter—chapter 2—is divided into four sections: 1—"The 'Jewish Question' "; 2—"*Pro* and *Contra*"; 3—"*Status in statu.* Forty Centuries of Existence"; 4—"But Long Live Brotherhood!" Chapter 3—the chapter of "reconciliation"—is divided into two sections: 1—"The Funeral of a 'Citizen of the World' "; 2—"An Isolated Case" (12: 76–95). Let us first consider chapter 2.

1. *"The 'Jewish Question' "*

Oh, don't imagine that it is really my intention to raise the "Jewish question"! I wrote down that title in jest. To raise a question of such magnitude as that of the situation of the Jews in Russia and *the situation of Russia*, which counts among its sons three million Jews—I'm not up to it. (12: 76)[1]

The flippant tone of the feuilletonist, from the outset, is hardly in keeping with the gravity of the subject Dostoyevsky is about to embark on. And yet, there is more than a kernel of truth in this preamble. At no time does he deal with the "Jewish question"; the only question he sees and is willing to see is the "Russian question," that of the survival of the nation that numbers "three million Jews" among its population. To put it in another way, the problem for Dostoyevsky is to find a way of disarming a people endowed with such vitality, energy and intelligence and imbued with a spirit of such solidarity and to render it harmless to the society that has given it shelter. Thus, by a curious reversal of the dialectic, Dostoyevsky transforms Solovyov's aphorism *"the Jewish question is a Christian question"*[2] into "the Christian [Russian]

question is a Jewish question." He puts the question in the following terms: to what extent are the Jews capable of breaking with
their traditional exclusiveness, of turning their backs on materialism and, in their relations with the Christian world, of acting in
accord with lofty ethical principles? Within this context, Dostoyevsky sets out to expose his grievances against the Jews. If there
still could be any doubts about his belonging to the anti-Semitic
camp, he now proceeds to dispel them himself. It is no longer the
hapless Kovner who is the principal witness for the prosecution, it
is his illustrious correspondent. The more Dostoyevsky denies the
allegations made against him, the deeper he sinks into the mire of
anti-Semitism.

Before acquainting the reader with the text of Kovner's letter of January 26 (which constitutes the better part of section 1),
Dostoyevsky expresses his astonishment at the accusations of hatred against the Jews leveled against him recently by other "educated" and even "high-class" Jews. Might the reason for this be
that "I sometimes refer to a Jew as 'a Yid'?" (12: 77):

> But, in the first place, I never thought that it was so offensive, and,
> secondly, as far as I remember, I always used the word "Yid" to
> denote a certain idea: "Yid, Jewdom, the reign of the Yids" and the
> like. It denoted a certain concept, a trend, a characteristic of the
> times. You can quarrel with the idea, you don't have to agree with
> it, but you can't be offended by a word.

Dostoyevsky was not wrong in suspecting that his use of *zhid* or
"Yid" might have put the Jews off, the more so since, notwithstanding his disingenuous assertion, he used it not "sometimes"
but almost always—in his novels, in his journalistic writings, in his
private correspondence. And why, then, this imprecise precision,
this innocent admission that he "sometimes" used *zhid* instead of
yevrei if, after all, he didn't feel that the term was all that "offensive"?[3]

There is no need to dwell on this point. Some fifteen years
earlier, Dostoyevsky had fully clarified the true implications of the
use of the term *zhid* in *Time* ("The Polemical Incident between
Foundation and *Zion*," December 1861), and the question, it will
be remembered from chapter 3, had been widely discussed in the
press of the period. As for his second argument—"Yid" as the ex-

pression of a *concept*—it is tantamount to an irrevocable verdict against the Jews and the ideas they allegedly incarnate that are responsible for the ills and evils of contemporary civilization. While it is true that Dostoyevsky implies that some non-Jews, too, have let themselves be corrupted by avarice, materialism and so forth, the fact of the matter remains that it is the Jews, the purveyors of these ideas and practices, who are the principal culprits. Nor is it by any means a foregone conclusion that the image conjured up by Dostoyevsky of "the reign of the Yids" is simply a figure of speech to characterize anyone—Jew and non-Jew alike—who worships at the altar of Mammon and is preparing the way for his triumph.[4] For would not Dostoyevsky, until the end of his life, persist in the belief that the Jews alone would come out unscathed, if not even stronger, from the future cataclysm they would bring upon mankind?[5]

In the final analysis, Dostoyevsky considers the charges of anti-Semitism brought against him so absurd as not even to warrant refutation. At best, they were the result of a regrettable misunderstanding that a few words of explanation would suffice to clear up. And with this he breaks off the dialogue to which Kovner had invited him.

Dostoyevsky seeks, rather, to turn Kovner's letter of January 26 to his own advantage, using it as a springboard for a new and incendiary attack against the Jews. Taking "the vehemence of the attack and the degree of touchiness" of his correspondent as a pretext, Dostoyevsky assumes the right to retaliate without any sense of restraint or moderation. The fury shown by Kovner ("an educated and gifted man") in his letter was clear evidence, Dostoyevsky tells his readers, of how the Jews feel about the Russians. "What, then," he asks, "is to be expected from uneducated Jews, of whom there are so many, what are their feelings toward the Russians?" If there is discord between Russians and Jews, "maybe the Russians are not solely to blame" and "it still remains to be seen which side is more at fault" (12: 78).[6] A qualification of pure formality: Dostoyevsky had no intention of drawing up a balance sheet, of weighing the *pro* and the *contra*, as section 2 purports to do. On the contrary, he now proceeds to put the Jewish people in the dock, making all the traditional charges against them and, notably, their exclusive allegiance to the cult of Mammon and, in the process, their undermining of the fundaments of the society that had given them refuge.

2. *"Pro* and *Contra"*

The admission, from the outset, that "it is terribly difficult to fathom the forty-century–long history of a people like the Jews" loses all meaning in the face of the accusations that Dostoyevsky multiplies against them (12: 79–80):

1. ". . . there is certainly no other people in the whole world who complains so much about their own lot . . . their humiliation, their sufferings, their martyrdom."

2. Think what you will, but is it not the Jews who "are reigning in Europe, is it not they who control the stock exchanges . . . and, hence, the policy, the domestic affairs, the moral conduct of the states?"

3. The Slav question would long ago have been resolved in favor of the Slavs and not the Turks "were the Jewish idea not so powerful in the world."

4. ". . . the Russian muzhik and the Russian common man, in general, are virtually more downtrodden than the Jew."

5. There's no use exaggerating the hardships suffered by Jews because of residence restrictions (as Kovner does in his letter of February 22); the sufferings of twenty-three million Russians at the time of serfdom were incomparably worse.

6. And, finally, what has happened to the people since the Emancipation, "who were the first to fall upon them as upon a prey . . . who enmeshed them in their age-old commerce of gold . . . ?"

There follows a long passage about the pernicious influence of the Jews on the Russian economy: the ruin of the peasants, the ruin of the lands the Jews had taken over from their former proprietors. The latter, "at least, had tried not to ruin their peasants." But was there anything surprising about this! "Those pure angels," look what they have done in the southern states of the United States, "they have already swept down in droves on the millions of Negroes who were given their freedom." But there is no need to cast your eyes so far: why right here at home, as the *New Time* (no. 371) reports from Kovno, " 'the Jews . . . have swept down on the local Lithuanian population and all but ruined them with vodka.' " You may object that the newspapers cited lack objectivity. But just pick up any newspaper, you'll find the same stories. Whence the conclusion: "this universal hatred, it surely means something."

After noting once again that the Jews enjoy considerable freedom of movement in spite of the law that curbs it, Dostoyevsky introduces a new theme, that of Jewish particularism, a subject he would elaborate on in section 3. For the moment he simply, but vigorously, argues that it is the Jews—and the Jews alone—who are responsible for their isolation: "our common people have no preconceived, a priori, blind, religious hatred of any sort toward the Jew, such as: 'He's a Judas, he sold out Christ' " (12: 80–82).

In support of that highly dubious statement, Dostoyevsky takes the reader back to the time of his Siberian exile. He would have done better to find a more convincing argument, for his own testimony in *The House of the Dead* gives the lie to his mollifying words. (Had the years dulled his memories or, worse than that, did Dostoyevsky knowingly distort them?) He insists on the kindness and religious tolerance of the convicts toward their Jewish fellow prisoners: "no one *despised* them, no one ostracized them, persecuted them. When they prayed (and the Jews pray shrilly, donning a special garment), no one found that strange, no one bothered them or ridiculed them. . . ." In a word, the Russians are "pure angels," to borrow, with no less irony, Dostoyevsky's characterization of the Jews. If anything, it was the Jewish convicts who were guilty of malice and intolerance toward the Russians: "it was the Jews themselves who, in many ways, shunned the Russians, were reluctant to eat with them, all but looked down upon them . . . and who, in general, manifested their aversion and repugnance toward the Russian, the 'indigenous' people" (12: 82).

Is this the picture that Dostoyevsky left of his life in Omsk? Does one recognize in this composite portrait of the Jew (haughty, contemptuous, malicious) the figure of Isai Fomich? And those Russians, so full of magnanimity, tolerance and kindness toward Isai? It is enough to recall the day Isai Fomich arrived in the camp, the scenes of haggling with the convicts, the baiting of Luchka, the Sabbath observance, to state that all that Dostoyevsky now writes is the product of the wildest fantasy.[7] But he needs this imaginary scaffolding to support his major thesis, namely, that the Jews bear allegiance to an order that is their own, that they are governed by an "idea" that eludes the control of the law common to ordinary mortals, in short, that they form a state within the state. And he is haunted by another fantasy, one of an entirely different nature, which he has no hesitation to share with his readers, knowing that it will acquire the force of a truth in their minds. It is much more than a fantasy, it is a nightmare that plunges the reader from horror to horror to the bottom of the abyss (12: 82–83):

> . . . now and then I am visited by a fantasy: well, now, what would it be like if there were not three million Jews but three million Russians and eighty million Jews in Russia—what would become of the Russians and how would they treat them? Would they allow them to enjoy the same rights as they enjoyed? Would they allow them to worship freely in their midst? Would they not turn them directly into slaves? Or, worse than that, would they not strip them bare! Would they not reduce them to ashes, exterminate them completely, as they did in days of yore with alien peoples, throughout their ancient history?

On this innocent "fantasy" "*Pro* and *Contra*" comes to a close, a title chosen to amuse or rather bemuse. Having given absolution to the Russians and pronounced an anathema on the Jews, Dostoyevsky now set about to discover the source of the Jews' hatred of the Russians, that implacable hatred that, in his eyes, was the core of the problem.

3. "Status in Statu. *Forty Centuries of Existence*"

For the well-informed reader, the very title of the section at once revealed its tenor and reflected little credit on its author. It drew its inspiration from Yakov Brafman's *Book of the Kahal*,[8] which, as we have seen, upheld the thesis that the Jews constituted a foreign body isolated from the rest of the nation, a people that recognized no law but its own and thus stood above the law of the state.

This is the thesis that Dostoyevsky defends throughout the

section, from start to finish. There are reasons to suggest that it was not only inspired by Brafman's work but was written under its direct influence, that is, with the book at hand. Significant in this regard is the use in the title of the term *status in statu*, an expression practically unknown in Russia prior to the appearance of *Kniga kagala* in 1869. However, it was not the 285 acts of the Minsk *kahal* (covering the period 1794 to 1803!), reproduced by Brafman, that held Dostoyevsky's attention. He found more edifying the author's survey of the history of the Jews from biblical times to the present day that supplemented the second edition of his work, published the following year, a copy of which, it will be recalled, Dostoyevsky possessed in his private library. The concordances between the texts of the two authors are too striking to be regarded as the fruit of simple chance.

Let us stop first to consider the passage—as unusual in form as it is in substance—that sets the tone of the third section. After highlighting the salient features of the alleged *status in statu*—"alienation and estrangement elevated to the rank of religious dogma, inassimilability, the belief that there exists in the world but one national personality—the Jew, and that if there are others it is to be presumed that they do not exist"—Dostoyevsky *quotes* the following passage (12: 84):

> "Go thou forth from among the peoples and form thine own entity, and know that henceforth thou art *one before God*, exterminate the others or reduce them to slavery, or exploit them. Believe in thy victory o'er the whole world, believe that all will be humbled before thee. Hold all things in abomination and have no commerce with anyone in thy daily life. And even when thou shalt be bereft of thy land, of thy political personality, even when thou shalt be scattered o'er the face of the whole world, amongst all the peoples —take no heed—believe in all that has been promised thee, now and forevermore, believe that all this will come to pass and, meanwhile, live, loathe, unite and exploit and—be patient, be patient."

The tone, the style, the language of the text have a biblical quality: it is God or one of his prophets addressing the chosen people. This is certainly the effect Dostoyevsky sought to achieve. An artful technique, commonly used by the anti-Semite, who, by sustaining a certain ambiguity, often obtains the desired results. (As for the probity of the practice, that's another matter entirely.)

The "quotation" as such is not to be found either in the Old Testament or in the Talmud.[9] Authentic in certain aspects and unquestionably biblical in inspiration, it is, nonetheless, a pure and simple forgery.

The Old Testament abounds in passages—particularly when lifted out of context—that can be exploited against the Jews. And that is exactly what Brafman did. But what is interesting here is that Dostoyevsky, in fabricating his own "quotation," used precisely the same biblical references as Brafman. To be sure, he rearranged and supplemented them in his own way, the better to justify the thesis of *status in statu*, but the Brafman contribution is too tangible to be the result of pure coincidence.

Dostoyevsky's pseudo-citation, not to speak of section 3 in its entirety, is based on the following fifteen verses of the Old Testament: Leviticus xx, 26, and Deuteronomy vii, 1–3, 6–8; xx, 10–15; xxx, 4–5. All of these references are found, carefully assembled, in the first chapter of the *Book of the Kahal*, marshaling "evidence" of the election of the people of Israel, its particularism, its hatred for other nations and, finally, its right, granted by God, to enslave and even exterminate them.[10] The various verses contain *almost* everything "reproduced" by Dostoyevsky in his amalgam: only two elements are missing that cast doubt on the authenticity of the "quotation" from the start. First of all, the second sentence: "Believe in thy victory o'er the whole world, believe that all will be humbled before thee"; and second, a fragment of the final sentence: ". . . believe that all this will come to pass and, meanwhile, live, loathe, unite and exploit and—be patient, be patient."

The first exhortation—that prophesying the universal domination of Israel—obviously would have no place in the Old Testament: the "whole world" is a concept much too vast. At the same time, however, the "command" (like the second, as well) clearly bears the Brafmanian stamp, a precious indication in itself, which is immediately confirmed by Brafman's commentary in the same first chapter. He links up Deuteronomy vii, 6: "For thou art a holy people unto the Lord thy God: the Lord thy God has chosen thee to be his own treasure, out of all peoples that are upon the face of the earth" with Genesis xlix, 10: "The scepter shall not depart from Judah, Nor the ruler's staff from between his feet, As long as men come to Shiloh; And unto him shall the obedience of the peoples be." And he sees in the juxtaposition of these two verses "the solemn promise of the establishment for them [the Jews] of the eternal Jewish state under the scepter of the Messiah . . . that shall rule over all the peoples of the earth." A few lines on, Brafman defines "the fundamental religious dogma on which Judaism is based" as "the recognition of the Jews as the chosen people and the promise to establish their eternal state and their domination over all other peoples."[11] In endorsing this interpretation, Dostoyevsky reveals how much he is indebted to the Jewish apostate.

"There you have," writes Dostoyevsky, drawing the lesson from his own "quotation," "the essence of that *status in statu,* and then, of course, there are internal and, maybe, occult laws protecting that idea"—an unequivocal allusion to the laws of the *kahal,* which neither he nor Brafman can forgo without destroying the edifice of half-truths they took such pains to erect.

Thus, as Dostoyevsky sees it, the survival of the Jewish people over forty centuries of history can be attributed only to the *status in statu* and is, therefore, proof of its existence. This, then, would explain what Berdyayev would later term "the historical destiny of the Jews." But whereas, for him, that destiny would always remain an enigma: "The very preservation of that people is inscrutable and rationally unexplainable,"[12] Dostoyevsky believed he held the key to that mystery, and that was the *status in statu.* Yet the *status in statu* itself required an explanation; to what could it be attributed? Here Dostoyevsky had no ready answer. After dismissing the most conventional explanations, such as religious persecution, the instinct for self-preservation, inequality before the law, he suggests that its tenacity was due to "a certain driving and impelling idea, something universal and profound, about which, perhaps, mankind is not yet able to say its final word."[13] Dostoyevsky is inclined to see religion as the preponderant element, a view that allows him to broach the Messianic theme, already touched on lightly in the "quotation": "Believe in thy victory o'er the whole world, believe that all will be humbled before thee." Following the example of Brafman, Dostoyevsky now sets out to explore the Jews' age-old belief in the coming of the Messiah, but it is not the Messiah as the Jews conceived of him. Dostoyevsky goes along with the rather widespread interpretation that, for the Jews, the coming of the Messiah meant nothing else but the triumph and universal domination of Israel, a temporal victory and material hegemony. Actually, the Jews attributed a spiritual role to the Messiah; his coming would usher in the reign of God, the establishment of the universal theocracy, something that our author forgets or wishes to forget.

Not only does Dostoyevsky distort the Jewish Messianic idea, he deliberately ridicules it. Once again he reverts to that terrible weapon that had served him so well in the past (cf. Isai Fomich), the weapon of mockery. No more fitting time than this to evoke an "innocent" childhood memory (12: 84–85):

> When I was still a child, I read and heard a legend about the Jews to the effect that even then they were confidently waiting for the Messiah, every one of them, from the lowliest Yid to the highest and most scholarly amongst them, the philosopher and cabalist-Rabbi, that they all believed that the Messiah would gather them together again in Jerusalem and, with sword in hand, would humble all peoples before them; and that is, apparently, why the Jews —or, at least, the vast majority of them—prefer but one profession: dealing in gold or, at the very most, the fashioning of it, and all that, apparently, so that when the Messiah came, they should not possess a new homeland or be nailed down by possessions to an alien land, but own only gold and precious stones that could be easily carried away with them when
> The ray of dawn will glow, will shine:
> Cymbals, timbrels, flutes we'll bear,
> And silver, riches and sacred ware,
> To our ancient home, to Palestine.

As if to avoid any misunderstanding, Dostoyevsky repeats that he had heard all that "as a legend," but adds that it went to "the heart of the matter."

The verses he chose to illustrate the legend are in themselves revealing. He borrowed them from Nestor Kukolnik, a second-rate dramatist, all but forgotten today, who enjoyed a certain renown during the first half of the nineteenth century. Most of his many plays are set in Italy, Spain and Latvia of the fifteenth century. The strange world of Kukolnik is inhabited by knights, ecclesiastics, voivodes, merchants and a generous number of Jewish characters—traitors and schemers, well-versed in the occult sciences and the Cabala. The verses in question were taken from *Prince Daniil Vasilyevich Kholmsky* and are part of the song sung by the Jewess Rakhil, daughter of the rich Pskov merchant and cabalist Zakhary Moiseyevich Oznobin. Written in 1840, the play had its première at the Aleksandrinsky Theater in St. Petersburg on September 30, 1841. It is quite possible that Dostoyevsky saw a performance of this play since he frequented that theater during the winter of 1841–1842.[14] Had Rakhil's Song left such an indelible impression on his mind that thirty-five years later he was able to quote it *from memory?* This is a possibility and might explain two slight errors in Dostoyevsky's rendering of the text.[15]

The link Dostoyevsky established between Jewish Messianism, of religious inspiration, and the *status in statu* (with the persistence of the latter explained only by vitality of the former) undoubtedly warranted further elaboration. But at this crucial juncture in the narrative, the argumentation becomes increasingly muddled, to such an extent that it cannot even be wholly excluded that Dostoyevsky simply introduced the subject of Messianism to avail himself of an opportunity to tell, in all innocence, that startling little tale. At any rate, following that digression, he returns to the question of the *status in statu*, this time in the context of the debate concerning the civic equality to be granted to—or withheld from—the Jews. And it is at this point that one comes upon the phrase often quoted (out of context) by those who would like to obscure or wash away the anti-Jewish essence of Dostoyevsky's essay on the Jewish question.

Dostoyevsky, indeed, wrote the following: "It goes without saying that everything that is dictated by humanity and justice, everything that is dictated by human feeling and Christian law—all that must be done on behalf of the Jews" (12: 85).[16] (And he reiterated that statement in section 4.) But no sooner does he lay down that "inviolable" principle than he reduces it to nought (12: 85):

> But should they, fully armed with their organization and their particularism, their ethnic and religious insularity, fully armed with their codes and principles, diametrically opposed to the idea that up to now, at least, has shaped the development of the whole European world, should they demand full equality in the enjoyment of *all* rights enjoyed by the native population, would they not, then, enjoy something more than, something in addition to, something in excess of those enjoyed by the native population itself?

Dostoyevsky could very well have concluded this section on this word of warning, for what he has to say now he has said time and time again before. But he is determined to put the final touch on his portrait of the Jews, underscoring the trait that, in his eyes, epitomizes the Jews, and that is *bezzhalostnost*, mercilessness, implacable hatred of everything that is not Jewish. Can there be any doubt about it? "Why, just ask the native inhabitants in our border regions what drives the Jew and what has been driving him for so many centuries? Their reply will be unanimous: *merciless-ness*; 'the only thing that has driven him for centuries is his mer-cilessness toward us and his thirst for our sweat and blood' " (12: 86).

Before proceeding to the fourth and final section, Dostoyev-sky takes a last look at Europe and "the triumph of Jewry" there in every sphere: in finance, in domestic and foreign policy and, worst of all, in spiritual life. Like a fiery prophet, revealing the most impenetrable mysteries, he announces the end of the (Chris-tian) world: " . . . what the future holds, that the Jews know: their reign, their complete reign is approaching! Emerging fully trium-phant are ideas eroding feelings of brotherly love, the craving for truth, Christian feelings, national feelings and even the national pride of the European peoples. Materialism . . . is on the way. . . ." (12: 87).[17]

Suddenly, the tone changes, the exaltation wanes, and Dos-toyevsky embarks or seems to embark on the path of conciliation and reconciliation.

4. *"But Long Live Brotherhood!"*

The letter of another Jewish correspondent serves as the point of departure of this concluding section. Respecting, as he had to, the writer's anonymity—for the letter bore only the initials "T.B."—Dostoyevsky went right to the heart of the matter (12: 88):

> But what, then, am I saying, and why? Or am I really an enemy of the Jews? Is it really true, as one assuredly generous and educated young Jewish girl writes[18] (I'm sure she is, judging from her letter and the sincere and ardent feelings that permeate it)—is it true, then, that I am, as she puts it, an enemy of that "unhappy" people whom I (apparently) "never miss an opportunity to attack ferociously"? "Your despisal of the Yiddish people that [you claim] 'thinks only about itself,' etc., etc., is obvious."

"But long live brotherhood!" There is no reason for Dostoyevsky to be embarrassed by the title, for actually it bears no relation to anything that follows. It would make sense only if it were followed by an interrogation mark. In both substance and spirit, there is little that distinguishes this section from section 2 (*"Pro* and *Contra"*), except for the excess of cynicism and sophistry that pervades it. Without mitigating, in the least, his charges against the Jews, Dostoyevsky once again affirms that, in spite of everything, he is "resolutely in favor of the full extension of the rights of Jews in formal legislation and, if at all possible, the fullest equality of rights such as are enjoyed by the native population. . . ." (Let us break off the quotation here to show how Dostoyevsky's intentions can be misconstrued by detaching a sentence or a phrase from its context.) But he continues: ". . . (*N.B.*, although, perhaps, in certain cases, they already enjoy, even now, greater rights or, to put it better, greater *opportunities for exercising them,* than the native population)" (12: 88; the emphasis is Dostoyevsky's). In other words, what Dostoyevsky gives with one hand, he immediately takes back with the other; and in the process, as if regretting every concession made to the spirit of "brotherhood," he unleashes a fresh torrent of accusations.

Once again, as in *"Pro* and *Contra,"* Dostoyevsky gives free rein to his "fantasy" (12: 88–89):

> "Well, now, what if, for some reason or another, our rural commune, which protects our poor native-muzhik against so many ills, should collapse, well, now, what if, right then and there, the Jew should sweep down like a horde [*vsem kagalom*] on that liberated muzhik, so inexperienced, so incapable of resisting temptation . . . yes, what would happen? Why, in a trice, it would be the end of him: all of his property, all of his strength, the next day would be in the hands of the Jew, and this would be the beginning of an era that neither the time of serfdom nor even that of the Tatar yoke could hold a candle to."

Faithful to his method, Dostoyevsky follows through with his customary assurance that "I am, nevertheless, in favor of full and absolute equality of rights because that is Christ's law, because that is a Christian principle" (12: 89).

Dostoyevsky, thus, always returns to his basic idea, that the Jews are much more to blame than the Russians for the present state of affairs: today it is the Russians who are the persecuted and the Jews—the persecutors.

Things being what they are, how can the two peoples be reconciled and "brotherhood" be established? Dostoyevsky sees but one chance and that is that the Jews change, that they become "more tolerant and just" toward the Russians. But the odds are against it, unless, of course, the Jews' "haughtiness, their eternal 'peevish aversion' " toward the Russians is only "a prejudice," an "historical excrescence" and *"does not lie concealed in some much deeper recesses of their law and structure"* (12: 90; the emphasis is Dostoyevsky's). In other words, the Jews would remain what they always had been and harmony with the Russians would never be achieved. That did not prevent Dostoyevsky, however, from executing a final pirouette and advocating the extension of civic rights to all the Jewish people provided that—the game is always the same—"it proves itself capable of accepting and exercising such rights without detriment to the native population" (12: 90).

Such is Dostoyevsky's declaration of principles anent the Jewish question, such is the text that reflects honor on the views of the Brafmans and Grineviches and that added grist to the mill of anti-Semitic "thought" in the closing decades of the nineteenth century.

It is, admittedly, difficult to measure the influence exerted by this contribution—and by other articles in subsequent issues of *The Diary*—on the course of events in Russia, but certain disquieting parallels can be drawn. Thus, after the assassination of Alexander II in March 1881, a wave of anti-Semitism swept over Russia. In August of that year, Provincial Commissions were set up to examine and revise the legislation applicable to Jews. The proceedings of these commissions reveal the same apprehensions as those expressed by Brafman and given endorsement by Dostoyevsky. Thus, one reads in the report of the Vilno Commission:

> For the Jew, there is no fatherland, no state, no laws except their caste laws, no authority except that of their *kahal*. They represent a mobile state within the states against which they are waging permanent and relentless economic warfare.

And in the report of another commission:

> Any further extension of the rights of Jews at the present time

would be dangerous. Let the Jews repudiate their secluded way of life, let them reveal the secrets of their social organization . . . and when they do, we can then give some thought to opening up new spheres of activity to the Jews without fear that they are bent on taking advantage of the privileges of a nationality without being a part of the nation and without assuming their share of the national duties.[19]

Can one exclude altogether the possibility that Dostoyevsky exercised some influence on the ideological formation of Grand Duke Sergei, who, as governor-general of Moscow and commander of the Moscow Military District, would order the expulsion of 20,000 Jews from that city in 1891?[20]

Is there anything startling in the fact that twenty years after the publication of "The 'Jewish Question'" certain pamphleteers, like Anosov,[21] would invoke the name of Dostoyevsky to stir up public passions against the Jews at a time when pogroms were raging? Or that some thirty-five years after, at the famous ritual murder trial of the young Mendel Beilis, Chief Prosecutor O. Yu. Vipper would again invoke the authority of Dostoyevsky to rebut the arguments of Karabchevsky, one of the lawyers for the defense? "If I remind you," said Vipper, addressing the court, "of the prophetic words of the renowned Dostoyevsky, it is not because I wish to speak out against the Jews, but since they are being showered with such praise, something has to be said by way of refutation; he said: 'The Jews will destroy Russia.'"[22]

It matters little that the quotation is inexact, for it does not betray in the least the heartfelt conviction of the author of *The Diary*.[23]

And now, even today, the fear lingers on that some of the great writer's legacy may be mustered in support of anti-Semitism. Would that not be one reason why the Soviet literary authorities decided to exclude *The Diary of a Writer* practically *in toto* from the ten-volume popular edition of Dostoyevsky's *Collected Works* published in 1956 to 1958?[24] Is not that one reason why the deletions made in the fourth volume of Dostoyevsky's *Letters* (1959), as far as one can judge, affected only those passages—and even one whole letter—containing disparaging references to the Jews?[25] Is not that, too, one reason why *all* derogatory allusions to the Jews have disappeared from the *Correspondence* between Dostoyevsky and his wife, published in 1976?[26] Thus, one century after the death of Fyodor Mikhailovich Dostoyevsky, there is still apprehension over the influence some of his writings may have on Soviet readers, in particular, and on foreign readers as well.

Dostoyevsky bears a heavy responsibility, and there is no reason why he should be exonerated. Berdyayev was quite to the point when he wrote that "perhaps the most dismaying thing of all is that those who rejected the cross are the ones who bear it, while the very ones who accepted the cross have used it so often to crucify the others."[27]

What was the reaction of Avraam-Uriya Kovner, the man who had incited Dostoyevsky to take a public stand on the Jewish question? The first thing to be noted is that his letter of June 3, 1877,[28] was characterized by the utmost moderation—one is even tempted to say "Christian humility." There is no disdain, no "peevish aversion," no vindictiveness; moreover, his comments were remarkably laconic.

He began by expressing his profound gratitude to his correspondent for having accorded him the honor of a public response. However, he could not but take exception to the reversal of the situation imagined by Dostoyevsky in which a small minority of Russians were placed at the mercy of a huge majority of Jews. He wrote:

> To my mind, it is much worse to say such a thing about a people in public (or, rather, to harbor such a conviction) than to maintain that the vast majority of Russians are still pagans and idolators today. How can the Russian people help hating the Jews when their foremost representatives refer to them publicly as wild beasts? May you be forgiven for this thoughtless paradox, much-esteemed Fyodor Mikhailovich; I say "thoughtless" because, deep down in your heart, you are the finest of men (as you have proven for the thousandth time in your excellent chapter on a "Citizen of the World" in the same issue of your *Diary*).[29]

Kovner goes on to note that he shared many of Dostoyevsky's opinions about the Jews, but without elaborating on this point, and that he had originally raised the question "more out of a desire to clarify for myself the kind of person you were, in whom I descried the qualities of 'a citizen of the world,' than out of any love or compassion for the Jewish people, who really don't interest me at all." As to Dostoyevsky's remark that he found it hard to conceive of a Jew who did not believe in God, Kovner, noting that this was the case of many young Jews today, asked: "Would you advise them, perhaps, to convert to Christianity when they are unable to believe in any organized religion? Isn't it better for them to remain 'citizens of the world'?"[30]

With this, the Kovner-Dostoyevsky exchange on the Jewish question came to a close. The rest of this letter and Kovner's last two letters of June 30, 1877, and January 21, 1878,[31] dealt only with matters of a personal nature, in particular the question of manuscripts that Kovner had sent to Dostoyevsky in the hope that he would help find a publisher for them—a hope that would never materialize. The strange episode thus ended. But this brief epistolary encounter between this "fugitive" from the ghetto and the great writer sheds a revealing light on one of the most obscure and controversial aspects of Dostoyevsky's intellectual biography.[32]

Kovner was, of course, the most important of Dostoyevsky's Jewish correspondents, but he was not the only one. Others manifested themselves, but, unfortunately, not much is yet known—or, to put it more precisely, the information is withheld—about these correspondents and the contents of their letters.[33] Thus, soon after the appearance of "The 'Jewish Question,'" Dostoyevsky received a short, two-page anonymous letter, dated April 12, 1877; the envelope bears the annotation, written in his own hand, "On the Yids" (*O zhidakh*)[34]—the famous term, it will be remembered, that he did not consider "so offensive." Given the context, the very contrary would seem to be true.

In March 1877, Dostoyevsky received the first of a number of letters from a young gymnasium student in Vitebsk, one Vladimir Kazimirovich Stukalich. Did he belong to the small Polish minority of that city (five percent of the population) or was he a Jew of Polish origin (over one-half of the population of Vitebsk at that time was Jewish)? His letters—eight in all—dealt primarily with his personal situation (poverty, poor health, family matters). But in one twelve-page letter, probably written in the summer of 1877, Stukalich tackled the problem of social inequality and the Polish and Jewish questions. Whether this letter had any bearing on the March essay, we are unable to say. Be that as it may, Dostoyevsky, apparently, never replied to the young Stukalich.[35]

It is even more regrettable that we know next to nothing

about the twenty-page letter, written by Ruvim Moiseyevich Kulisher on April 21, 1877, that directly concerned Dostoyevsky's article on the Jewish question. (It may be safely assumed that it was
highly critical.) Kulisher (1828–1896) was a prominent dermatolo-
gist, a specialist in military health and hygiene and one of the few
Jews holding high rank in the Russian army; a prolific writer, he
wrote a number of important medical books as well as works on
Jewish life and education in both Yiddish and Russian. Dostoyevsky honored his illustrious correspondent with this laconic annotation on the envelope: "The Jewish question by a Jew" (*Yevreiskii
vopros ot yevreya*); [36] he never acknowledged the letter.

And finally, there was a short letter from one Kuznetsova,
writing from Odessa on May 9, 1877, in the same connection. Dostoyevsky filed it away after noting on the envelope: "Medical
treatment authorized." [37]

As to the Russian reaction to Dostoyevsky's public airing of
the Jewish question, there is not much that can be said in the light
of the available evidence. It seems inconceivable that such close
friends of Dostoyevsky as Ivan Aksakov, Prince Meshchersky,
Pobedonostsev or Putsykovich—who fully shared his views on the
question—should have kept silent on the issue, but (at least in their
letters of that period) there is nothing to indicate that the contrary
was true.[38] But there was assuredly nothing reproving in their silence. It is, of course, difficult to believe that Vladimir Solovyov,
to whom Dostoyevsky drew very close in 1877 (they had known
each other since 1873) did not raise and condemn, either privately
or publicly, either then or subsequently, Dostoyevsky's attitude
toward the Jews, but if he did, hardly any traces remain.[39] We do
know, however, thanks to Dolinin, that Dostoyevsky did receive
approving letters from readers. In his introduction to volume 3 of
Dostoyevsky's *Letters*, he notes that " 'true-blue Russians,' 'Muscovites,'[40] admirers of *Moskovskiye vedomosti* thanked him [Dos-
toyevsky] for 'keeping a vigilant eye on *age-old Russian interests*'
and solving 'in the Russian manner' the Polish and Jewish questions." [41]

It would be wrong (and equally dismaying) to think, however,
that there were no "true-blue Russians" who repudiated Dostoyevsky's position. Amid the paucity of evidence, the testimony of
Yekaterina Letkova (1856–1937), a young Moscow University stu-

dent in Dostoyevsky's day, acquires particular significance. In her *Reminiscences*, she tells of meeting Ivan Goncharov at the Makovskys in St. Petersburg in 1879 and of how the conversation at dinner turned to the subject of Dostoyevsky. Without departing from his customary calm, the author of *Oblomov* chimed in: "The young people have a weakness for him. They regard him as a prophet. But he despises them. In every student he sees a despicable socialist, in every girl student a . . ." "Goncharov didn't finish his sentence," Letkova continued. "Whether he had been about to say some vulgar word and then stopped himself short, remembering that I was a girl student, I cannot say."

Not long after, Letkova returned to Moscow. "I decided," she went on,

> I would say nothing about Dostoyevsky in class to avoid stirring up a heated argument about his reactionary views, his Slavophilism, everything that young people at the time reproached him for.
>
> But that was difficult. Dostoyevsky occupied too important a place in the political and social life of the day for his words and pronouncements not to provoke some sort of reaction among the youth. In student circles and meetings Dostoyevsky's name was constantly brought up. Every issue of *The Diary of a Writer* was the occasion of the most violent controversy. His position on the so-called "Jewish question," a position that for us was a kind of litmus test of decency . . . was wholly inadmissible and intolerable: "Yid, Jewdom, the reign of the Yids, the Yid idea taking over the whole world." All of these epithets made the young people's blood boil.[42]

Finally, it may be asked whether the March essay generated any comments in the Russian (and Jewish) daily and periodical press. Here, too, we are unable to give any satisfactory answer, although it may be presumed that it did.[43] Moreover, with the notable exception of Letkova, none of the numerous memoirists has evoked either the article in question or the broader problem of Dostoyevsky's attitude toward the Jews in general. The fact remains, however, that "The 'Jewish Question'" exerted a real and lasting influence on Russia and the Soviet Union.

Let us now take a look at chapter 3 of the March issue of *The Diary*. As mentioned earlier, it is composed of two sections: 1—

"The Funeral of a 'Citizen of the World'" and 2—"An Isolated Case." Like the preceding chapter, it, too, drew its inspiration from the letter of a Jewish correspondent. This time it was the letter of February 13, 1877, from Sofya Yefimovna Lurye, a young Jewish student from Minsk, with whom Dostoyevsky had been in both personal and epistolary contact since the previous year, a relationship that would continue until the end of 1877. Too little is known about this young girl of eighteen for us even to attempt to explain why Dostoyevsky was so taken with her.[44] But the fact remains that he was full of solicitude for her and showed her uncommon kindness and consideration. None of Dostoyevsky's other correspondents—and they were numerous at the time of *The Diary*—enjoyed such warm sympathy and gracious concern as this young Jewess.

Nine months earlier—in his *Diary* of June 1876—Dostoyevsky spoke for the first time of Sofya Lurye, devoting several glowing pages to her (11: 330–332). Without mentioning either her name or her Jewish origin, he tells of how "a young girl"—Sofya was then in St. Petersburg—visited him regularly every month during the winter of 1876 to discuss her problems and seek his advice.[45] Coming from a well-to-do or even wealthy family but reluctant to reconcile herself to her parents' milieu and their way of life (marriage, family, etc.), the shy, modest and reserved young Sofya was searching for another path, a path in which she could be useful to society.

One day, Dostoyevsky tells us, Sofya came by to tell him of her decision to abandon her studies momentarily and go to Serbia to care for the sick and wounded. He did all he could to dissuade her, but seeing that nothing could make her change her mind, he finally gave in to her and sent her on her way with his consent and blessings: "She left, her face radiant with happiness, and you can be sure in a week's time she'll be over *there*" (11: 332). As it turned out, however, her plans didn't materialize,[46] and after spending the better part of 1876 in St. Petersburg, she returned home to Minsk. Whether Dostoyevsky ever saw her after the meeting described in *The Diary* is not known.

Be that as it may, apparently not long after her return to Minsk, Sofya wrote her letter of February 13, 1877, the letter that served as the focal point of chapter 3 of *The Diary*, with its description of the funeral of Dr. Hindenburg. But that was not all it contained: Sofya also sought Dostoyevsky's advice on a matter of a purely personal nature (which shows how much confidence she had in him):

> Mummy definitely wants me to marry the doctor, he's hand-some, rich and a Court Counselor. . . . He's willing to wait for me as long as I want. But how can I marry him when I don't love him? I have great respect for him, but that's as far as it goes. Mummy . . . cried the whole evening. I'm going to tell him I don't love him, and then he won't want to marry me, of course. I am not even nineteen yet. . . .[47]

Dostoyevsky replied on March 11. He had found her letter "charming" and apologized for not answering sooner; he had in-advertently left it unopened for nearly a month.[48] As to the ques-tion of her marriage, he took her dilemma to heart like a father, showing understanding and devotion, his only concern being her happiness. Without knowing exactly why himself, he wanted her to like that man and hoped she would marry him. The difference in age was of absolutely no importance. And then, Dostoyevsky asked a question that, coming from him, was quite astonishing, especially in the light of his subsequent remark in *The Diary* that "Miss L. and I had practically never spoken about 'the Jewish question,' although I think she is a strict and pious Jewess" (12: 91). Toward the close of his letter, he wrote: "There's one thing you didn't mention: what is his religion? Is he Jewish? If he is Jewish, how come he's a Court Counselor? If I am not mistaken, the Jews only quite recently obtained the right to a rank in the civil service. To be a Court Counselor, he would have had to serve at least fifteen years."[49]

What is shocking here is precisely the fact that there is noth-ing at all shocking in the way in which Dostoyevsky broaches the question. At the very moment when he had, unquestionably, al-ready begun drafting his long essay on the Jews—where he would affirm that he never considered the word *zhid* "so offensive," where he would shamelessly flaunt his contempt for the educated Jew, where he would claim that the Jews enjoyed almost full equality of rights—at that very moment, without batting an eye-lash, he is capable of addressing himself in the most seemly and friendly manner to a young Jewish girl whom he esteems. And because he is so utterly sincere, it is all the more astonishing that his feelings toward this young girl had no effect whatever on his attitude toward the community of which she was a part.

The question must, therefore, be asked whether Sofya Lurye was not for Dostoyevsky that classic "Jewish friend" whom he needed to convince himself and to convince others of the preposterousness and groundlessness of the charge that he was an "unconditional" anti-Semite.[50]

This at once conscious and subconscious desire for exoneration might also explain, to some extent, at least, Dostoyevsky's decision to add, as a postscript to "The 'Jewish Question,'" the story of the burial of the good Dr. Hindenburg. Was this not an easy way out, a convenient ploy to shelter himself from the truth of his own feelings and from the accusations of others?

The story of Dr. Hindenburg is the story of a German obstetrician who devoted his whole life to the service of the poor, in a spirit of complete self-abnegation, making no distinction between Orthodox, Jew or Protestant. Not only did he refuse to accept a fee from those who could not pay, but he often left them money and provided them with food.

Sofya Lurye described in her letter—and Dostoyevsky after her in his *Diary*—the emotion that gripped those who stood around the bier of the doctor who had led the life of a saint and who was given the funeral of a saint: "While his body still lay in the coffin (in the church), there was not, I believe, a single person who did not come to weep over him and kiss his feet, especially the poor Jewish women whom he had helped so much; they wept and prayed that he go straight to Paradise" (12: 92). Although it was forbidden by Jewish law (when a non-Jew was being buried), some young Jewish boys chanted psalms. "In all synagogues prayers were said for his soul, and the bells in *all* the churches tolled as the cortège passed by." And Sofya Lurye concluded her account with the poignant image of the priests of different denominations united in their affliction: "At his grave orations were delivered by a pastor and a rabbi, and they both wept . . ." (12: 92).[51]

Against this backdrop Dostoyevsky sets "An Isolated Case," a rather clumsy effort, it must be said, to lecture his public. The example to be followed is, of course, that of the "citizen of the world" Dr. Hindenburg. He is impelled to see in it "something like the beginning of a solution to the whole question . . . why, yes, that same 'Jewish question,' the title I gave to the second chapter of this *Diary"* (12: 93).

Dostoyevsky thereupon takes up his brush to paint, in the highly realistic manner so characteristic of him, the tableau suggested by Sofya Lurye's story: the night cold and forbidding; a wretched hovel; a poor Jewish woman in childbirth; a child born in the flickering light of a sputtering candle; an old doctor, tearing his shirt into strips, to swaddle the infant: "The poor little newborn Jewish babe [*yevreichik*] lies squirming before him on the bed, the Christian takes the tiny little Jew in his hands and wraps him in the shirt torn from his own back." Dostoyevsky exultantly exclaims: "The solution of the Jewish question, gentlemen. . . . All that Christ sees from on high, and the doctor knows it: 'this poor little Yidling [*zhidok*] will grow up one day and perhaps take the shirt off his own back and give it to a Christian, remembering the story of his own birth,' the old man thinks to himself with naive and noble faith" (12: 94).[52]

Will the old doctor's dream come to pass, Dostoyevsky asks? Probably not, but, after all, you never can tell.

An isolated case, a unique case—the case of Dr. Hindenburg —but "the drip-drop of water wears away the stone" and "prejudices will pall before every isolated case and, ultimately, will vanish altogether" (12: 95). Thus, Dostoyevsky places his faith in the "isolated case"; therein lies the key to the unification of all peoples.

If he insists so much on the idea of the exemplary force of the "isolated case," the reason is that he sees in it an effective argument against the liberals, the "politicos," who see the solution of problems, in general, and the Jewish problem, in particular, in the reform of laws and institutions. Using the example of Dr. Hindenburg as a pretext, Dostoyevsky cites the case of another doctor in South Russia who refused to go to the aid of a drowned man who had just been taken from the water. The curious lesson he draws from this incident reveals what he really thinks: "And yet he [the doctor] may have been an educated man, imbued with new ideas, a progressive, but a man who 'rationally' demanded new general laws and rights for everyone, disregarding the isolated cases" (12: 95). In other words, Dostoyevsky is saying, better not rush things, legal reforms are not enough to improve the situation, everything depends on the evolution of human relationships.

There was, indeed, a lesson to be drawn by Dostoyevsky from the life and death of Dr. Hindenburg, from his meetings with the young Sofya, who had but one idea—to serve humanity, just as there was a lesson to be learned from the death of that other young Jew on the Serbian battlefields.[53] And that lesson was that "cases," isolated or not, were not the issue, the issue was human beings; that the Jews, as human beings, were entitled to the same rights and subject to the same duties as their fellows, that no "cases," no matter how exemplary, would ever solve the Jewish question so long as an entire human community was subjected to the law of contempt and exposed to "insult and injury."

That the "drip-drop of water" would in time wear away the granite of mutual distrust and hostility the author of "The 'Jewish Question'" could not himself believe, let alone convince others. Thus, this third chapter was as ineffectual an antidote against the redoubtable effects of the chapter that preceded it—Dostoyevsky's major contribution to the anti-Jewish cause—as it was against everything else he had written earlier in the same *Diary* or elsewhere. Nor is there any evidence that in his subsequent writings— whether in *The Diary*, his letters or his last novel—Dostoyevsky found any inspiration in the example of Dr. Hindenburg. On the contrary, he would resume and even intensify his campaign against the Jews. The drop of water would be lost in a sea of lies.

As for Dostoyevsky's subsequent relations with Sofya Lurye, the following is known from the material that is available. She answered Dostoyevsky's letter of March 11, 1877, on March 28/29, that is, a few days prior to the publication of the March issue of *The Diary*. Something of the contents of her letter (which remains unpublished) is known from Dostoyevsky's reply of April 17.[54] After thanking her for her friendship and saying that he hoped he had caused her no trouble by publishing the story about Dr. Hindenburg, he touched on matters she had raised in her letter: her disagreement with her parents on the question of her marriage, some to-do over her dowry that indisposed her toward her fiancé and the like. Dostoyevsky advised her to be more flexible and show her parents greater understanding. She also wrote of her enthusiasm for Victor Hugo (*Les Misérables*), whom she compared to Goethe and Shakespeare (an opinion that Dostoyevsky did not share). And Dostoyevsky ended his letter with a promise to send Sofya the address where he could be reached after leaving St. Petersburg in May. That letter, unfortunately, is the last to have come down to us.

Sofya continued to write Dostoyevsky rather regularly until the end of 1877: May 7 (her future plans, her passion for Hugo's poetry, fragments of her French translation of Dostoyevsky's "A Gentle Spirit"); July 14 (her hope to enter the university and to lead an independent life); September 3 (an answer to Dostoyevsky's letter, which was a terrible disappointment to her, her reading of Danilevsky's works, her meeting with the poet Minsky-Vilenkin);[55] and, finally, her last known letter sent from Riga in the fall of 1877, in which she thanked Dostoyevsky for his help and told him of her plans to go abroad to continue her studies.[56]

It would surely be of interest to learn what it was in Dostoyevsky's lost letter (probably of August) that she found so distressing. It would also be interesting to learn how and why Dostoyevsky helped her. Sofya's letters would, undoubtedly, shed light on these questions, but their secrets remain locked in Soviet archives. But despite the lacunae that exist, it is clear that the relations between Sofya Lurye and Dostoyevsky were marked by genuine and profound sympathy. The episode remains unprecedented in the life of the great writer: Sofya Lurye was the only person of her race to whom Dostoyevsky extended the warm hand of friendship. And yet, for him to recognize in that people anything else but the *zhid*, decidedly much more was needed than this "isolated case."

8. *Dostoyevsky's Last Years: The Anti-Jewish Theme in His* Diary—*His Letters—His* Notebook—The Brothers Karamazov

BEFORE PROCEEDING to the period of *The Brothers Karamazov*, let us take a look at the issues of *The Diary of a Writer* that appeared between April and December 1877, when Dostoyevsky announced to readers that he was interrupting its publication in order to devote himself once again to purely literary activity.

In April, Russia went to war against Turkey, a war that Dostoyevsky had earnestly desired and now fervently supported in every successive issue of *The Diary*.

The whole first chapter of the April issue was a paean to war, a stentorian call to arms: "War. We Are the Strongest of All"; "War Is Not Always a Scourge, It Is Sometimes Salvation"; "Does Spilled Blood Redeem?" Those who believe or want to believe in the weakness of Russia are sadly deluded. The nation is strong and united. Those who envied and maligned it took heart, imagining that Russia "would put up with anything and everything, down to the last and ignominious slap in the face," rather than go to war (12: 99):

> The hearts of our age-old enemies and detractors, whom for two centuries we have been exasperating in Europe, began to quiver, the hearts of thousands of European Yids and, with them, of millions of Judaizing "Christians" began to quiver, and the heart of Beaconsfield began to quiver....

Let everyone understand, once and for all, that Russia, "strong in the spiritual unity of our people" and our "national consciousness," is invincible (12: 100):

> That we are not France, which is all in Paris, that we are not Europe, at the mercy of the stock exchanges of its bourgeoisie. . . . They do not understand and do not realize that if we *want to*, neither the Yids of all Europe combined nor the millions of their gold will vanquish us. . . .

With an obstinacy verging on an obsession, Dostoyevsky persisted in believing—or, at least, in proclaiming—that European policy was dictated by the Jews. What better way than this could be found to inflame the patriotic ardor of the nation, to forge its will to stand firm and to triumph? And will, resolution and determination were now more necessary than ever in that summer of 1877 when the Russian armies began to suffer huge losses at the battle of Plevna, the strategic Turkish-held Bulgarian fortress, which would resist assault upon assault until it fell in December. Military reverses led to growing disenchantment—even in high governmental spheres—with the Panslav idea.[1]

Until the end of 1877, Dostoyevsky fought relentlessly against this mood of defeatism. *The Diary* dedicated itself entirely to the defense of Panslavism; the Jewish question faded into the background, though it was not wholly forgotten. In the September issue, for example, Dostoyevsky vituperated against those who were ready to abandon their Slav brothers. If their voices were heeded, Russia would be doomed. Returning to a theme he had broached in December 1876—that of the "Judaizers" and the "Europeanizers" (11: 503; see chapter 6)—Dostoyevsky wrote (12: 261):

> Now, hardly anyone but the blindest of Russian Europeans and, with them, to their shame, the small-time speculators, fails to perceive and recognize that idea [the Slav idea]. . . . They are now clamoring in chorus about the stagnation in trade, the crisis in the stock exchange, the fall of the ruble. But if these small-time operators of ours were farsighted enough to see beyond their noses, they would realize that if Russia had not begun the present war, things would be even worse for them. If there is to be "business," even stock-exchange business, the nation has to live, genuinely live, that is, lead a really active life and fulfill its natural destiny, and not be a galvanized corpse in the hands of the Yids and speculators.

Although it is true that after the *coup de théâtre* of March 1877 Dostoyevsky spoke less and less about the Jews in his *Diary*, it was not because the subject no longer interested him. On the contrary, he considered the subject to be of such importance that he envisaged the idea of treating it on a regular and permanent basis. In a notebook entry, dated December 24, 1877, under the heading "*Memento* for the rest of my life," he listed his literary projects for the years ahead (they would never be realized). Apart from a few literary works ("a Russian *Candide*," "a book about Jesus Christ," "my memoirs"), he planned the publication of a monthly journal that would contain seven sections, the second being a "Chronicle of Events," in which he would cover and comment on such matters as "the railroads, the Yids, the Poles in Russia, the seminarians, etc. The whole thing with a moral lesson." The third section would be his *Diary of a Writer*.[2]

At first glance, Dostoyevsky's anti-Semitism, as it manifested itself, particularly in his correspondence, during the last three years of his life, seems to be at once banal and inoffensive. Banal —in the sense that it reveals nothing more than a visceral antipathy for the Jew as such; inoffensive—in the sense that it is confined to the sphere of private correspondence. His feelings emerge mainly on the pages of the letters he wrote to his wife Anna Grigoryevna from Ems, where he went rather regularly to take the cure (for emphysema); they bristle with denigrating remarks about the Jews it was his misfortune to come into contact with. But for all their banality, his feelings are nonetheless significant. For they reveal an *état d'âme*, a mood, that colored certain passages of *The Brothers Karamazov*, which he was working on at the time, and place them in more meaningful perspective.

I shall also stop to consider other letters from Dostoyevsky: one to N. E. Grishchenko, a reader of *The Diary*; another to five students at Moscow University; and a third to V. F. Putsykovich, editor of *Grazhdanin*. I shall also again touch briefly on Dostoyevsky's letter of August 1879 to Pobedonostsev.[3] These letters reveal Dostoyevsky's concern over two new aspects of the Jewish question—the role and influence of the Jews in the Russian press and, more especially, in the Russian revolutionary movement. He would deal publicly with that second aspect in the last two issues of *The Diary*, published in August 1880 and January 1881, the month of his death.

Starting in 1874, Dostoyevsky was a frequent visitor to Ems, where he went to take the waters.[4] Many of his letters to Anna Grigoryevna[5] date from his sojourns in Germany, which, though beneficial, perhaps, to his physical health, were detrimental to his mental state. He suffered from being separated from his wife and children, his environment, his country; he disliked the Germans and held himself aloof from the Russians who were there for the cure or were living there. He was continually short of money and had to stay in second-rate hotels. He lived in constant fear of epileptic attacks that would leave him for days on end in a state of utter exhaustion. The waters did not agree with his digestion, an additional cause of discomfiture. The result of all this was increasing nervousness, irritability and touchiness. Naturally enough, he gave vent to his feelings in his letters, especially those to his wife, for good husband that he was, he kept her informed of the humdrum of his daily life. When things were going badly, he had to take it out on someone—sometimes it was the Germans, sometimes the Russians, but most of the time, especially in 1879, it was the "Yids" who bore the brunt of it all.[6]

On July 28/August 9, 1879, a week after his arrival in Ems, Dostoyevsky was, as usual, complaining in a letter to his wife about how expensive things were, but also about his entourage:

> Things are horribly expensive here, you can't buy anything <Yids galore>. I bought some paper (writing) and some lousy penpoints, paid a fistful of money, you'd think we were on some desert island. <The Yids are all over the place. Why, close to a third of the summer visitors are newly rich Yids from every corner of the earth. Although the Russians are represented by a good thirty names (judging from the Resort Register), they're all unknown: a certain Semyonov from Petersburg, a certain Prince Meshchersky (but not ours). Chicherin is apparently here. There are a few princesses and countesses with their families (Dolgorukaya, Obolenskaya, Radziwill)—but I'm not acquainted with any of them. Furthermore, all the other Russian names are, for the most part, those of wealthy Russian Yids. In the room right next door to mine in the [*Hôtel*] *d'Alger*, there are two rich Yids, a mother and her son, a twenty-five–year-old Jew-boy—and they are making my life miserable: they talk to each other from morning to night, loud, long and with no letup, which prevents me from either reading or writing. After all, you'd think that in the twenty-five years since she'd had him they would have talked themselves out; but no, they keep at it night and day, not like normal human beings, spouting whole pages (in German or Yiddish), as if they were reading a book; and all that with the vilest Yiddish intonation, which, in my irritable condition, has exasperated me more than anything else. What's more, they

don't stand on ceremony, they don't talk, they shout, as if they were the only ones in the hotel.> Yesterday I got down to work. . . .[7]

In his letter of July 30/August 11, it was still a question of that mother and son who continued to poison his existence, but, to make matters even worse, Dostoyevsky lost his umbrella:

I went and bought a very shoddy one, I think, in silk of course, for fourteen marks (six rubles in our money). The shopkeeper who sold it to me <(a miserable Yid)> said to me: Did you inquire about your umbrella at the police?—The police, at the Casino?— Yes, there's a branch there. Well, the thought had never occurred to me. I went over there, inquired, and they immediately gave me back my lost umbrella that they had picked up some time ago. What a pity! I offered the execrable shopkeeper two marks if he would take back the umbrella and refund me twelve marks, but he refused. What a misfortune, the only thing that goes is money. <The third incident was with my Yid neighbors in the *Hôtel d'Alger*. For four days I sat there and endured their (the mother's and son's) chatter next door; they talk pages, whole volumes of talk, endlessly, without the slightest respite; and worst of all, when they are not shouting, they are screaming, like in a *kahal*, a prayer hall, completely oblivious to the fact that they're not the only ones in the house. Although they are Russian (wealthy) Yids, they're from somewhere in the western regions, from Kovno. Since it was already 10 o'clock and time to turn in, I yelled *as I was getting into bed*: "Ah, those damned Yids, will they ever let you sleep!" The next day, the landlady *Mme. Bach* came by and told me that her Yids had complained to her that I had offended them, that I had called them *Yids* and that they were checking out of their room. I told the landlady that I myself was planning to leave because her Yids were driving me crazy: you couldn't read, write or even think. The landlady was terribly upset by my threatening to leave and said that she preferred to get rid of the Yids, but she offered me a splendid room upstairs that will be available in a week's time. I know the room, really a fine one, and besides it's two talers a week cheaper. I agreed, and even though the Yids haven't shut up and persist in their loud talk, still they've stopped yelling and for the moment things are bearable.> That's that for my adventures.[8]

A few days later (letter of August 4/16), Dostoyevsky was feeling so depressed that he was comparing his life at Ems with the life he had once led at Omsk: "My life here, Anya, is unbearably hard and grim, scarcely any easier and no worse than the penal servitude I endured. And I say this *without exaggeration.* Alone, not a single familiar face <, nay, only those repulsive mugs of the Yids>." Things, however, had taken a turn for the better as far as his noisy neighbors were concerned: <"The Yids are bothering me less, but it looks very much as if I'll be moving upstairs into another room.">[9] But in his letter of August 7/19, he was able to tell his wife that he wouldn't be changing rooms after all, because <"my neighbors the Yids are checking out next week">.[10] In that same letter, he complained again about the rising cost of living, and, of course, it was the "Yids" who were responsible for it. Moreover, they were manipulating the rate of the ruble: <"(The local Yids are giving only 212 marks for 100 rubles and the rate has begun to fluctuate terribly again.)">[11]

The theme of the Jewish presence and influence in Germany was, as we saw in chapter 6, a major element in Dostoyevsky's letter written a few days later (August 9/21) to K. P. Pobedonostsev. But this letter was also permeated with a feeling of sadness and anxiety for his family, for he had a clear premonition that his death was near at hand, "a year or two" hence. He complained bitterly, too, about his isolation, the alien atmosphere, "the riffraff from all over Europe," and the Russians from the borderlands, a transparent reference to the Jews.

When he wrote to Anna Grigoryevna the following day, his mood was still one of deep despondency and his grievances were the same as ever: "On all of my previous visits to Ems, I always found a few Russians whom I knew—this time, there's nobody, just those disgusting <Yid and English> mugs, silence and solitude. . . . Mugs and ugly pusses at the baths, especially women's, <and the Yids and Yidenehs,> and the crowds, and the pushing and the devil knows what!"[12]

As for the shopkeepers, Dostoyevsky wrote his wife on August 16/28, they were all scoundrels the likes of which were unknown in Russia. He was, of course, talking about the Jews: <"Yids everywhere, the Yids have taken over everything, and there's no limit to their swindling; they literally swindle.">[13] He would write her two other letters before rejoining her at Staraya Russa at the beginning of September but would say no more about the Jews.

As noted earlier, three other letters of the period also merit

consideration; they were all written in 1878. The first—Dostoyevsky's letter of February 28 to Nikolai Epifanovich Grishchenko—
is unique in more than one respect. On February 16, Grishchenko
wrote to Dostoyevsky from Kozelets, Chernigov Province, expressing regret over the author's decision to suspend publication of *The
Diary of a Writer*. In his reply, Dostoyevsky touched—for the first
and only time—on a new theme, that of the growing and nefarious
influence of the Jews on the Russian press,[14] and he also scored
the "Europeanizers" and the "liberals" who were abetting them.
Although the original is not, apparently, extant, this letter was
published three times by Suvorin's reactionary and anti-Semitic
organ *New Time* (*Novoye vremya*), in 1891, 1901 and 1903. It
has the further "distinction" of having been *completely* suppressed by Soviet censorship. In view of the importance of this
letter, it is reproduced below in the version as published by *New
Time* (no. 5406, March 18/30, 1891) "in full except for portions of
no particular interest": [15]

> Yes, there are lots of people who don't believe in literature any-
> more, i.e., in its sincerity, and they expect something new, and yet
> they are the very people who fail to notice what is happening. You,
> for example, complain about the Yids in Chernigov Province, but
> in our own literary life right here at home there are already nu-
> merous publications, newspapers and magazines that are financed
> and put out by the Yids (more and more of them are making their
> way into our literature), and the editors, who are hired by the Yids,
> merely lend their names to the newspaper or magazine—and that's
> the only thing Russian about them. To my mind, this is just the be-
> ginning, and the Yids are going to take over an even bigger share
> of the literary market, to say nothing of their involvement in life,
> in various aspects of everyday affairs: the Yid is spreading like
> wildfire. And I don't have to tell you that the Yid and his *kahal*
> when you come right down to it, constitute a conspiracy against
> the Russians.
>
> There are many old, hoary liberals who never liked Russia to
> begin with and even hated her for her "barbarity" but still have the
> sincere conviction that they love both Russia and the people.
> They're all a bunch of dreamers whose entire education and Euro-
> peanizing boils down to a "tremendous love for mankind," but *only
> as a whole*. Whenever they come into contact with a man *in flesh
> and blood*, who has a face, they can't even stand looking at that

face or remaining in its presence, so repugnant is it to them. It is much the same way with them when it comes to nations: mankind they love, but if ever it manifests itself in the demands, needs and desires of a nation, they regard it as prejudice, backwardness, chauvinism. They are all unreal people, they feel no pain, and they live their lives basically in blissful serenity, no matter how great the ardor of their writings. The editors of the *Word*—they're retarded liberals quite oblivious to the fact that they've outlived their time, become obsolete, instinctively hating everything that is new and fresh. What's more, they are not even capable of understanding the new things that are happening and their implications for the future. They come out in support of the Yids, in the first place, because at one time (in the eighteenth century) it was something novel, something liberal, because it was the thing to do. What care they if today the Yid is triumphant and oppressing the Russian? As far as they are concerned, it is still the Russian who is oppressing the Yid. But, fundamentally, it is a question of faith: their hatred of Christianity has brought them to love the Yid; and mind you, it is not because they regard the Yid as a nation that they defend him but only because they suspect in others a national revulsion and hatred toward the Yid. As a result of this, they castigate the others as a nation.

Another myth that was beginning to be propagated at the time was that of the Jewish character of the nihilist and revolutionary movement. This new fable was given wide currency, notably by Suvorin in *New Time* and Meshchersky in the *Citizen*. And it was this myth that Dostoyevsky sought to give substance to in his letters to five students at Moscow University and to V. F. Putsykovich, dated April 18 and August 29, respectively. The truth of the matter was that in the seventies the Jews played a decidedly minor role in the struggle against the established order. Few Jews were involved—and, with the exception of Mark Natanson, only in a subordinate capacity—in the Chaikovsky Circle that engaged in the dissemination of "legal literature" and in nonviolent agitation among factory workers and was in the vanguard of the "going-to-the-people" movement in the years 1873 to 1876. Nor were the Jews prominent in other radical groups of the period. Not a single Jew was implicated in the major political trials of the first half of the decade of the seventies—those of the Dolgushintsy, Dyakov-Siryakov and Semyanovsky, among others. And in the second half of that decade, the *narodniki* and terrorists counted few Jews in their ranks. During the period 1879 to 1889, which abounded in acts of terrorism, no more than a dozen or so Jews were incriminated.[16] Not a single Jew, for example, was involved in the affair of Vera Zasulich (March 1878), whose trial Dostoyevsky followed with keen interest; or in the Mirsky affair (March–April 1879), to which Dostoyevsky alluded in another letter to Putsykovich.[17] And finally, while it is true that a Jewess, Gesya Gelfman, would be involved in the assassination of Alexander II, her role was limited to that of an accomplice.

But Dostoyevsky was not interested in facts. What counted was his conception and whatever could be found to validate or seemed to validate his thesis. Such substantiation he found in the case of "the demonstration at Kazan Square" that was tried before the Petersburg court in January 1877. On December 6, 1876, a group of young people had gathered at the Kazan Cathedral for the purpose of holding a service to honor the memory of those who had died in prisons or in Siberian exile. On being told that it could not be held, since December 6 was "the tsar's Day" (Saint Nicholas), they decided, after consulting with the priest, to say a prayer for Chernyshevsky (still languishing in exile). But at the last minute, they were ordered to vacate the premises, whereupon a demonstration took place in the square; it was brutally put down by the police.[18]

Among those who were apprehended and inculpated were three young Jews,[19] and for Dostoyevsky this was the salient fact. He seized upon this "isolated case"—this was the first time that Jews had been implicated in a political trial in Russia[20]—to give substance to his new myth.

Dostoyevsky spoke of the Kazan demonstration on two occasions, the first, in his letter of reply of April 18, 1878, to the Moscow University students who had written to him after the clash between students and shopkeepers in Okhotnyi Ryad a few weeks earlier. Asked to take a public stand on the issue of relations between the intelligentsia and the people and to answer the question of "Who was to blame?" for the widening rift as reflected in the recent outburst of violence, Dostoyevsky carefully avoided placing sole responsibility on the students. He situated the problem in a broader context: society was in a state of crisis, the most serious symptom of which was the gulf between the educated classes and the common people (a constant preoccupation of Dostoyevsky ever since his return from Siberia). If the gap continued to widen, the fault lay entirely with the upper classes, influenced by European ideas or beguiled by illusory theories like the "going-to-the people" movement, which by no means prevented the intelligentsia from still treating the people with aristocratic disdain. The youth, the repository of Russia's hope for the future, were undeniably thirsting for the truth but were looking for it everywhere except where it was to be found: in the people, in their native soil, in *pochvennichestvo*. In a word, instead of drawing nearer to the people, the young were drawing further apart from them. And Dostoyevsky recalled the events of December 6 in St. Petersburg:

> Last winter during that Kazan incident of ours, a crowd of young people desecrates a national shrine, smokes cigarettes in the sanctuary, provokes a scandal. "Look here," I would have said to these Kazaners (and I told some of them to their face), "you don't believe in God, that's your business, but what right have you to offend the people by desecrating their shrine?" And the people spoke of them as "young swells" and, worse still, referred to them as "students," although there were lots of nondescript Jews and Armenians among them (it was proved that the demonstration was political, inspired from outside).[21]

These, then, are the only "facts" Dostoyevsky considered noteworthy in the Kazan affair. He went even further than the bill of indictment, which made no mention of any act of desecration.[22] Did he do so willfully? Perhaps. Had he not made a similar insinuation in *The Possessed* to stigmatize Lyamshin, capable if not guilty of committing an act of sacrilege?

Dostoyevsky returned briefly to the Kazan affair in his letter to Putsykovich of August 29, 1878, the complete text of which is known only from its first publication in 1887. Though full of platitudes, this letter nonetheless represents the culmination of Dostoyevsky's thinking on the Jews. Initially nothing more than objects of scorn and derision, peddlers, small-time moneylenders, Jews were too ridiculous to be really hated. But, by the end of the sixties, they had become financiers and manipulators, occult masters of the stock exchanges and state treasuries dedicated to the destruction of the foundations of Christian civilization. And now, they had become nihilists, the driving force behind the revolutionary movement and agents of socialist subversion.[23] It is the Jew in this guise that Dostoyevsky flayed in his letter to Putsykovich:

> You write that the assassins of Mezentsov [the head of the Third Section] are still at large and that it is surely the work of the nihilist scum. Why, of course. No doubt about it. But will we ever get over our apathy and get out of the rut we're in? Come, now, you know better! Your story about how you sent Mezentsov an anonymous letter from some Odessa socialists who had made a threat on your life for writing against socialism is superb in its originality. You had absolutely no reply and your letter was lost for posterity—and that's that! <A propos: when will people finally realize how much the Yids (by my own observation) and perhaps the Poles are behind this nihilist business? What a collection of Yids were involved in the Kazan Square incident, and then the Yids throughout Odessa history. Odessa, the city of the Yids, is the center of our rampant socialism. In Europe, the very same situation: the Yids are terribly active in the socialist movement, and I'm not speaking now about the Lassalles and the Karl Marxes. And understandably so: the Yid has everything to gain from every radical cataclysm and coup d'état because it is he himself, *status in statu*, that constitutes his own community, which is unshakable and only gains from anything that undermines non-Yid society.>—The articles in our press about the murder of Mezentsov are the height of stupidity. . . .[24]

Thus, Dostoyevsky remains faithful to the "idea" that Versilov was the first to give expression to in *A Raw Youth* where he announced the coming "reign of the Yids." The same vision reappeared in *The Diary of a Writer*, sharpened by the concept of *status in statu*; and it would be given further definition and refinement in the single issue of *The Diary* that came out in 1880, the same issue in which Dostoyevsky's famous speech on Pushkin appeared with its appeal for the "unity of all humanity" (12: 389).[25] In the article entitled "Two Halves," he prophesied the fate awaiting Europe for having strayed from the path of Christianity and sunk into the mire of materialism: the end of civilization, the advent of the proletarian era and the crumbling of the whole social structure (12: 411):

All these parliamentarisms, all currently espoused civic theories, all accumulated riches, the banks, the sciences, the Yids, the whole lot will come crashing down in a twinkle and without leaving a trace—except for the Yids who even then will find a way out and even turn things to their advantage. All this is "near at hand, at the doorstep."

But Dostoyevsky gave far more explicit and revealing expression to his thoughts and innermost feelings in the following entry in his "Notebooks," made in the course of the same year:

> *Yid.* The Bismarcks, the Beaconsfields, the French Republic and Gambetta, etc.—the power they all represent is nothing but an illusion. And increasingly so with each passing day. Their master, the master of all, the master of Europe is the Yid and his bank. And now mark my words: one fine day he'll put his *veto* and Bismarck will go flying like a wisp of straw. The Yid and his bank are now reigning over everything: over Europe, education, civilization, socialism—especially socialism, for he will use it to uproot Christianity and destroy its civilization. And when nothing but anarchy remains, the Yid will be in command of everything. For while he goes about preaching socialism, he will stick together with his own, and after all the riches of Europe will have been wasted, the Yid's bank will still be there. The Antichrist will come and stand above the anarchy.[26]

Thus Dostoyevsky unites in one sublime synthesis two opposing tendencies—capitalism and socialism. The cement that binds them is Jewdom or, more specifically, that *status in statu* that forges the Jewish community into a power capable of weathering and emerging triumphant over all the vicissitudes of history.

To protect Russia from such a fate, Dostoyevsky zealously cautioned it against any liberal sentimentality toward its Jewish minority. For, fortified by its internal organization and cohesion, Russian Jewry would not fail to turn to its own advantage any concessions that might be accorded it. In the same "Notebook" for 1880, Dostoyevsky inserted another entry that can only be described as harrowing:

> *The Yids.* And even were they to hold sway over all Russia—with their *kahal* and machinations—and suck the Russian muzhik dry; oh, no, don't breathe a word about it! Otherwise, some *illiberal misfortune* may occur. What won't people say then! That we con-

sider our religion superior to Judaism and oppress them out of religious intolerance. And then what would happen? You can just
imagine what would happen![27]

No assessment of the final years of the writer's life, from the
particular standpoint of this study, would be complete without
consideration of *The Brothers Karamazov*, the crowning achievement of Dostoyevsky's literary career. He got down to work on it
toward the middle of 1878 and submitted the final installment to
the *Russian Herald* in November 1880, a few months before his
death.

The references to the Jews in the hundreds of pages of this
monumental novel can, so to speak, be counted on the fingers of
one hand. At first glance, this is surprising in view of Dostoyevsky's preoccupation, if not to say obsession, with the Jewish question in his correspondence, *The Diary* and "Notebooks" of the
same period. But the blows he strikes, few and far between as they
may be, are nonetheless stunning. And, as we shall see, in one instance at least, the Jewish theme bursts in with such brutality and
insidious design as to break the natural flow of the narrative, elec-
trifying the attention of readers and causing their hair to stand on
end.

What more ingenious way could have been found to convey
the rapacity of the old Karamazov, Fyodor Pavlovich, than to set
his early life in Odessa, that "city of the Yids," as Dostoyevsky put
it in his letter to Putsykovich of August 29, 1878, the very moment
when he was working on the first chapters of his novel? Here is
the famous portrait of that old reprobate (XIV: 21):

> A word now about Fyodor Pavlovich. . . . Three or four years
> after the death of his second wife, he left for the south of Russia
> and finally turned up in Odessa, where he lived for a number of
> years. At the start, he made the acquaintance of, in his own words,
> "a bunch of Yids, Yidels, Yiddishers and Yidlings,"[28] but even-
> tually ended up being received not only by the Yids but "by the
> Jews as well." It was presumably during this period of his life that
> he developed a knack for making and extorting money.

But even before making his way to Odessa (had it slipped
Dostoyevsky's mind?), Fyodor Pavlovich had already displayed
shrewdness and dexterity in money matters by associating him-

self with a "Yid." It was during a business trip to the provinces, "in the company of some Yidel or other," that he married his second wife. Though he was "a carouser, drunkard and debauchee, he never neglected putting his capital to work and operated always successfully, though, of course, almost always unscrupulously" (XIV: 12).

In a similar vein, Grushenka's shrewdness, her acumen and prowess in "business" (Dostoyevsky borrows the German and Yiddish word *Geschäft*) qualified her for being labeled a "real Yideneh" (*sushchaya zhidovka*). And, Dostoyevsky went on to explain, "It was not that she lent out money at interest, but it was common knowledge, for example, that, in partnership with Fyodor Pavlovich Karamazov, she had for some time now been busy buying up notes for a song, at one-tenth of their face value, and afterwards sold some of them at their full value" (XIV: 311).[29]

Other allusions to the "Yids" could be cited, but they are of no particular interest.[30] Let us rather cut through to the heart of the matter.

Near the beginning of book 11, written in the spring of 1880, Dostoyevsky subjects the reader to one of the most terrifying scenes he ever conjured up, the scene of Alyosha's final meeting with young Liza Khokhlakova. He finds "the little demon" in a state of overexcitement, bordering on hysteria, which was, moreover, as Dostoyevsky tells us, the normal condition of this pathologically sick and abnormal adolescent. The conversation that ensues between Alyosha and Liza plunges the reader directly into the demonic world of an Hieronymus Bosch. An abominable, hallucinatory vision rises up out of the demented mind and tortured soul of Liza—but is it out of hers alone?—and opens onto a bottomless abyss, an abyss that swallows not only Liza, but Dostoyevsky and his beloved hero Alyosha in her wake.

Even to the twentieth-century reader familiar with all that is now known about the field of psychopathology, Dostoyevsky's Liza is not quite convincing: it is hard to imagine that a fourteen-year–old girl, living in the last century, regardless of how sick and deranged she was, could have behaved and spoken in the manner of Liza. But let us leave aside our own reservations, mindful of the fact that, for Dostoyevsky, Liza symbolized the moral decadence and degeneration of the new intelligentsia just as the old Karamazov symbolized the passions and amorality of the old generation. Let us admit, then, that such a pathological, sadomasochistic type could exist, that a child could wish to suffer and be miserable, to do injury to herself and to others, and even be capable of killing. And finally, let us even admit that Liza could have had the following conversation (XV: 24):

> "Alyosha, is it true that at Passover the Yids steal and slaughter children?"
> "I don't know."
> "You see, in one book I have, I read about some trial someplace and about how a Yid got hold of a four-year–old boy and cut off all the fingers of both hands and then fastened him to the wall, hammered nails into him and crucified him, and afterwards he told the court that the child had died quickly, in a matter of four hours. That's fast, all right! He said the child moaned and moaned all the while and he stood there feasting his eyes upon him. That's great!"
> "Great?"
> "Yes, great. I sometimes imagine that it was I who crucified him. He would hang there moaning and I would sit opposite him eating pineapple compote. I adore pineapple compote. How about you?"

Now, even if there is a remote possibility that a Liza could have harbored and expressed such thoughts, Alyosha's "I don't know" staggers the mind. Those few terrible words bring down discredit upon the author. How could Dostoyevsky have dared to put these words in the mouth of his Alyosha, Alyosha, the incarnation of charity, the symbol of Russia's spiritual regeneration? No, an Alyosha could never have spoken those words.[31]

How could Dostoyevsky who, for all his novels and especially for *The Brothers Karamazov*, spared no efforts to ensure by means of the most painstaking and exhaustive research the authenticity of the facts he incorporated and the human and psychological truth of the characters he portrayed, how could he have brought himself to violate in so flagrant a manner the principle he had elevated to the status of a moral law: respect for the artistic integrity of each and every one of his characters?[32] What demonic force incited him to betray Alyosha the pure, the virtuous, the godlike, his Alyosha who, in other circumstances, responded with a ringing No to the question: would you be willing to edify the future happiness of all mankind on the tears of a single baby (XIV: 224)?

All this gives rise to another question: what gave Dostoyevsky the idea of introducing into *The Brothers Karamazov* the monstrous theme of ritual murder? Today, thanks to the invaluable research of Leonid Grossman,[33] the answer to that question is, at least, known. Dostoyevsky, it will be recalled, was an avid reader of the daily press, constantly on the lookout for material or ideas that lent themselves to artistic treatment (as, for example, the Nechayev affair, which provided him with material for *The Possessed*). This time his attention was arrested by the Kutaisi affair. On April 4, 1878, Passover eve, Sarra Modebadze, a young peasant girl from the Georgian village of Perevisi, disappeared; two days later, her body was discovered; wounds were found on her hands. An inquest was held; the coroner concluded that her death was accidental: "drowning during a torrential rainfall"; the wounds on her hands, subsequent to her death, were inflicted by rodents and birds of prey. Despite the official findings of the coroner, the judicial authorities claimed that she had been the victim of a crime, the date of her disappearance being conclusive evidence thereof. Shortly thereafter nine Jews from the neighboring village of Sachkheri were apprehended and indicted for murder. The defendants were brought to trial on March 5, 1879, in Kutaisi; the case created a considerable stir since it revived the medieval legend of ritual murder committed by the Jews. Not only that, it was the first ritual murder trial ever to be held in Russia. On March 13, the court handed down its verdict: all the defendants were declared not guilty and were acquitted. The appeal introduced by the state prosecutor in the Tbilisi court was dismissed in April 1880.[34]

During the pretrial investigation, the extreme right-wing press launched a campaign seeking to accredit the legend of the ritual crime; the anti-Jewish movement was assuming alarming proportions. The eminent Orientalist and professor at St. Petersburg University Daniil A. Khvolson, author of a remarkable study entitled *Concerning Certain Medieval Accusations against the Jews* (1861), fearing that the second edition of this book that he was then preparing would appear too late, hastily brought out a brochure summarizing the main points of his larger work and refuting the infamous legend.[35]

One of the journals Khvolson pointed an accusing finger at was Prince Meshchersky's organ the *Citizen* (Dostoyevsky, it will be recalled, had been its editor in 1873–1874).[36] In the summer of

1878, the *Citizen* began publication of a series of incendiary articles that sought to give credence to the myth. By a curious coincidence—Grossman calls attention to it—the *Citizen* (nos. 23–25, August 1878) published alongside a feuilleton of Dostoyevsky's ("From Kuzma Prutkov's Strolls in the Countryside") the first article in that series: "Information on the Killing of Christians by Jews for the Purpose of Procuring Blood . . ."[37] Grossman considers it an absolute certainty that Dostoyevsky was acquainted not only with the article adjoining his own but also with the whole series that continued into the following year, all of which centered around the Kutaisi affair. Moreover, Grossman conclusively proves that Dostoyevsky was *directly* inspired by these articles, pointing out striking textual concordances between Liza's account and certain passages in the series published by the *Citizen*. He cites, in particular, the following excerpt from the article that led off the series in the August 1878 issue and that contained the "confession" of one Jew: "I ordered one child to be fastened to the cross and he lived a long time; I ordered another one to be nailed to it and he quickly died."[38]

After setting forth the facts, Grossman places them in their moral context. Did Dostoyevsky have the *right* to use such a theme? For the eminent critic, the question does not even arise. Dostoyevsky, he writes, the apostle of *universal* harmony, the defender of the insulted and the injured, "the great writer whose voice was passionately listened to by vast numbers of readers, stood up and affirmed 'I don't know.'" But he could not but have known that "in that alarming and incandescent atmosphere . . . the slightest equivocation . . . could lead to the condemnation of innocent people and, possibly, an untold number of bloody consequences."[39]

Alyosha's evasive reply is not justifiable on either human or artistic grounds. If, at least, the artistic truth had been respected, if, for example, it had been the old Karamazov who uttered the words, "I don't know," it would, of course, have been regrettable that Dostoyevsky chose so unsavory a theme to shed further light on his character, but the matter would have to be left at that. But it is because the reply is artistically false that the betrayal—the double betrayal Dostoyevsky was guilty of—stands out so blatantly.

For in betraying Alyosha, Dostoyevsky betrayed himself. Driven by a blind hatred against a people, ostracized and execrated in the country of their adoption—the only homeland they knew—Dostoyevsky, humanist and Christian, in the twilight of his life, did not shrink from endorsing, with all the authority he commanded as both man and writer, an ignominious myth and odious lie. Thus, he knowingly and willfully incited his people, the "God-bearers," against the "people of the Book."

In the final analysis, this terrible and bloody confrontation between two peoples, a confrontation that throughout his lifetime Dostoyevsky refused to debate on the plane of ideas, was the inevitable consequence of his Great Russian Messianism. The profound but arrogant and exclusive love he bore for Russia inspired in him a no less profound hatred for a community whose very existence constituted in his eyes a formidable challenge to his nation and the "God-bearing" mission he claimed for it.

Conclusion

SUCH, THEN, was one of the spiritual itineraries traveled by Fyodor Mikhailovich Dostoyevsky over nearly four decades of intense literary activity. It started, as we have seen, with his finished, but never found, drama *The Jew Yankel*, prefiguration, in a way, of the few Jewish characters later portrayed by Dostoyevsky (Isai Fomich Bumstein, Lyamshin) and of other anonymous figures who would make a fugitive appearance now and then on the pages of his novels, embodying the image he had of the Jewish people. It ended on a note of high drama, his celebrated speech on Pushkin, in which Dostoyevsky called for the unity of all mankind . . . except for the Jews, a terrible disqualification that revealed the great gulf that he had put between his own people and the Jewish people, who, in his eyes, had ceased to exist as a people.

In exploring the development of Dostoyevskyan thought on the subject of the Jews, I drew on the writer's literary and journalistic works, his "Notebooks," his correspondence, the memoirs of contemporaries and a vast body of critical literature. I chose a chronological method advisedly: it seemed preferable to any other for tracing the evolution of the author's thinking in this particular domain in its interaction with the general evolution of his ideas in a Russia that was undergoing prodigious transformations in the ideological, social and economic spheres.

It is clear from the foregoing chapters that Dostoyevsky attached particular interest and considerable importance to the Jewish question, more so than any other novelist of nineteenth-century Russia. Roturier though he was, Dostoyevsky stood squarely in the aristocratic tradition of Russian literature of his day, which had nothing but contempt for the city, its small industries, trade, merchants and shopkeepers, and its emerging bourgeoisie. This contempt became even more pronounced after the Emancipation of the Serfs, and some of the most illustrious representatives of Russian literature now could be seen casting a critical if not reproving eye at the Jews, in whom they discovered all of the vices of that growing class of merchants that they held in abhorrence.

Therein—in that prevailing climate of opinion—lies one of the sources of Dostoyevsky's anti-Semitism. It can, therefore, be said that he was anti-Semitic *a priori* or, at any rate, that at the time he embarked on his literary career he—like other members of his class—had no particular liking for the Jews. It is even quite possible, as I have suggested, that before his banishment to Siberia Dostoyevsky had never really met a Jew, except in the pages of Russian and foreign literature. Thus, the disparaging remarks about the Jews in his writings prior to his arrest (1849) may be attributed to a kind of innate, visceral, stereotyped anti-Semitisim or, as Gornfeld put it, "banal" anti-Semitism.

"Economic" anti-Semitism, it can be supposed, existed in a latent or embryonic state in the young Dostoyevsky. But in 1848–1849, the period in which he frequented the Petrashevsky Circle, Dostoyevsky discovered a theme he later tried—with little success, however—to develop (in *The Idiot, A Raw Youth* and in the rough drafts of *The Brothers Karamazov*): the Rothschild theme in juxtaposition with the Christ motif. This literary failure would be largely compensated by the scope given to the theme in *The Diary of a Writer*, with much more blatant anti-Semitic overtones.

As for "religious" anti-Semitism, it played a secondary role in Dostoyevskyan thought. It will be recalled that Dostoyevsky wrote (in *The Diary of a Writer*, March 1877) that "amongst our common people there is no preconceived, a priori, narrow-minded, religious hatred of the Jew," an affirmation I disputed, citing his own testimony in *The House of the Dead*. But there is no tangible evidence of "religious" anti-Semitism in Dostoyevsky himself, even in his pastiche of Isai Fomich's religious practices. That, like the whole caricatured portrait of Isai in *The House of the Dead* and the burlesque treatment of Lyamshin in *The Possessed*, is part and parcel of the author's general attempt systematically to denigrate not Judaism itself but the Jewish people, denigration that he needed (or so he thought) to establish Russia's Messianic claim and, therefrom, the exclusive rights of the Russian people to Christianity (the "Russian Christ").

It was through the mouth of his hero Shatov (*The Possessed*) that Dostoyevsky proclaimed that Christianity was not or, rather, was no longer a universal truth but "the truth of one chosen people, the Russian God-bearing people, the new Israel." Dostoyevskyan logic or, as Merezhkovsky put it somewhat extravagantly, "his national-exclusive, narrow, 'circumcised,' Judaizing Orthodoxy,"[1] led him to demolish and then deny any claims the Jews might have to being the chosen people. This brings us to the heart of the problem: the deep, the pathological roots of Dostoyevsky's anti-Semitism are to be sought in his arbitrary and absolute refusal to acknowledge the election of the Jewish people.

Dostoyevsky zealously set about the task of denigration his doctrine demanded especially during the last ten years of his life. Nothing could be allowed to shake his conviction that the Russians were the theophoric people. Trite, commonplace, "banal" anti-Semitism he left far behind him. The time had come to square accounts with the Jewish people and eliminate them as rivals for all times.

Even several years before the outbreak of the Russo-Turkish War, Dostoyevsky had drawn close to governmental circles and the most reactionary elements of Russian society for whom out-and-out anti-Semitism was an article of faith. And the war, when it came, fed the flames of anti-Jewish feelings. Who was to blame for Russia's isolation if not the European financiers and Lord Beaconsfield—all Jews? And what about the Jewish war-profiteers in the capital? And the Jewish tavernkeepers in the Pale of Settlement who were bleeding the people dry? The theme of the Jew-predator-and-parasite assumed new proportions under the pen of Dostoyevsky (*The Diary of a Writer*) and a host of second-rate yellow journalists and pamphleteers. More shocking even than what he wrote—poisonous grist from the anti-Semitic mill—was that Dostoyevsky lent his moral authority to endorse an incendiary campaign that could only have—as it did have—grievous consequences for the future.

But the infernal logic of his doctrine had to be fueled by more extravagant allegations. The Jews, he now insisted, were not striving for economic power as an end in itself. They were commanded by occult laws, they formed a state within the state (the Brafmanian thesis that became a linchpin of Dostoyevskyan ideology) and their ultimate goal was *political* hegemony (Versilov in *A Raw Youth*). And shortly before his death, in a "Notebook" entry that was partially worked into one of the chapters of his *Diary* ("Two Halves," August 1880), Dostoyevsky made an ingenious attempt to reconcile the irreconcilable, averring that Jewish finance and the nihilist movement were marching hand-in-hand, paving the way for the triumph of socialism and anarchy, the collapse of Christian civilization, the establishment of the "Kingdom of the Jews," and . . . the advent of the Antichrist.

And yet, Dostoyevsky did not lose all hope. In the final issue of *The Diary*, written and published in the last month of his life (January 1881), he expressed the conviction that his people "will ultimately be saved by a *universal communion in the name of Christ*."

In a remarkable essay entitled "The Spirit of Israel and the World Today," Martin Buber attempted to determine the profound source of anti-Semitism. He wrote:

> If we consider all the reasons for anti-Semitism advanced by the Christian nations, we find that they are all superficial and transitory. But if we go deeper, we find that there is one deep and unconscious reason that is true for all periods of the exile. It is, that there has entered and become dispersed among them a people carrying a charge from heaven which is written in a book which became sacred for them too when they became Christians.[2]

For Dostoyevsky, this book, this charge from heaven, no longer belonged, nor could belong, to the fallen people. It had passed with full title to the new Israel, to Holy Russia.

Notes

Introduction

1. See A. G. Dostoyevskaya, *Bibliograficheskii ukazatel sochinenii i proizvedenii iskusstva, otnosyashchikhsya k zhizni i deyatelnosti F. M. Dostoyevskovo* . . . *1846–1903* (St. Petersburg, 1906); N. A. Sokolov (comp.), *Materialy dlya bibliografii F. M. Dostoyevskovo,* in A. S. Dolinin (ed.), *F. M. Dostoyevsky: Stati i materialy,* 2 vols. (Moscow-Leningrad, 1924), vol. 2, pp. 1–121 (second pagination); *Bibliografiya proizvedenii F. M. Dostoyevskovo i literatura o nyom 1917–1965* (Moscow, 1968).

2. For example, the publication of Dostoyevsky's notebooks and copybooks for the period 1860 to 1881 in *Literaturnoye nasledstvo,* no. 83 (Moscow, 1971); the appearance in 1972 of the first volumes of the new critical edition of Dostoyevsky's *Complete Works* in thirty volumes; the publication of new materials and research in *Literaturnoye nasledstvo,* no. 86 (Moscow, 1973); and, most recently, the correspondence between Dostoyevsky and his wife edited by S. V. Belov and V. A. Tunimanov, *Perepiska* (Leningrad, 1976).

3. M. Gorky, "Yeshcho o 'karamazovshchine,' " *F. M. Dostoyevsky v russkoi kritike* (Moscow, 1956), pp. 393–399.

4. A. G. Gornfeld, "Dostoyevsky, Fyodor Mikhailovich," *Yevreiskaya entsiklopediya,* 16 vols. (St. Petersburg, 1906–1913), vol. 7, pp. 310–313.

5. D. S. Merezhkovsky, *Prorok russkoi revolyutsii,* in *Polnoye sobraniye sochinenii,* 24 vols. (Moscow, 1914), vol. 14, pp. 208–210.

6. L. P. Grossman, "Dostoyevsky i yudaizm," *Ispoved odnovo yevreya* (Moscow-Leningrad, 1924), pp. 165–181.

7. A. Z. Steinberg, "Dostoyevsky i yevreistvo," *Vyorsty,* no. 3 (Paris, 1928): 94–108.

8. P. Berlin, "Dostoyevsky i yevrei," *Novyi zhurnal,* no. 83 (New York, 1966): 263–272.

9. D. I. Zaslavsky, "Dostoyevsky o yevreyakh," *Yevreiskii vestnik,*

no. 1 (Petrograd, 1922): 6–10; idem, "Yevrei v russkoi literature," *Yevreiskaya letopis*, no. 1 (Moscow-Petrograd, 1923): 59–86.

10. M. Schwarz, "Dostoievsky and Judaism," *Jewish Review*, no. 4 (London, 1933): 57–73; Nina Gourfinkel, *Dostoïevski notre contemporain* (Paris, 1961), pp. 115–120; D. V. Grishin, *Dostoyevsky—chelovek, pisatel i mify* (Melbourne, 1971), pp. 138–156; idem, "Byl li Dostoyevsky antisemitom?" *Vestnik russkovo khristianskovo dvizheniya*, no. 114 (Paris, 1974): 73–88.

11. O. F. Miller and N. N. Strakhov, *Biografiya, pisma i zametki iz zapisnoi knizhki F. M. Dostoyevskovo* (St. Petersburg, 1883), pp. 3–352 (second pagination).

12. See A. S. Dolinin's editorial note in *Pisma*, vol. 4, p. xix.

13. See my article "Rewriting Dostoyevsky's Letters," *American Slavic and East European Review*, no. 2 (1961): 279–288; idem, "Peredelka pisem Dostoyevskovo," *Novyi zhurnal*, no. 65 (1961): 111–120.

14. Speeches made in February 1881, 1882 and 1883, subsequently published as *Tri rechi v pamyat Dostoyevskovo*.

15. In his article written in 1891, "Russkii natsionalnyi ideal," reprinted in *Sochineniya* (St. Petersburg, 1901–1903), vol. 5, p. 379, Solovyov wrote: ". . . we can in no way condone the outbursts of . . . Dostoyevsky against the 'Yids,' the Poles, the French, the Germans, against all Europe, against all alien faiths." (I am indebted to Jean Laloy for having called my attention to this reference.)

16. See Vladimir Seduro, *Dostoyevski in Russian Literary Criticism—1846–1956* (New York, 1957).

17. For example, S. Borshchevsky, *Shchedrin i Dostoyevsky* (Moscow, 1956); V. Ya. Kirpotin, *Dostoyevsky i Belinsky* (Moscow, 1960); Ya. E. Golosovker, *Dostoyevsky i Kant* (Moscow, 1963); N. F. Belchikov, *Dostoyevsky v protsesse Petrashevtsev* (Moscow, 1971); A. A. Gozenpud, *Dostoyevsky i muzyka* (Leningrad, 1971); V. S. Nechayeva, *Zhurnal M. M. i F. M. Dostoyevskikh "Vremya"—1861–1863* (Moscow, 1972); idem, *Zhurnal M. M. i F. M. Dostoyevskikh "Epokha"—1864–1865* (Moscow, 1975).

18. See above, note 6. The German edition of this book—*Die Beichte eines Juden* (Munich, 1927)—is more complete than the Soviet edition.

19. "Dostoyevsky i pravitelstvennyye krugi 70-kh godov," *Literaturnoye nasledstvo*, no. 15 (Moscow, 1934): 83–162.

20. A. S. Dolinin (ed.), *F. M. Dostoyevsky—Materialy i issledovaniya* (Leningrad, 1935), p. 49.

21. Ibid., p. 24.

22. *Pisma*, vol. 3, pp. 255–258.
23. The new Soviet edition of Dostoyevsky's *Complete Works* will contain six volumes (xxv–xxx) of his letters. *All* inimical references to the Jews will be deleted from this collection; the omissions will, however, be indicated by ellipses enclosed in angle brackets. This procedure was adopted by the editors of *F. M. Dostoyevsky–A. G. Dostoyevskaya: Perepiska* (Leningrad, 1976) to signal excisions.
24. V. S. Nechayeva (ed.), *Opisaniye rukopisei F. M. Dostoyevskovo* (Moscow, 1957).
25. Letter of A. S. Bushmin, December 12, 1959. The letters have never been published.

1. *The Emergence of a "New Talent"*

1. For the most complete information on this subject, see M. P. Alekseyev, "O dramaticheskikh opytakh Dostoyevskovo," *Tvorchestvo Dostoyevskovo* (Odessa, 1921), pp. 41–62.
2. Ibid., p. 49; see also the memoirs of A. E. Riesenkampf, in *F. M. Dostoyevsky v vospominaniyakh sovremennikov*, 2 vols. (Moscow, 1964), vol. 1, pp. 112–113. Dostoyevsky himself never spoke of them.
3. *Pisma*, vol. 1, p. 69.
4. *Pisma*, vol. 1, p. 73; Alekseyev, in *Tvorchestvo Dostoyevskovo*, p. 53.
5. Alekseyev, in *Tvorchestvo Dostoyevskovo*, p. 54.
6. D. I. Zaslavsky, "Yevrei v russkoi literature," *Yevreiskaya letopis*, no. 1 (Moscow-Petrograd, 1923): 59–86.
7. A play by the second-rate but popular dramatist Nestor Kukolnik. Like so many of his plays, *Prince Kholmsky* is set in the Middle Ages, and its action is based on the intrigues and plots of Jewish cabalists. It had its première at the Aleksandrinsky Theater on September 30, 1841, and was performed regularly during the fall and winter season 1841/42, a time when Dostoyevsky frequented that theater (cf. L. P. Grossman, *Zhizn i trudy F. M. Dostoyevskovo* [Moscow-Leningrad, 1935], p. 35). The play left a lasting impression on him.
8. Alekseyev, in *Tvorchestvo Dostoyevskovo*, p. 54.
9. Riesenkampf, in *F. M. Dostoyevsky v vospominaniyakh sovremennikov*, vol. 1, pp. 117–118.
10. D. D. Bregova, *Doroga iskanii* (Moscow, 1962), p. 2.
11. Ibid., p. 247.

12. The Jews were expelled from St. Petersburg in 1826 by order of Nicholas I; see "Saint Petersburg," *Yevreiskaya entsiklopediya*, 16 vols. (St. Petersburg, 1906–1913), vol. 13, p. 941.
13. *Pisma*, vol. 1, p. 76.
14. Bregova, *Doroga iskanii*, pp. 259–261.
15. From September 1842 (or 1843) to March 1844, Riesenkampf and Dostoyevsky shared the same apartment (cf. Grossman, *Zhizn i trudy*, pp. 38–39). The latter was working on *The Jew Yankel* during that period.
16. Dostoyevsky was, in fact, a day-boarder at Drashusov's School in 1843 (cf. A. M. Dostoyevsky, *Vospominaniya* [Leningrad, 1930], pp. 64–65). But there is no trace of either a Vinnikov or a Marya Mikhailovna in Dostoyevsky's correspondence, memoirs of contemporaries or elsewhere. Are they simply a figment of Bregova's imagination or did she discover their names in unpublished documents?
17. Bregova, *Doroga iskanii*, p. 261.
18. Riesenkampf, in *F. M. Dostoyevsky v vospominaniyakh sovremennikov*, p. 117.
19. Dostoyevsky often modeled his characters on real-life prototypes.
20. *Peterburgskaya letopis: Chetyre stati 1847 g.* (Petersburg-Berlin, 1922), p. 19. There is some controversy over the attribution of the feuilleton of April 13 to Dostoyevsky. Joseph Frank (*Dostoevsky—The Seeds of Revolt, 1821–1849* [Princeton, 1976], note, p. 218) agrees with Tomashevsky and Khalabayev, the editors of the first Soviet edition of Dostoyevsky's *Complete Works* (vol. 13, 1930), that it was written by Dostoyevsky's close friend Pleshcheyev. The French scholar Gustave Aucouturier, however, "n'exclurait pas la participation" of Dostoyevsky (Dostoïevski, *Oeuvres*, 7 vols. [Paris: Bibl. de la Pléiade, 1969], vol. 6, p. 1677, and he accordingly included the piece in that volume (pp. 239–242). The concordances between the disputed feuilleton and those of April 27 and May 11 (anent Ernst) and between the former and *Netochka Nezvanova* indicate, at the very least, Dostoyevsky's collaboration in the writing of that article. Most recently, the venerable Soviet scholar V. S. Nechayeva (*Rannii Dostoyevsky 1821–1849* [Moscow, 1979], pp. 192–208) definitively attributes the feuilleton of April 13 to Dostoyevsky.
21. See the articles on Ernst in *Larousse de la musique*, 2 vols. (Paris, 1957), vol. 1, p. 311, and in Adolf Kohut, *Znamenityye yevrei v istorii kultury chelovechestva*, 2 vols. (Odessa, 1902), vol. 1, pp. 133–136.

22. *Peterburgskaya letopis*, pp. 30–31.
23. Among the celebrated artists who performed in Russia during the period 1842 to 1847—Liszt, Berlioz, Rubini, Blas, Ole Bull, Ernst— only the last mentioned was Jewish.

2. The House of the Dead

1. In his letter of September 26, 1880, to N. N. Strakhov, cited by N. N. Gusev in *Yasnopolyanskii sbornik* (Tula, 1960), p. 115.
2. A "Jew Bumstein" makes a fleeting apparition in *Uncle's Dream* (1859). In this novella full of mordant humor, the *zhid Bumstein*, like his homonym Isai Fomich, is cast in the role of moneylender. Marya Aleksandrovna Moskalyova, the heroine of the story, turns to him to obtain the money she needs to buy back a letter compromising the honor of her daughter, Zina. Marya describes this poignant scene: "Wearing a pair of light shoes, I myself ran through the snow to the Jew Bumstein and pawned my brooch, a keepsake of my saintly mother!" (II: 323). With one masterful stroke, Dostoyevsky assembles all the melodramatic effects he requires: a defenseless woman, her loyalty to a loved one, the hostility of the elements, a rapacious Jew.
3. Szymon Tokarzewski, "F. M. Dostoyevsky v Omskoi katorge," *Zvenya*, 9 vols. (Moscow-Leningrad, 1936), vol. 6, p. 507.
4. I. D. Yakubovich, one of the authors of the "Commentary" to volume IV, told Professor Robert L. Jackson of Yale University, who was in Leningrad in 1974/75, that a "mistake" had been made, that Bumstehl was *not* of the Greek Orthodox faith (letter from Jackson to the author, February 3, 1977).
5. In Dostoyevsky's time, the word *zhid* was no longer used by the educated classes except in a derogatory sense. By the end of the reign of Catherine the Great (1762–1796), the term had been replaced by *yevrei* (etymologically: Hebrew) in all official documents (cf. *Yevreiskaya entsiklopediya*, 16 vols. [St. Petersburg, 1906–1913], vol. 7, pp. 497, 587). However, the two terms continued to co-exist in the press and in literature until the accession of Alexander II (1856). By 1860, *zhid* was definitely considered a term of opprobrium.
6. The majority of Dostoyevsky critics have paid scant or no attention to the character of Isai Fomich. Even in his major study of *The House of the Dead*, "Pogibshiye i pogibayushchiye" (reprinted in *F. M. Dostoyevsky v russkoi kritike* [Moscow, 1956], pp. 96–161),

Pisarev mentions him only in passing (p. 118), noting that the interest rates charged by Bumstein (516% per annum) were moderate in comparison to those practiced in the seminaries. Pierre Pascal, the eminent French Dostoyevsky scholar, provides some interesting comments on Isai in his excellent translation: *Récits de la Maison des Morts* (Paris, 1961).

7. A. G. Gornfeld, "Dostoyevsky, Fyodor Mikhailovich," *Yevreiskaya entsiklopediya*, vol. 7, pp. 310–313.

8. D. I. Zaslavsky, "Dostoyevsky o yevreyakh," *Yevreiskii vestnik*, no. 1 (Petrograd, 1922): 6–10; idem, "Yevrei v russkoi literature," *Yevreiskaya letopis*, no. 1 (Moscow-Petrograd, 1923): 59–86.

9. L. P. Grossman, "Dostoyevsky i yudaizm," *Ispoved odnovo yevreya* (Moscow-Leningrad, 1924), pp. 165–181.

10. A. Z. Steinberg, "Dostoyevsky i yevreistvo," *Vyorsty*, no. 3 (Paris, 1928): 94–108.

11. P. A. Berlin, "Dostoyevsky i yevrei," *Novyi zhurnal*, no. 83 (New York, 1966): 263–272.

12. Joshua Kunitz, *Russian Literature and the Jew* (New York, 1929).

13. Robert L. Jackson, "A Footnote to *Selo Stepančikovo*," *Richerche Slavistiche*, vols. 17–19 (Florence, 1970–1972): 247–257.

14. According to Tokarzewski, the Poles and the Circassians befriended Bumstein "to protect him from the jibes and abuses of the entire prison" (cited by Jackson, "A Footnote," *Richerche Slavistiche*, p. 248).

15. The use of *zhid, zhidok, zhidovka* is artistically justified. The caricature lacks originality: Saltykov-Shchedrin's Jews were also comical, looked like plucked chickens and spoke gibberish (cf. Kunitz, *Russian Literature and the Jew*, pp. 88–94).

16. Dostoyevsky had, of course, every right to treat his characters as he wished or as he apprehended them. He offers profoundly human and humane portraits of Akim Akimych, Sirotkin, Dutov, Orlov, Alei and even of the Polish prisoners, of whom he was not particularly fond. Isai Fomich is the only character who titillated his comical verve.

17. *Pisma*, vol. 4, p. xvii.

18. D. I. Zaslavsky, "Zametki o yumore i satire v proizvedeniyakh Dostoyevskovo," *Tvorchestvo Dostoyevskovo* (Moscow, 1959), pp. 453–457.

19. At the time this paragraph was first written, I was unaware of Robert L. Jackson's study on this particular question. While not altogether dismissing a Gogolian influence on the portrait of Opiskin, he persuasively argues that Isai Fomich "lurks behind the conception of Foma Fomič," whereas I suggest the converse.

20. N. V. Gogol, *Sobraniye khudozhestvennykh proizvedenii*, 5 vols. (Moscow, 1959), vol. 2, p. 180.

21. As Pierre Pascal (*Récits*, p. 184) has noted: "tout cela ne correspond à aucun rite, et le crachat pendant la prière est considéré comme sacrilège."

22. Isai Fomich, like the Jewish characters of Nekrasov, Saltykov-Shchedrin, Pisemsky and so forth, speaks Russian with a Jewish accent; and it is likely that he spoke in the manner Dostoyevsky parodies. But it is significant (as will become clear later) that Dostoyevsky refrained from parodying the speech of his young friend Alei, a Daghestan Tatar, whom he taught to read and write Russian.

23. The numerous repetitions in the novel may be due to the fact that it was first published serially and to Dostoyevsky's desire to accommodate readers who may have missed earlier installments. But Pierre Pascal (*Récits*, p. lxvi) feels that the "désordre [est] trop visible pour ne pas avoir été voulu."

24. According to Article 468 of the *Ustav o soderzhashchikhsya pod strazheyu*, "Jews in correctional institutions can remain in their quarters for prayer"; according to Article 1036 of the same statute, "Jews in disciplinary battalions are exempted from work on Saturdays for prayer" (see *Alfavitnyi ukazatel k svodu zakonov rossiiskoi imperii izdannomu v 1857 godu* [St. Petersburg, 1860], p. 312). I have been unable to ascertain whether these provisions—or some other regulation—authorized Jews to leave the grounds of a prison to attend Sabbath services in a neighboring community (in this instance, Omsk). There was no synagogue in Omsk until the year 1855 (see *Yevreiskaya entsiklopediya*, vol. 12, pp. 92–93); the events described by Dostoyevsky are anterior to that date: Dostoyevsky was released from prison in February 1854. But it is possible that prayers were held in some private house in Omsk prior to 1855, in which case Dostoyevsky's account could be true. It is furthermore clear that he was well acquainted with the provisions of the statute governing Jewish convicts.

25. Grossman, *Ispoved*, p. 171.

26. Dostoyevsky, apparently, did not himself witness Isai Fomich's arrival in the camp, which, he tells us, was related to him by one of the Polish prisoners. Whether this was actually the case or whether this was simply a convenient device for him to avoid personal responsibility for his description of the event cannot be determined.

27. See Dostoyevsky's "Siberian Notebook" (IV: 238—items 91 and 92).

28. Grossman (*Ispoved*, p. 172) dwells at length on this passage. He does not take issue with the convicts' attitude toward Isai, which he finds quite natural, but he does take issue with the attitude of "the great writer and passionate advocate of brotherly love" who has the effrontery to declare that "nobody offended him." "With startling candor," Grossman observes, "Dostoyevsky reduces the Jewish convict to the state of a dumb animal, incapable of feeling offense, insults. . . . " Not only does Dostoyevsky fully sympathize with the way the convicts taunt Isai Fomich, he even derives a certain satisfaction from it. He "forgets that the convicts treated their domestic animals much better than Isai Fomich; neither the universally loved Gnedko nor the garlanded goat Vaska was exposed to the torrent of offensive abuse that showered down upon the Jewish convict."

29. Ibid., pp. 172–173. Zaslavsky is either blindly insensitive or simply dishonest when he writes: "And Dostoyevsky himself, with his humorous description . . . of [Isai Fomich's] droll, semi-burlesque prayer and of the feeling of bliss he procured from his performance, arouses sympathy and compassion for Isai Fomich; he loves him for his simple-heartedness" (see "Zametki o yumore," *Tvorchestvo Dostoyevskovo*, p. 452). For the editors of the new Soviet edition of Dostoyevsky's *Complete Works*, the scene is also "full of humor" (IV: 284).

    Behind the comic element in Dostoyevsky's characterization, Robert L. Jackson discerns the "serious" role played by Isai Fomich in the author's "general ideological design"—in his juxtaposition of "the Jew Isaj Fomič with the Tartar Alej," contrasting "on the symbolic-ideological plane of the novel the *Christ-like* figure of Alej . . . with the Jew who, in the words of one of the convicts, 'sold Christ' " ("A Footnote," *Richerche Slavistiche*, note 1, p. 250).

30. Both Steinberg and Pascal have noted these inaccuracies and tried to find an explanation for them. The only plausible reason, according to Steinberg, is that Dostoyevsky "in regarding a Jew in the flesh, did not, as it were, see him at all, or rather saw him only through some preconceived formula" ("Dostoyevsky i yevreistvo," *Vyorsty*, p. 97). Pascal suggests the possibility that, because Isai was obliged to work on Saturdays, he put on phylacteries to show that this day was no longer a holiday (*Récits*, note 4, p. 83). But that hypothesis is contradicted by Dostoyevsky himself, who wrote of Isai that "on Saturdays, he went . . . to the prayer house in town" and "as if it were today, I can still see Isai Fomich loitering about the prison on Saturdays, trying his level best to do nothing" (IV: 93, 96).

31. See above, note 21. It is curious to note the incongruity of Dostoyevsky's lexicon. For *tallith*, he uses the word *riza* or chasuble, the outer vestment worn by the Orthodox (or Roman Catholic) priest; for phylacteries (or, more precisely, the leather thongs that serve to attach them)—*naruchnik* or maniple, which, in the Western church alone, is one of the Eucharistic vestments, consisting of a strip of stuff worn suspended from the left arm.

32. See chapter 4, note 13.

33. Only a fragment of the original manuscript of *The House of the Dead* is extant, and the letters written by Dostoyevsky during this period make no mention of Isai Fomich. His "Siberian Notebook" (*Sibirskaya tetrad*) does, however, contain several entries revealing a contemptuous attitude toward the Jews, though not specifically toward their religion (cf. IV: 238–242—items 91, 92, 113, 181, 202, 203, 250). Dostoyevsky incorporated them all into the narrative, except for the last mentioned (250), an anecdote of dubious quality and taste. Apparently judging it too good to waste, he managed—and the artifice is transparent—to graft it on a polemical article in his journal *Time* (*Vremya*) against Katkov's *Russian Herald* (*Russkii vestnik*); I shall return to this article in chapter 3 (see note 39). It is also interesting to note that the same issue of *Time* (no. 10, 1861) contained the first publication of chapter 9 of *The House of the Dead*, the chapter incorporating most of Dostoyevsky's observations on the Jews that he had jotted down in his notebook.

34. That short sentence speaks volumes about the national exclusiveness and religious intolerance of the Jews, a favorite latter-day theme of Dostoyevsky's.

35. Dostoyevsky found this little chant "absurd and ridiculous." Isai, apparently, swore to him that "this was the same song . . . that was sung by six hundred thousand Jews . . . when they crossed the Red Sea, and that it is decreed that every Jew should sing this melody at the moment of triumph and victory over his enemies" (IV: 95). Commenting on this passage, Pierre Pascal wrote (*Récits*, note 1, p. 183) that "ce chant, mal exécuté par Isaïe Fomitch, dans un cadre peu approprié, pouvait paraître 'ridicule et absurde.'" This view, in my opinion, errs on the side of indulgence, but it is interesting to note that the eminent French scholar felt impelled to clarify this point.

36. Grossman, *Ispoved*, p. 173.

37. Ibid. This nuance escaped the attention of the authors of the two most authoritative translations of *The House of the Dead*. Pascal (*Récits*, p. 105) translates this passage by "Il avait été envoyé pour assassinat": Mongault and Désormonts (*Oeuvres* [Paris: Bibl. de la

Pléiade, 1950], vol. 1, p. 975)—"Il était là pour meurtre." As for Constance Garnett (London, 1948, p. 61), she is more faithful to the original: "He had been sent here charged with murder." There is obviously a nuance, but whether it is filled with all the significance Grossman accords it is another question.

38. Grossman, *Ispoved*, p. 174.
39. Ibid.
40. Ibid., p. 175.
41. Ibid.

3. Time *and the "Jewish Question"*

1. For a summary of these and other legislative reforms, see Louis Greenberg, *The Jews in Russia*, 2 vols. (New Haven, 1944), vol. 1, pp. 74–78.
2. S. M. Dubnow, *History of the Jews in Russia and Poland*, 3 vols. (Philadelphia, 1918), vol. 2, p. 166.
3. Greenberg, *The Jews in Russia*, vol. 1, p. 77; see also *Yevreiskaya entsiklopediya*, 16 vols. (St. Petersburg, 1906–1913), vol. 1, p. 812.
4. Greenberg, *The Jews in Russia*, vol. 1, p. 77; D. I. Flisfeder, *Yevrei i ikh ucheniye ob inovertsakh* (St. Petersburg, 1874), p. 131. Stroganov's memorandum is cited *in extenso* by Yu. Gessen, "Popytka emantsipatsii yevreyev v Rossii," *Perezhitoye* (St. Petersburg, 1908), vol. 1, pp. 158–163.
5. S. Ginzburg, "Zabytaya epokha," *Voskhod*, no. 5 (1896): 137.
6. Understandably so, since the major issue of the day was Alexander's reforms and the debates over the path of Russia's development as reflected in the competing doctrines of Slavophilism, liberal Westernism and radical Westernism.
7. Looking back nostalgically on this period in his article "Literaturnyi krizis" (*Sovremennik*, nos. 1–2, 1863), M. A. Antonovich, dismayed by the apathy toward the growing conservatism of the Russian press, observed that "at the present time you will not find a single conservative issue to which the literary world would react with such unanimity as it did . . . to the insult leveled at the Jews by Zotov." See Antonovich, *Literaturno-kriticheskiye stati* (Moscow-Leningrad, 1961), p. 106.
8. *Voskhod*, no. 5 (1896): 141; also cited in Greenberg, *The Jews in Russia*, vol. 1, p. 78.
9. For the most complete information on this entire episode, see *Voskhod*, no. 5 (1896): 130–159; see also R. Vydrin, "Iz istorii

russko-polsko-yevreiskikh otnoshenii," *K yevreiskomu voprosu v Polshe* (Moscow, 1915), pp. 237–249.

10. Although Yevgeny Korsh's *Atenei* was short-lived (January 1858–May 1859), it counted among its contributors a number of distinguished writers, among them Turgenev, Saltykov-Shchedrin, S. Solovyov, Buslayev and Chernyshevsky. The fact that a new journal did not hesitate to become identified with the cause of Jewish reform is itself highly indicative of the mood prevailing at the time.

Martin Isayevich Gorvits (1837–1883) subsequently became a noted professor of obstetrics and gynecology in St. Petersburg. A convert to Russian Orthodoxy, he nevertheless maintained close relations with the Jewish community.

11. The complete text of the protest along with the full list of signatories can be found in *Voskhod*, no. 5 (1896): 131–133. As impressive as the list was, it did not include the names of such prominent literary figures as L. N. Tolstoy, Saltykov-Shchedrin, Goncharov, Pisemsky, Ostrovsky, Herzen or Dostoyevsky.

With regard to Dostoyevsky and Tolstoy, the following may be noted: Dostoyevsky could not possibly have signed since he had not yet returned from exile, and Tolstoy, throughout his life, was reluctant to take a *public* stand on the Jewish question. As for Herzen, he was already in London, and it is even more significant that he made known his views from there. In his "Otvet na pismo iz Polshi," *Kolokol*, no. 37 (March 1, 1859): 300 (facsimile edition [Moscow, 1962], vol. 2, p. 300), after accusing the Poles of "a Catholic feeling of hatred toward the Jews that . . . is nonexistent in Russia," he made the following explicit reference to the protest: "All literary Moscow and Petersburg, irrespective of party differences, extended a friendly hand to the Jews and rose up against the unseemly attack of a certain journalist."

12. One writer of the period viewed it as "a protest against the use of the word *zhid* in journalism" (cf. Flisfeder, *Yevrei i ikh ucheniye*, p. 8). The conclusion is not unwarranted: following the protest, Zotov himself felt constrained to write that "we see nothing denigrating in the term *zhid*" (cf. *Yevreiskaya entsiklopediya*, vol. 2, p. 735).

13. Greenberg, *The Jews in Russia*, vol. 1, p. 78; *Voskhod*, no. 5 (1896): 139.

14. In addition to the names already cited (Annenkov, Chernyshevsky, Nekrasov, Zhemchuzhnikov): A. D. Galakhov, A. A. Golovachov, S. S. Gromeka, K. D. Kavelin, I. E. Zabelin.

15. See V. M. Solovyov, *Yevreistvo i khristianskii vopros* (Moscow, 1884).
16. Cited in *Voskhod*, no. 5 (1896): 137–139; this unsigned article has been attributed to E. P. Karnovich, author of *Russkii yevrei* (1863).
17. "Polemicheskii sluchai s *Osnovoi* i *Sionom*," *Vremya*, no. 12 (December 1861): 114–116. Grossman has suggested that Dostoyevsky may very well have been the author of this article, an opinion not shared by Tomashevsky and Khalabayev, who felt that "there was not sufficient evidence to include it" in their edition of Dostoyevsky's works (13: 611). The most recent research on *Time*—V. S. Nechayeva, *Zhurnal M. M. i F. M. Dostoyevskikh "Vremya"—1861–1863* (Moscow, 1972)—sheds no light on the paternity of this article.

    Osnova (1861–1863) was a South Russian, Russian-language sociopolitical monthly, published in St. Petersburg by P. A. Kulish, fervent advocate of Ukrainian nationalism. For this and the whole-hearted support it gave to the Emancipation of the Serfs, it was severely criticized by *Sovremennik* and the Revolutionary-Democrats (who took a dismal view of the way in which the agrarian reform was being implemented).

    Sion (1861–1862) was a weekly, published in Odessa by E. Soloveichik and L. Pinsker, militant organ of Russian Jewry, relentless in its exposure of anti-Semitism.
18. With reference to the term *zhid*, Dostoyevsky would write later that "I didn't think that there was anything so offensive about it" (12: 77).
19. A point of view to which Dostoyevsky would fully subscribe in the late seventies.
20. It is especially the language of this final paragraph that lends support to the theory attributing authorship of this article to Dostoyevsky. Such phrases as *sovremennyye peredovyye lyudi, vysokoye nachalo vseobshchevo primireniya narodov, nepritvorno, so vseyu iskrennostyu zhelali by my primireniya* clearly bear his lexical and stylistic hallmark.
21. Aksakov published widely on the Jewish question in *Den* and *Moskva* in the sixties and in *Rus* in the early eighties. All of these articles are available in I. S. Aksakov, *Sochineniya*, 8 vols. (Moscow, 1886), vol. 3, pp. 687–844. A useful summary of his views will be found in Kritikus (S. Dubnow), "I. S. Aksakov i yevrei," *Voskhod*, no. 2 (1887): 1–17. (Dostoyevsky's essay on the Jewish question in *The Diary of a Writer* unmistakably shows the influence of Aksakov.)

22. "Devyatnadtsatyi numer *Dnya*," *Vremya*, no. 2 (1862): 164–168. Tomashevsky and Khalabayev (13: 611) dispute the opinion of the Finnish scholar Oskar von Schulz, who attributes this article to Dostoyevsky. Purportedly relying on the editorial records of *Time*, they find it more plausible to ascribe authorship to Strakhov. Such is not the view of Nechayeva (cf. *Zhurnal M. M. i F. M. Dostoyev- skikh*, pp. 272–273, and note 6, p. 273), who attributes it to M. I. Vladislavlev. Nechayeva, too, relies on *Time's* editorial records and, in particular, on Mikhail Dostoyevsky's letter of January 17, 1862, to Vladislavlev, in which the former wrote: "P. S. It would be a good idea to analyze the newspaper *Day*. Let me know—I'll send it to you." Be that as it may, on the basis of stylistic and other con- siderations, I am inclined to the view attributing paternity of the article to Dostoyevsky. It contains a number of phrases or allusions curiously reminiscent of certain passages in Dostoyevsky's first ar- ticle (signed) on Aksakov's weekly: "The Latest Literary Events— The Newspaper *Day*," in the November 1861 issue of *Time* (13: 145–154).

The other considerations suggesting Dostoyevsky's authorship are these:

a. *All* of the other unsigned articles devoted to *Day* have been definitively attributed to Dostoyevsky.

b. The article was prepared in great haste and under the pres- sure of a deadline. In his memoirs of a later day, Strakhov de- scribed Dostoyevsky's aptitude for journalism and his extraordinary ability to write under pressure, contrasting this with his own in- ability to do so (see O. Miller and N. Strakhov, *Biografiya, pisma i zametki iz zapisnoi knizhki F. M. Dostoyevskovo* [St. Petersburg, 1883], pp. 216, 220).

c. On more than one occasion, Dostoyevsky felt constrained to moderate the conservative tone of Strakhov's articles (ibid., p. 235). It is not conceivable that Strakhov would ever have written a word in favor of communists or materialists, unlike, as will be seen, the author of this article.

23. The May issue of *Time* actually came out on June 3. Aksakov's reply to the criticism touched off by his February editorial ap- peared in the May 26 issue of *Day*. I shall come back to this article later.

24. "Otvet g. A. Aleksandrovu (25 N° *Dnya*)," *Vremya*, no. 5 (1862): 60–78. Although not identified as such, Lyakub was a Russian- Jewish journalist and contributor to *Rassvet* (*Dawn*) and its succes- sor *Sion* until the latter ceased publication in April 1862.

25. No attempt need be made here to examine the programs of these parties. The point at issue was the path of development that Russia was to follow. Fundamentally conservative, the Slavophiles saw Russian history in terms of Orthodoxy, Muscovy and the *mir*. One of their leading spokesmen was Ivan Aksakov and his newspaper, *Day*.

    Representing the school of Westernizing liberalism with a program patterned on the English constitutional monarchy was Mikhail Katkov and his journal, the *Russian Herald*.

    The radical Westernizers or Revolutionary-Democrats (as they are customarily designated by Soviet authors) drew their inspiration from French eighteenth-century thought and, particularly, from French radical thought of the nineteenth century. Their principal spokesmen were Chernyshevsky, Nekrasov and Dobrolyubov and their journal, the *Contemporary*.

26. One of this group of Jewish intellectuals was Avraam-Uriya (Arkady Grigoryevich) Kovner, who was to be called the "Jewish Pisarev." His letters to Dostoyevsky in the late seventies led to the latter's essay on the Jewish question in *The Diary of a Writer* (see chapters 6 and 7 of the present study).

27. *Pisma*, vol. 1, p. 264 (October 11, 1859).

28. Ibid., vol. 1, p. 268.

29. Antonovich, *Literaturno-kriticheskiye stati*, p. 97.

30. *Pisma*, vol. 1, pp. 312–313.

31. "Obyavleniye o podpiske na zhurnal *Vremya*" (13: 498).

32. The first manifestation of Dostoyevsky's Slavophile sympathies is found in his oft-quoted letter of January 19, 1856, to Apollon Maikov. It is more patriotically bombastic in tone, more traditionally Slavophile than his *pochvennichestvo*. This is understandable: Dostoyevsky was writing not only *to* Maikov but also *for* the censors. But even so, he manifested a certain sympathy toward the Westernizers: "Possibly you have been somewhat disturbed recently by the influx of French ideas amongst that class of society that is thinking, feeling and studying. . . . But you yourself will agree that all men of common sense, that is, those who set the tone, had been considering French ideas solely from a scientific angle . . . while still remaining Russian" (*Pisma*, vol. 1, p. 166).

33. In his letter of February 24, 1861, to M. de Poulet, Mikhail Dostoyevsky wrote: "I think you agree with *Time*'s orientation; we are not Westernizers nor are we Slavophiles, we are Russians" (A. S. Dolinin, ed., *F. M. Dostoyevsky: Stati i materialy*, 2 vols. [Petersburg (*sic*), 1922], vol. 1, p. 509).

34. To Strakhov's article on Apollon Grigoryev in the September 1864 issue of *Epoch*, Dostoyevsky appended a long—and revealing—editorial note in which he underscored the need for exercising journalistic tact (13: 351):

> Apollon Grigoryev very often made mention of Khomyakov and Kireyevsky in *Time*, and he always spoke about them as he wished since the editorial board of *Time* fully shared his views. But what was unfortunate was that he often *lacked discrimination* in his remarks about them; he would speak of them gratuitously. The mass of readers at the time were oriented in quite another direction. The only thing they knew about Khomyakov and Kireyevsky was that they were *reactionaries*. . . . It was imperative to acquaint the readers with them, but to do so cautiously, *with discrimination*, gradually and diffuse their spirit and ideas rather than discredit them with loud and hollow praise. . . . But Grigoryev never understood those demands. He simply did not possess that tact, that flexibility that any journalist or *purveyor of ideas* must have.

35. Strakhov has written that *pochvennichestvo* was "a Russian, patriotic trend seeking definition and, as logic demanded, finally merging with Slavophilism. But for a short while it held itself apart, for two reasons: first, the desire for independence, faith in its own strength; second, the desire to carry its ideas to the public with as much success as possible, to capture its interest, to avoid clashing with its prejudices" (see Miller and Strakhov, *Biografiya*, p. 207).

36. *Pochvennichestvo* had, in fact, nothing in common with the declining liberalism and growing aristocratic conservatism of the *Russian Herald*. A liberal organ at its inception in 1856, by the beginning of the sixties, in reaction to the growth of the radical movement, it had veered sharply to the right to become the defender of the landed nobility, a class that Dostoyevsky was not particularly fond of.

37. "*Svistok i Russkii vestnik*," *Vremya*, no. 3 (1861), reprinted in 13: 186–198.

38. "*Otvet Russkomu vestniku*," *Vremya*, no. 5 (1861), reprinted in 13: 199–220.

39. "Po povodu elegicheskoi zametki *Russkovo vestnika*," *Vremya*, no. 10 (1861), reprinted in 13: 227–235.
    Dostoyevsky thereupon introduced the following parable:

> Once upon a time a Jew [*zhid*] hired a workman to chop wood. The muzhik chops and grunts under each blow. The Jew looks on

and asks: "Why are you grunting?" —"It's easier that way."
—"Well, then, you chop and I'll do the grunting for you," says the
Jew. With every swing of the muzhik's axe, the Jew joins in with a
grunt. After having finished the job, the muzhik asks for his money,
but the Jew gives him less than had been agreed on. —"How's that
now," says the muzhik, "after all, I finished chopping the wood,
didn't I?" —"But I did the grunting," says the Jew, "and that made
it easier for you." The Jews are a cunning lot! And are you not
wasting your time grunting?

(Cf. chapter 2, note 33, of the present study.)

40. "Poslednyye literaturnyye yavleniya—Gazeta *Den*," *Vremya*, no.
11 (1861), reprinted in 13: 145–154.

41. Antonovich, "O pochve," *Literaturno-kriticheskiye stati*, pp. 14–34.

42. S. S. Borshchevsky, *Shchedrin i Dostoyevsky* (Moscow, 1956), p.
61.

43. *Epoch* began publication in January 1864 and bore a close affinity
to the *Russian Herald* and *Day*.

44. Reference is made to the following articles in *Time*: "Primer apa-
tii" (no. 1, 1862); "Mikroskopicheskiye nablyudeniya" (no. 2, 1862);
"Nechto ob opalnom zhurnale" (no. 5, 1862). The first was in reply
to Antonovich's "O pochve" (December 1861); the second—to
Chernyshevsky's "Materialy dlya biografii N. A. Dobrolyubova"
(January 1862); and the third—to Antonovich's "O dukhe *Vremeni*
i o g. Kosits kak nailuchshem yevo vyrazhenii" (April 1862). The
controversy between the two journals subsided in May when the
Contemporary was closed down for eight months. Antonovich revived it in January 1863. The polemics between Shchedrin and
Dostoyevsky likewise commenced in January but were interrupted,
in turn, by the closure of *Time* in April 1863. The controversy that
was resumed with full force with the appearance of *Epoch* bears
no relevance to the present study.

45. "Dva lagerya teoretikov," *Vremya*, no. 2 (1862), reprinted in 13:
235–253.

46. "Slavyanofily, chernogortsy i zapadniki," *Vremya*, no. 9 (1862), reprinted in 13: 253–258.

47. L. P. Grossman, *Zhizn i trudy F. M. Dostoyevskovo* (Moscow-
Leningrad, 1935), p. 109.

48. M. S. Gus, *Idei i obrazy F. M. Dostoyevskovo*, 1st ed. (Moscow,
1962), p. 181.

49. This was the article in which Dostoyevsky made the following
allusion to *Time*'s February article on the Jewish question (13:
254):

An editorial office like that of *Day* can hardly be suspected of in-sincerity. We respect it, although to this day, for example, we can-not recall without laughing *Day*'s supposition about a Jew's be-coming Procurator of the Holy Synod. (We think our readers will recall that fantastic Procurator from among the Jews. The point at issue was the equalization of the rights of Jews and Russians in Russia. "If there are equal rights, it is not to be excluded that one day you'll see a Jew occupying the post of Procurator of the Holy Synod: what are we headed for!" *Day* exclaimed, and in the light of the possibility that there could be a Jewish Procurator, it con-cluded that it was impossible to accord certain rights to Jews!) But differences like these of our journal with *Day* can in no way, of course, undermine our personal esteem for it.

50. Aksakov, *Sochineniya*, vol. 3, p. 694.

4. *Svidrigailov's Suicide—Shatov's Credo—The "Rothschild Idea"*

1. *Pisma*, vol. 2, p. 81 (February 18/March 1, 1868).
2. Ibid., vol. 2, p. 31 (August 16/28, 1867).
3. For the sake of completeness, let me call attention to the few other scattered and quite conventional allusions to the Jews in *Crime and Punishment*: the moneylender Alyona Ivanovna (Raskolnikov's vic-tim, who is not Jewish) is "rich as a Yid" and "a terrible bitch" (VI: 53); Razumikhin describes Luzhin as "a spy and profiteer . . . a Yid and charlatan" (VI: 156); Svidrigailov (!) deplores the moral de-generation of St. Petersburg: "The common people are boozing, the educated youth . . . are wasting themselves in impossible dreams and visions . . . ; the Yids have moved in from God knows where and are stashing money away, and all the rest is debauchery" (VI: 370); and "a Yid" makes a fleeting appearance as a fence (VI: 384). The influx of the Jews into the cities of Holy Russia accom-panied by the subjection of the populace to their financial domina-tion would become one of Dostoyevsky's favorite themes, but he shows little perspicacity in making Svidrigailov the spokesman for this view.
4. V. B. Shklovsky, *Za i protiv* (Moscow, 1957), p. 220.
5. M. S. Gus, *Idei i obrazy F. M. Dostoyevskovo* (Moscow, 1962), p. 268.
6. A. Z. Steinberg, "Dostoyevsky i yevreistvo," *Vyorsty*, no. 3 (Paris, 1928): 104–105. In Dostoyevsky's eyes, the Jews, originally the

chosen people of God and the repository of universal truth, were no longer worthy of this sacred trust and had become, in the words of Shatov-Dostoyevsky, "ethnographical material," a view that will be examined more fully in the present chapter.

7. Ibid.

8. Except for the three authors mentioned, the scene of Svidrigailov's suicide has not arrested the attention of other observers. Neither Professor Pierre Pascal, the eminent French Dostoyevsky scholar nor the well known émigré critics, the late Wladimir Weidlé and the late Georges Adamovitch—in private conversations with the author—recognized any particular symbolic significance in this scene.

9. Though Svidrigailov's "Opinion" is not given explicit expression in the final version of the novel, it finds implicit expression in the suicide scene.

10. To what extent can Dostoyevsky be identified with Shatov? The least that can be said is that they share strikingly concordant views on the "exclusive role" of Russia, as evidenced by Dostoyevsky's letters of the period. And if any doubts subsist, they are thoroughly dispelled by one passage in *The Diary of a Writer* (January 1877), in which Dostoyevsky espouses Shatov's credo almost verbatim: " 'Every great people believes, and must believe if it aspires to a long life, that it and it alone holds the key to the salvation of the world, that it lives to stand at the head of [other] peoples, to draw all of them unto itself as one and to lead them in unison to the final goal preordained for all of them' " (12: 22).

This passage has given rise to numerous commentaries, either direct or indirect. In addition to those of Berdyayev and Steinberg, let us note the reactions of Vladimir Solovyov, Tolstoy, Volynsky, and Merezhkovsky:

Solovyov (*Tri rechi v pamyat Dostoyevskovo* [Berlin, 1925], p. 21: second allocution of February 1, 1882):

... he [Dostoyevsky] considered Russia the chosen people of God, chosen not to rival with other peoples nor to dominate nor have primacy over them, but to serve all peoples without reward and to realize, in fraternal concourse, true universalism and ecumenism.

Tolstoy (letter of July 5, 1890, to Solovyov, published in F. G[etz]., *Slovo podsudimomu* [St. Petersburg, 1891], p. xi):

In theory I have always recognized that the lofty spirit of Christian teachings was accessible to all peoples, particularly to the Jewish people from whom they derived. As I see it, the principal stumbling block is the exclusiveness, the special mission, which the Jews attribute to themselves. For a people to claim they have a mission . . . is not only not (possible) necessary, it is harmful. A man and a people must follow their calling, but not define it since it is indefinable down to the grave. . . .

. . . Moreover, all arguments about the mission of the Jewish people that sets them apart from other peoples make the Jews repugnant to me; to me, at any rate, Anglo-Saxonism, Germanism, Slavism (particularly Slavism) are as repugnant as the belief in Jewish specificity.

Volynsky (*Dostoyevsky* [St. Petersburg, 1909], pp. 304–305):

Shatov's populistic fanatacism supplants religious feelings . . . by a kind of blind belief in the exclusiveness of his own people, it transforms religion into idolatry. . . . One might even say that Shatov's belief . . . is nothing else but a variety of human unbelief, for true spiritual belief ends the moment a spiritual vocation is denied to other peoples. . . . At this point, the idol of nationalism eclipses the ideal of the divine, and no matter how inspired the words that are pronounced, no matter how entrancing the rapturous ravings of none other than Dostoyevsky, hiding behind the figure of Shatov, one can detect nothing of that Christian spirit that, on the symbolic day of Pentecost, was wafted from the humble hearth of a Jewish abode throughout the world, intelligible to all and breaking down the barriers among peoples.

Merezhkovsky (*Prorok russkoi revolyutsii*, in *Polnoye sobraniye sochinenii*, 24 vols. [Moscow, 1914], vol. 14, p. 209):

There still might be some doubt whether Dostoyevsky shared the thoughts of his hero had he not reiterated them in *The Diary of a Writer*. . . . Accordingly, Orthodoxy, which is the true Christianity in Dostoyevsky's opinion, is "the great presumption" of the Russian people, its faith in its own self as in God, because the Russian God, "the Russian Christ" is nothing less than "the synthetic personality" of the Russian people. Instead of the old formula "The Russian people is all in Orthodoxy," a new one, the converse, is obtained: All Orthodoxy is in the Russian people. Only when Russia, by its God, by its Christ "triumphs over and drives from the world all other Gods and Christs" will the "Russian Christ" become universal.

11. N. A. Berdyaev, *Dostoevsky* (New York, 1959), p. 182. For a Christian, the Hebraic Messianic idea was fulfilled with the coming of Christ. Reconciled in Christ, the nations found their unity in Christendom. Judaism, of course, does not recognize Christ as the Messiah.

12. Steinberg, "Dostoyevsky i yevreistvo," *Vyorsty*, no. 3 (1928): 103.

13. A parallel may be drawn between this imaginary scene and a real incident in Dostoyevsky's life, which is described in a letter to his wife written from Wiesbaden in April 1871. After heavy losses at the roulette table, Dostoyevsky fled from the casino in a state of extreme emotional agitation and sought the solace of a priest: "As I hurried along the unfamiliar streets in the darkness, the thought kept running through my mind that he is God's pastor, it's not like speaking to a private person but rather like going to confession. But I lost my way in the city and when I reached a church that I took for the Russian church, I was told in a shop that it wasn't a Russian church but a synagogue [*zhidovskaya*]. I felt as if someone had poured cold water over me. I came running home" (*Pisma*, vol. 2, p. 347). Does not this letter reveal an almost pathological revulsion?

14. Katz had fond memories of Dostoyevsky and his solicitude toward him. See A. V. Skandin, "F. M. Dostoyevsky v Semipalatinske," *Istoricheskii vestnik*, vol. 1, 91 (1903): 201–225; N. I. Yakushin, *Dostoyevsky v Sibiri* (Kemerovo, 1960), p. 113.

    Unfortunately, almost nothing is known about Dostoyevsky's relations with his Jewish neighbors in the apartment house (Alonkin's House) he lived in from August 1864 to January 1867 except that they lacked cordiality (cf. *Pisma*, vol. 2, p. 23; July 1/12, 1867). The Dostoyevskys didn't have much luck, either, on their return from abroad in July 1871. The only accommodations they were able to find were some "miserable *chambre-garni* [*sic*]. Very expensive, uncomfortable and with wretched Yid landlords" (*Pisma*, vol. 2, p. 367; July 18, 1871).

15. L. P. Grossman, *Zhizn i trudy F. M. Dostoyevskovo* (Moscow-Leningrad, 1935), p. 343.

16. *Dnevnik A. G. Dostoyevskoi—1867* (Moscow, 1923).

17. Ibid., p. 7.

18. Ibid., p. 8.

19. Ibid., p. 10.

20. Ibid., pp. 226, 230–232, 241–242, 246, 248–249, 261–262, 283–284, 287–289, 291, 297, 305–307, 326, 331, 333–334, 336–337, 340, 345.

21. Ibid., p. 306.

22. Gus, *Idei i obrazy*, p. 392, citing *Delo Petrashevtsev*, 3 vols. (Moscow, 1940), vol. 1, p. 93. In his notes to *L'Adolescent* (Dostoïevski, *Oeuvres*, 7 vols. [Paris: Bibl. de la Pléiade, 1956], vol. 5, p. 1102), Pierre Pascal mentions that Petrashevsky "propageait activement un pamphlet français intitulé *Rothschild, roi des Juifs.*" It would also be interesting to know to what extent the Petrashevsky, in general, and Dostoyevsky, in particular, had been influenced by the anti-Semitic current in the Fourierist movement. (For an excellent study on the relationship between the socialist movement and the problem of anti-Semitism, see George Lichtheim, "Socialism and the Jews," *Dissent*, vol. 15, no. 4 [1968]: 314–342).

23. Gus, *Idei i obrazy*, p. 391.

24. Here, for the first time, Dostoyevsky juxtaposes the Rothschild theme and the Christ motif. In the "Notebooks" for *The Brothers Karamazov* the two ideas are invariably linked together.

25. As G. M. Fridlender has noted, the allusion to the inscription on the cross "Jezus Nazarenus, Rex Judaeorum [*Tsar* Iudeiskii]" is rendered by Ganya as "*korol* Iudeiskii," an unmistakable reference to the "king" of the Stock Exchange, Rothschild. He provides some original insights on the genesis and commingling of the Christ and Rothschild themes in Dostoyevsky's writings, tracing the phenomenon directly back to Heine, who juxtaposed the two themes in his *Zur Geschichte der Religion und Philosophie in Deutschland*, the translation of which appeared in Dostoyevsky's *Epoch* in 1864 (nos. 1–3). See Fridlender, *Realizm Dostoyevskovo* (Moscow-Leningrad, 1964), pp. 286–288.

26. Dostoyevsky implies that the Jews were untidily dressed.

27. It is interesting to compare this passage with the corresponding one in the "Notebooks" for *A Raw Youth* (XVI: 279–280). The final version is identical to the original draft in all but one significant respect: the fragment printed in italics (mine) replaced the following, rather obscure, phrase: "there will be a forced oxidation accompanied by a complete awareness of one's own fermentation." The idea of the Jews' taking over power became one of Dostoyevsky's favorite themes in the seventies. It is found on a number of occasions in his *Diary of a Writer* and in his letters of the period.

28. That Dostoyevsky attributed cardinal significance to the "Rothschild idea" is confirmed by this entry of September 6, 1874, in his "Notebooks": "*VERY IMPORTANT* Never, throughout the whole course of the novel, does the Adolescent entirely abandon his idea about Rothschild. This *idea fixa* is his *way out* of *everything*, of all problems and difficulties. . . .' Steer the novel through in such a

way as to give this idea *primordial* importance in the novel. Primordial importance in the sense that it never lets go of the Adolescent, latches on to him. . . ." (XVI: 105–106).

29. A. S. Dolinin (ed.), *F. M. Dostoyevsky—Materialy i issledovaniya* (Leningrad, 1935), p. 374.

5. The Possessed

1. The Russian title is *Besy* or, literally, *The Demons,* but we have retained the English title by which it has come to be known.

2. This is by and large true even of the critics who have been concerned with the problem of Dostoyevsky and the Jews. Grossman in "Dostoyevsky i yudaizm" (*Ispoved odnovo yevreya* [Moscow-Leningrad, 1924], pp. 165–181) makes no mention whatever of Lyamshin. Steinberg in "Dostoyevsky i yevreistvo" (*Vyorsty,* no. 3 [1928]: 94–108) makes only a scant reference to him. Gornfeld in his article on Dostoyevsky (*Yevreiskaya entsiklopediya,* vol. 7, pp. 310–313) is, of necessity, brief in his evaluation of Lyamshin but indicates the importance he attaches to him. And finally Zaslavsky in "Dostoyevsky o yevreyakh" (*Yevreiskii vestnik,* no. 1 [1922]: 6–10) dismisses him as a decidedly episodic character who, for no very good reason, just happens to appear in the novel. He notes, not quite correctly, that "there is nothing specifically Jewish about Lyamshin" and, quite correctly, that "he speaks a flawless Russian." He is a complete nonentity, "a toy in the hands of real 'demons,'" he is "incapable of playing an independent role or leading the movement." People like Lyamshin, Zaslavsky concludes, "cannot 'destroy' Russia." All this is, of course, true, but it sheds no light either on Lyamshin's character or on his place in the novel.

3. Steinberg (*Vyorsty,* no. 3 [1928]: 97) assumes, without explaining why, that Lyamshin was a convert. He possibly inferred this from the fact that Lyamshin was a postal employee, a position not normally held by a Jew. However, the Law of November 27, 1861, would have made it possible for a Jew with a university degree to occupy a post in the civil service.

4. See XII: 209. It goes without saying that Dostoyevsky radically and freely transposed the events as well as the characters. As he wrote Katkov in October 1870: "I take only the bald fact. My fantasy can differ in the highest degree from the reality as it was. . . ." (*Pisma,* vol. 2, p. 288).

5. Not much, unfortunately, can be gleaned from the "Notebooks" for

The Possessed. Dostoyevsky introduces the character of Lyamshin unnamed—in notebook no. 2, p. 3, in an entry dated the beginning of March 1870. Listing the members of the *"Nechayev clique,"* he noted: "Possibly a fourth one (a pickpocket and windbag)" (X: 129). On page 40 of the same notebook, he reappears, still unnamed, as: "one vile little man," which is closely followed by a parenthetical notation "(Blasphemy and sacrilege in the church)" (XI: 85); the date of this entry has not been established; it may even antedate the previous one by a few weeks. Lyamshin is mentioned by name for the first time in notebook no. 4, page 5: "Lyamshin will denounce" (XI: 294), an entry dated June 1872. Thereafter he appears under his name in the few other references that are made to him throughout the "Notebooks" (XI: 297, 298 and 302). Not once is there the slightest indication of Lyamshin's Jewish origin, even in those entries that are subsequent to January 1871, when serial publication of the novel began in *Russkii vestnik.* It is, therefore, even more curious to note that Lyamshin appeared as *"zhidok Lyamshin"* in the very first installment of the novel, that is, almost a year and a half before he was named for the first time in the "Notebooks."

6. Cf. Lev Deich, *Rol yevreyev v russkom revolyutsionnom dvizhenii* (Berlin, 1923).
7. For Utin's biography, see *Literaturnoye nasledstvo*, no. 62 (Moscow, 1955): 606–625.
8. Dolinin even adds that "it would be well to keep this [eventuality] in mind in analyzing *The Possessed"* (*Pisma*, vol. 2, p. 402). There is the further possibility that Dostoyevsky had met Utin as early as 1862 at Chernyshevsky's. It is known that the writer visited Chernyshevsky sometime after the middle of May and that Utin visited him three times between May 18 and May 31 of that year. (Cf. L. P. Grossman, *Zhizn i trudy F. M. Dostoyevskovo* [Moscow-Leningrad, 1935], pp. 112–113; *Literaturnoye nasledstvo*, no. 62 [Moscow, 1955]: 612.)
9. *Pisma*, vol. 2, p. 31.
10. Suslova leaves no doubt about the nature of her relationship with Yevgeny Utin. In her diary she wrote: "Utin was here just now. He spoke very *frankly.* I told him that he could be very distracting but that I could not love him" (A. P. Suslova, *Gody blizosti s Dostoyevskim* [Moscow, 1928], p. 117).

   Less is known about Suslova's relations with Nikolai Utin. It is clear, however, that the latter held her in the highest esteem, since he devoted more than half of his long letter to Ogaryov of Novem-

ber 23, 1863, to Suslova, commending her to the considerate attention of both Ogaryov and Herzen. Utin also has some interesting
things to say about Dostoyevsky (*Literaturnoye nasledstvo*, no. 62
[Moscow, 1955]):

> I am anxious to make it plain, however, that I for one have
> seen very little of her [i.e., Suslova] and that it is extremely
> unlikely that she would get on with me for the very simple
> reason that she is very close to F. Dostoyevsky and, as might
> be expected, fully shares his views. As for me, I would find it
> impossible to get on with Dostoyevsky—I could not accept his
> mysticism and . . . moralizing; that does not prevent me from
> respecting him for suffering for his beliefs or respecting him
> *as a person.* He must have considered me an insolent kid; that
> is certain, but sad . . . ."

11. Acts of arson and sacrilege, which played an important role in the
final version of the novel, are mentioned several times in the
"Notebooks" (XI: 85, 212, 278–279). But none of these acts, in the
"Notebooks," is attributed to Lyamshin (with the possible exception of the first mentioned: see above, note 5).

12. An interesting case has been made by M. S. Altman for seeing in
Karl Levy, a gifted pianist of the period, one of the prototypes of
Lyamshin. It is based on the following passage in V. A. Sollogub's
Reminiscences (first published in 1865): "Once, at the home of one
of Poland's most fervent patriots, he [Levy] was asked to play
something. He sat down at the piano. . . . The notes of *Jeszcze
Polska nie zginela* resounded, but while his left hand was busy
'rolling out' the phrases of 'To the Fatherland,' his right hand was
tripping lightly over the high notes rendering one of the most beloved and soul-stirring Russian melodies. . . . " Altman draws a
parallel between Levy's musical divertissement and Lyamshin's *La
Marseillaise/Mein Lieber Augustin* caprice and suggests that Dostoyevsky, a frequent guest at Sollogub's *soirées*, may very well
have seen Levy's performance or, at least, heard or read about it.
(See M. S. Altman, "Iz arsenala imyon i prototipov literaturnykh
geroyev Dostoyevskovo," *Dostoyevsky i yevo vremya* [Leningrad,
1971], pp. 212–213.)

13. In adding this unexpected touch to Lyamshin's composite portrait,
Dostoyevsky may have patterned him after Pavel Isayevich Veinberg, a past master in the art of Jewish mimicry, who, in the seventies, gave frequent public performances in which he parodied the
Jews and other minorities. The author of *Scenes from Jewish Life*
(six editions were published between 1870 and 1878), Veinberg

"contributed a great deal to the building up of anti-Jewish feeling in Russia" (cf. *Yevreiskaya entsiklopediya*, vol. 5, pp. 381–382).

While there is no direct evidence that Dostoyevsky was acquainted with Pavel Veinberg, he may very well have met him through his brother Pyotr, a prominent and respected literary historian, whom Dostoyevsky knew very well from their many years of working together in the Literary Fund.

14. Dostoyevsky would later implicate the Jews (and the Armenians) in the profanation of the Kazan Cathedral in St. Petersburg during the student demonstrations in December 1876. Cf. *Pisma*, vol. 4, p. 18.

15. In a very real sense, this scene symbolizes the immolation of Shatov even before his physical annihilation. The poor devil is already so disfigured by the ugly realities of life that he is no longer recognizable as the eloquent defender of the faith, the prophet of the sacred mission of his people. Is not the Jew Lyamshin an integral part of this ugly, inescapable reality? Is not the confrontation between Shatov and Lyamshin the confrontation between Dostoyevsky and the phantom he cannot elude, which, even in the pitiful figure of a Lyamshin, is the negation of the election of the Russian people and its *exclusive* Messianic role?

16. Is Dostoyevsky implying that Lyamshin wanted to save Shatov, warning him of the impending danger? If that be so, it would seem to indicate a certain degree of sympathy toward the former.

17. Yet Dostoyevsky the man is unwilling to concede to Lyamshin the human grandeur that his integrity as a writer compelled him momentarily to confer upon him.

18. It is entirely conceivable that Dostoyevsky deliberately cast Lyamshin in the role of informer because he was a Jew. For he could very well have assigned the role to Virginsky without any radical revamping of the plot (or even to Shatov, which would have necessitated a fundamental revision). But the author was loath to cast a Russian (indigenous) in that role; he considered denunciation as a morally reprehensible act even when dictated by the highest ethical and civic motives. The problem is raised a number of times in the "Notebooks" for *The Possessed* (XI: 74, 108, 298–299), but the most revealing evidence of Dostoyevsky's position is found in the reminiscences of the publisher Aleksei Suvorin. He recounts that on the day of Mlodetsky's attempt on the life of General Loris-Melikov (head of the Supreme Executive Committee, an antiterrorist organ) he was at Dostoyevsky's apartment. Dostoyevsky raised the question of whether Suvorin would inform the police if he got wind of a plot to blow up the Winter Palace. The latter

replied that he would not. "Nor would I either," Dostoyevsky said. "Why? It is, after all, a terrible thing. It's a crime. We could, perhaps, avert it. . . . I have mulled over all the reasons that would compel me to speak out—they are cogent, sound. And then I thought about the reasons that would prevent me from doing so—they are utterly insignificant. Simply the fear of being taken for a stool pigeon" (*Dnevnik A. S. Suvorina* [Moscow-Petrograd, 1923], pp. 15–16).

19. What makes this entry even more surprising—and, thus, even more significant—is the fact that, with the exception of this detail, the final version of the scene of Shatov's murder follows very closely the version in the "Notebooks."

20. The only critic, to my knowledge, to have commented on Lyamshin's act of denunciation was A. L. Volynsky. His final conclusion, however, differs radically from my own. He writes that "a conscious-stricken Lyamshin 'ran to the authorities' in order to unmask the assassins. He ran to the authorities as if to a source of absolution and redemption and—strange and uncanny as it may seem—Dostoyevsky manifests here a certain sympathy toward the pitiful Lyamshin, so violent was his hatred against Russian nihilism" (Volynsky, *Dostoyevsky* [St. Petersburg, 1909], p. 344).

21. While the program of Dostoyevsky's Nechayev has much in common with that of the real Nechayev, we have not been able to determine whether the mobilization of the Jews for revolutionary ends was actually a part of Nechayev's program; it quite conceivably could have been. It is to be noted that Dostoyevsky uses the term *yevrei* and not *zhidi* (in the first edition of the "Notebooks," E. N. Konshina, ed. [Moscow-Leningrad, 1935], p. 274, the word is underscored). Dostoyevsky's intention, however, is not at all clear. If he is distinguishing here between the assimilated and Russified Jew (who was beginning to appear in the revolutionary movement at this time) and the Jewish masses whose culture was Yiddish (*zhidi*, as he would describe them), the meaning of the sentence still remains equivocal: "To stir up" implies an action on the masses, not on an élite.

6. *Dostoyevsky as Journalist:* The Citizen, The Diary of a Writer—*Correspondence with A. G. Kovner*

1. F. M. Dostoyevsky, *Dnevnik pisatelya,* vols. 11 and 12 of *Polnoye sobraniye khudozhestvennykh proizvedenii* (Moscow-Leningrad, 1929).

2. See V. V. Vinogradov, *Problema avtorstva i teoriya stilei* (Moscow, 1961), pp. 487–611; also his article "Iz anoninmovo felyetonnovo naslediya Dostoyevskovo," *Issledovaniya po poetike i stilistike* (Leningrad, 1972), pp. 185–211.

3. In his preface to *The Diary* (11: iii–xxvi), Desnitsky came out against the Pereverzev school, which dominated Soviet literary criticism until 1929. Pereverzev by and large rejected the idea of any interaction between the two genres: "to look for Dostoyevsky's philosophy, his political and religious ideas in his [literary] works . . . is like asking a baker for a pair of boots." Such views were to be found only in his journalistic articles and not in his stories and novels that depict "life and living characters that possess universal, objective value" (V. Pereverzev, *Tvorchestvo Dostoyevskovo*, 3rd ed. [Moscow-Leningrad, 1928], pp. 59–61). But at the same time Pereverzev was obliged to acknowledge that whenever Dostoyevsky "wants to express some personal and intimate thought, he does so not by way of some [personal] reflection, but invariably by placing it in the mouth of this or that hero, at times even unconcerned whether it jibes with his character or not" (cited by Desnitsky, 11: xii). (Earlier chapters have shown the perspicacity of this observation.)

4. Cf. Shatov's and Dostoyevsky's credo: see chapter 4, note 10.

5. *The Raw Youth* falls chronologically in this period, but it has already been discussed in chapter 4.

6. This is the thesis of the study by L. P. Grossman, "Dostoyevsky i pravitelstvennyye krugi 70-kh godov," *Literaturnoye nasledstvo*, no. 15 (Moscow, 1934): 83–162.

7. L. P. Grossman, *Zhizn i trudy F. M. Dostoyevskovo* (Moscow-Leningrad, 1935), p. 198.

8. Grossman, "Dostoyevsky," *Literaturnoye nasledstvo*, no. 15: 149.

9. On this subject, see Konstantin Konstantinovich Romanov's letter to Dostoyevsky of May 4, 1880 (*Literaturnoye nasledstvo*, no. 15: 162). In this letter—the last of a series of six addressed to Dostoyevsky—the young Romanov invited him to a small private reception on May 8. It is not known whether Dostoyevsky attended it, but it is known that he was received by the tsarevich in December of the same year (ibid., p. 92). The chances are, therefore, that they saw each other on more than one occasion.

10. *Pisma*, vol. 3, pp. 49–50. Only one other letter from Dostoyevsky to Alexander is extant, that of November 16, 1876, in which the writer solicits the privilege of sending the tsarevich *The Diary of a Writer* (*Pisma*, vol. 3, pp. 251–252).

11. Grossman notes ("Dostoyevsky," *Literaturnoye nasledstvo*, no. 15:

86) that at the end of the seventies, Dostoyevsky "was in regular contact with Countess S. A. Tolstaya (widow of the poet Aleksei Konstantinovich); Ye. A. Naryshkina; Countess A. Ye. Komarovskaya, wife of the director of the Chief Administration on Press Affairs, Yu. F. Abaza; Princess Volkonskaya, wife of the prominent diplomat S. P. Khitrovo; I. P. Kornilov, former superintendent of the Vilno School District; General Chernyayev, known for his Slavophilism; I. A. Vyshnegradsky, future Minister of Finance; Ye. A. Shtakenschneider, daughter of the palace architect; Countess Ye. A. Geiden, president of the Order of St. George; Yu. D. Zasetskaya, president of the Society of Doss Houses, et al."

12. See A. G. Dostoyevskaya, *Vospominaniya*, 2nd ed. (Moscow, 1971), pp. 213–214.
13. Grossman, "Dostoyevsky," *Literaturnoye nasledstvo*, no. 15: 86.
14. Edward Crankshaw, *The Shadow of the Winter Palace* (London, 1976), p. 236.
15. See Dostoyevsky's letter to Maikov of January 18, 1856, in *Pisma*, vol. 1, pp. 163–168, and note thereto, pp. 519–520.
16. See Dostoyevsky's letter to Maikov of October 26/November 7, 1868, in *Pisma*, vol. 2, pp. 140–145, and note thereto concerning Samarin, pp. 433–434.
17. Samarin maintained that the German liberals who supported the *Kulturkampf* were controlled by the Jews. In his letter to Baroness de Rahden, a close Petersburg friend, he wrote the following from Berlin on February 21/March 4, 1876: "Quant à l'autre parti, celui de la kämpfende Cultur, il est juif—c'est tout dire. Vous savez certainement qu'aujourd'hui il n'y a presque plus de Berlin, il y a une Jérusalem nouvelle qui parle l'allemand. Quand il est question de judaïsme, qui trône à la chambre, que Bismarck *subit*, tout en se donnant les airs de s'en servir, qui dirige le haut enseignement . . . qui paie et inspire la majorité des journaux—il ne s'agit, bien entendu, ni de l'Ancien Testament, ni d'une nationalité élevée à la hauteur d'une race élue. C'est quelque chose d'impalpable et d'insaisissable dans son ensemble, c'est l'extrait le plus complet qui ait jamais existé de tous les éléments foncièrement hostiles à un ordre moral et social chrétiennement constitué" (*Correspondance de G. Samarine avec la Baronne de Rahden—1861–1876*, 2nd ed. [Moscow, 1894], pp. 241–242; published earlier in *Pravoslavnoye obozreniye*, 1877).

Dostoyevsky held precisely the same views about the preponderance of Jewish influence in Germany: cf. his letter to K. P. Pobedonostsev of August 9/21, 1879, cited further in the text.

18. I. S. Aksakov, *Sochineniya*, 8 vols. (Moscow, 1886), vol. 4, pp. 213–315.

19. Dolinin regretted, at the same time, that the subject had not been given the study it warranted; see *Pisma*, vol. 2, pp. 414–415 (comments on letter no. 301).

20. Grossman, "Dostoyevsky," *Literaturnoye nasledstvo*, no. 15: 83–162.

21. V. P. Meshchersky, *Moi vospominaniya*, part 2 (1865–1881) (St. Petersburg, 1898), p. 174. And he added: "I had never seen or met before such a total and complete conservative. . . . in his conservatism, Dostoyevsky had the austerity of an ascetic and the fanaticism of a neophyte" (p. 179).

    We shall not dwell on Meshchersky's views on the Jewish question: he was a rabid anti-Semite (see *Dnevnik knyazya V. P. Meshcherskovo* for 1889 and 1890: pp. 15–18, 165–168, 176–178, 271, 418–421). Dostoyevsky possessed a number of the prince's books in his personal library (see L. P. Grossman, *Seminarii po Dostoyevskomu* [Moscow-Petrograd, 1922], p. 26).

22. Robert F. Byrnes, "Dostoevskii and Pobedonostsev," *Essays in Russian and Soviet History* (New York, 1963), p. 87.

23. For the period 1873 to 1880, fifty letters are known, forty-two of them written by Pobedonostsev; the latter have all been published in *Literaturnoye nasledstvo*, no. 15: 124–148.

24. *Krasnyi arkhiv* (Moscow-Petrograd, 1922), vol. 2, p. 244. The passage enclosed in angle brackets was deleted from *Pisma*, vol. 4, p. 94.

25. Quoted in Grossman, "Dostoyevsky," *Literaturnoye nasledstvo*, no. 15: 142. Grossman notes (p. 143) that there was absolutely nothing "Jewish" about the first three periodicals mentioned.

26. It is likewise noteworthy that Pobedonostsev—in his letter of June 6, 1881, to Alexander III—registered strong disapproval of the pogroms that had taken place in the Ukraine in the spring of that year, stigmatizing the clergy for inciting the populace against "the landlords and the Jews" (see *Pisma Pobedonostseva k Aleksandru III*, 2 vols. [Moscow, 1925], vol. 1, p. 344). In his preface to this volume, the eminent historian Pokrovsky characterized Pobedonostsev as being "more composed and even-tempered than Dostoyevsky the journalist" (p. vi).

27. The work is in two parts: (1) an introduction and commentary by Brafman and (2) a compendium of the statutes of the Minsk *kahal* (the Hebrew word for "community") at the end of the eighteenth century. The *kahal* was abolished by law in 1844, a fact

that he conceals. Basing his "thesis" on the statutes and records of a defunct institution, Brafman alleges that the Jews recognize only Talmudic law and do not consider themselves bound by the laws of the empire; that they form a state within a state, a "Talmudic republic" that exploits and enslaves the non-Jewish populations living around them.

The book enjoyed at least four editions in Russia: 1869 (1st ed., Vilno); 1870, 1875 (2nd ed., part 1, Vilno; part 2, St. Petersburg); 1882 (2nd ed. [*sic*], part 1, St. Petersburg); 1888 (3rd ed. [*sic*], St. Petersburg). Moreover, the first and third editions were published in French (in Russia) under the more explicit title of *Livre du Kahal: Matériaux pour étudier le judaïsme en Russie et son influence sur les populations parmi lesquelles il existe.*

28. Grossman, *Biblioteka Dostoyevskovo* (Odessa, 1919), p. 158.

29. V. S. Nechayeva, *Opisaniye rukopisei F. M. Dostoyevskovo* (Moscow, 1957), p. 524.

30. The March issue was approved by the Censor's Office on April 2 (cf. Grossman, *Zhizn i trudy F. M. Dostoyevskovo*, p. 268).

31. It is a tragic twist of irony that Friedrich Schiller, who was so dearly loved by the young Jewish intelligentsia of the time for the humanity that permeated his writings, should have been used in a spirit so alien to him. But Brafman was well versed in the art of lifting quotations out of context and turning them to his own unscrupulous designs. He undoubtedly took his "citation" from Schiller's essay "Die Sendung Moses," which, translated into Yiddish in 1866, described the life of the Jews during their four-hundred–year exile in Egypt (F. Schiller, *Sämtliche Werke*, 5 vols. [Munich, 1960], vol. 4, pp. 784–785):

During their long sojourn, they lived apart from the Egyptians, isolated from them not only in the sense that they lived in their own dwellings but also in the sense that their nomadic way of life made the Jews an abomination to all the inhabitants of the country and excluded them from all participation in the life of the community. They governed themselves in the manner of nomads. . . . The father ruled over the family, the prince of the tribe over the tribes and, in this way, they formed a state within a state [der Hausvater die Familie, der Stammfürst die Stämme, und machten auf diese Art einen Staat in Staate aus], whose inordinate growth at length aroused the concern of the kings.

See also *Yevreiskaya entsiklopediya*, vol. 16, pp. 29–30.

32. In her *Reminiscences (Krasnyi arkhiv*, 3 [1923]: 276), A. G. Dostoyevskaya recalls that in the fall and winter of "1872" her husband

"was a frequent guest at the dinners of Pr. Meshchersky, at the receptions of N. P. Semyonov and at the Saturday gatherings of the deeply esteemed I. P. Kornilov, where the élite of the literary, scientific and bureaucratic world met." (Inexplicably, in the subsequent editions, in book form, of her *Vospominaniya*—1925, p. 256, and 1971, p. 354—the visits to Kornilov are put in the winter of "1879/1880.") The "deeply esteemed" Kornilov considered "the Poles and the Jews as a greater evil for Russia than the Mongols were" (cf. Louis Greenberg, *The Jews in Russia,* 2 vols. [New Haven, 1944, 1951], vol. 1, p. 93).

33. *Yevreiskaya entsiklopediya,* vol. 4, p. 918.

34. Greenberg, *The Jews in Russia,* vol. 1, p. 96, who cites Yu. Gessen, *Istoriya yevreiskovo naroda v Rossii,* 2 vols. in 1 (Leningrad, 1925), vol. 2, pp. 204–205; the latter believed that Grigoryev had "undoubtedly" been influenced in his views by *The Book of the Kahal.*

35. A. G. Dostoyevskaya, *Vospominaniya,* 2nd ed. (Moscow, 1971), p. 219; Dolinin has suggested that students of Dostoyevsky "in determining the sources of his views as a journalist must certainly consider the possibility of his having been influenced by Grigoryev at least insofar as the Eastern question is concerned" (*Pisma,* vol. 3, p. 298).

36. *Pisma,* vol. 3, p. 190.

37. *O tletvornom vliyanii Yevreyev na ekonomicheskii byt Rossii i o sisteme yevreiskoi eksploatatsii:* see Grossman, *Seminarii po Dostoyevskomu,* item 404, p. 46. Nothing is known about Grinevich; histories of the Jews in Russia make no mention either of the man or of his work. There is one scant reference to it in the Jewish periodical *Voskhod,* no. 1 (1881): 51–61, in the section "Current Events," where it is simply noted that the work is "beneath criticism."

38. Grinevich also went to great lengths in his effort to substantiate the accusations made against the Jews charging them with ritual murder crimes (pp. 38–50). It would be astonishing that this was not enough to discredit the work in the eyes of Dostoyevsky were it not for the even more disturbing fact that the latter, as will be seen in chapter 8, himself gave credence to this monstrous allegation.

39. M. S. Gus, *Idei i obrazy F. M. Dostoyevskovo,* 1st ed. (Moscow, 1962), p. 370.

40. Joshua Kunitz, *Russian Literature and the Jew* (New York, 1929), p. 62.

41. The article was accompanied by an editorial note: "For our part

we would add that the non-Jewish tavernkeepers are certainly no better than the Jewish tavernkeepers" (13: 586). The note has been attributed to Dostoyevsky, an attribution that appears highly dubious in the light of Dostoyevsky's persistent denunciation of the *zhidy-kabatchiki* in this very issue and in subsequent issues. Moreover, the expression *yevrei-kabatchik* was *never* employed by him.

Particularly relevant in this regard is the testimony of Mikhail Katkov. In an article written in April 1882 (*Moskovskiye vedomosti*, no. 110), he discredited the myth that held the Jewish tavernkeeper responsible for the ruin of the Russian people:

All of a sudden we discovered that it was the Yid-tavernkeeper who was to blame for the ruin of Russia and the miserable condition of the peasantry. Is that not a lie? Is it true that the Yid-tavernkeeper . . . is ubiquitous in Russia? There is not a single one in the provinces of Moscow, Tula, Ryazan, etc. The Yid-tavernkeeper is to be found only in the regions west of the Dnepr. Well, just ask the people who know where the most drinking is done and where the peasant is most impoverished—in the provinces of Kovno, Vilno, Kiev, Volyn or in our regions where Jews are forbidden to settle and where spirits are sold to the people by tavernkeepers or Orthodox kulaks? . . . Not only is drunkenness less widespread in the western provinces than in the rest of Russia, but the peasants there live better, not worse. In the western regions, there is, indeed, terrible, indescribable poverty, but it is the poverty of the Jews, not of the peasants.

(Cited by Vladimir Solovyov in a letter to F. Getz and published by the latter in his book *Slovo podsudimomu* [St. Petersburg, 1891], p. xvii.)

42. Compare with the apocalyptic vision of Versilov in *The Raw Youth* (chapter 4, note 27, of the present study), where this idea is given universal application; Dostoyevsky would return to this theme in the August 1880 issue of *The Diary* (see chapter 8 below).

43. The inappropriateness of this interpolation, so alien to the spirit of the article, is self-evident. Be that as it may, Dostoyevsky greatly exaggerated the importance of Jewish migration from the Pale of Settlement to the two capitals. During the period 1871 to 1880, the Jewish population of St. Petersburg increased by about 2,650 to reach just under 17,000 or 2 percent of the total population at the end of 1881; the percentage of Jews in Moscow was about the same (cf. *Yevreiskaya entsiklopediya*, vol. 13, p. 947; vol. 9, p. 335).

The reference to "exalted Yids of Judaic and Orthodox persuasion" is obscure, although it is clear that Dostoyevsky was more disdainful of the latter than of the former. The number of conversions during the seventies was not very significant—about 460 annually; it is true, however, that the converts included a number of people prominent in the financial, professional, intellectual and cultural life of Moscow and Petersburg. Broadly speaking, the motivation was not religious: conversion paved the way for professional advancement (see *Yevreiskaya entsiklopediya*, vol. 11, pp. 883–895; Greenberg, *The Jews in Russia*, vol. 1, pp. 172–178).

44. From January 1876 on, Dostoyevsky published *The Diary of a Writer* on his own.

45. D. V. Grishin (*Dostoyevsky-chelovek, pisatel i mify* [Melbourne, 1971], pp. 150–152) suggests that Dostoyevsky's animosity toward Disraeli may have been prompted by his reading of the latter's book *Lord George Bentinck: A Political Biography* (1852), which included a chapter on the Jewish question that was wholly unrelated to the principal theme of that work. (According to Sir Edward Clarke, *Benjamin Disraeli—The Romance of a Great Career* [New York, 1926], p. 122, the chapter had been written at an earlier date and then incorporated in a somewhat clumsy fashion in the book.) In that chapter, Disraeli lavished praise on the Jews (it was the Jews who were the founders of Christianity, etc.), and he refuted the allegations of those who claimed that the Jews were the guiding force behind secret societies bent on the destruction of the Christian order and on the establishment of Jewish hegemony throughout the world.

Grishin also suggests that Dostoyevsky's essay on the Jewish question in the March 1877 issue of *The Diary* was in some ways a direct rejoinder to Disraeli's chapter.

While many of Disraeli's works were published in Russian translation at the time, I have not been able to establish whether *Lord George Bentinck* or, at least, the chapter in question was among them.

46. In French in the original.

Some twenty years before, at the time of the Crimean War, Dostoyevsky invoked the image of the crucified Christ to denounce the European powers for supporting the Turks against the Russians and thus betraying Christ:

Look, ye all—He is crucified unto this day,
His sacred blood flowing anew!
But where is the Yid, crucifying Christ today,
Betraying again Eternal Love? . . .

Villainous deed, sinful and inglorious!
Christian with Turk against Christ!
Christian—Mohammed's defender!
Be ye ashamed, forsakers of the Cross,
Who have snuffed out the Divine Light!
But God is with us! Hoorah! Our cause is sacred,
And who for Christ his life willingly would not give! . . .

(Fragment of the poem "Na yevropeiskiye sobytiya v 1854 godu,"
written by Dostoyevsky in May 1854, reprinted in Miller and Strakhov, *Biografiya, pisma i zametki iz zapisnoi knizhki F. M. Dostoyevskovo* [St. Petersburg, 1883], pp. 17–20, addendum.)

47. The vampire image is used on a number of occasions by Dostoyevsky, but it is not clear whether he did so purely for literary effect
or also sought to take advantage of a superstition that was preva-
lent in Slav lore.

48. Nechayeva, *Opisaniye rukopisei F. M. Dostoyevskovo*, pp. 340–341,
404–405, 412, 413, 418–419, 491–492, 521, 523.

49. On the March issue, see page 101, above. In one section of the
April issue entitled "On Behalf of a Dead Man," Dostoyevsky reacted with vigor to a passage from the obituary of the historian
Afanasy Shchapov (published in the *Cause* and reprinted in *New
Time*), which he found deeply offensive to the memory of his
brother Mikhail. The alleged incident, related by the author of the
obituary, dated back to 1862, when Mikhail was publisher of
Vremya and Shchapov was one of its regular contributors. Hard
pressed for money, M. M. Dostoyevsky was unable to pay Shchapov his honoraria, badly needed by the latter to purchase some
warm clothing. He offered, however, to have Shchapov fitted out
by a Jewish tailor of his acquaintance who did work on credit;
Mikhail would defray the cost and charge it against past and future honoraria owing to his collaborator. Shchapov agreed to the
arrangement. As it turned out, the clothes were not only of dubious quality, but their price was exorbitant. Disputing the veracity
of the story and underscoring the deep humanity and compassion
of his brother Mikhail for those in need, Dostoyevsky concluded
his article as follows: "And this is the man whom people now seek
to portray in cahoots with some Jew tailor [*s kakim-to yevreyem
portnym*] in order to swindle Shchapov, split the profits with the
tailor and pocket a few rubles. Ugh, what utter nonsense" (11:
271–281).

50. See, for example, Kh. D. Alchevskaya, *Peredumannoye i perezhi-*

toye: Dnevniki, pisma, vospominaniya (Moscow, 1912), pp. 79–80.

51. The fascinating story of the extraordinary life of this not wholly typical representative of the Jewish intelligentsia of the second half of the nineteenth century has been told by Leonid Grossman in his book *Ispoved odnovo yevreya* (Moscow-Leningrad, 1924) and even more completely in the German edition of this work: *Die Beichte eines Juden*, edited by René Fülöp-Miller and Friedrich Eckstein (Munich, 1927). The latter publishes the full texts of the six known letters from Kovner to Dostoyevsky whereas the former gives the full text of his first letter of January 26, 1877 (also reprinted in *Pisma*, vol. 3, pp. 377–382), and only brief excerpts of four of the five remaining letters; Kovner's letter of June 3, 1877, his last, containing his comments on Dostoyevsky's March essay on the Jewish question, is blithely omitted. For more understandable reasons, the materials on Kovner's relations with Rozanov and their correspondence are not fully treated in the Russian edition.

On Kovner's childhood and adolescence, see his autobiography: A. G. [Kovner], "Iz zapisok yevreya," *Istoricheskii vestnik*, vol. 91, no. 3 (1903): 977–1009, and no. 4 (1903): 126–154.

52. Grossman, *Ispoved odnovo yevreya*, pp. 65–66.

53. Ibid., pp. 99–111; *Pisma*, vol. 3, pp. 377–382.

54. The analogy between the crimes of Kovner and Raskolnikov was made by Grossman (*Ispoved*, pp. 71–93); see also Nina Gourfinkel, "Dostoïevski jugé par Raskolnikov," *Mercure de France*, no. 858 (March 15, 1934): 531–542.

55. In his article "Berlin and Jerusalem," published in the early seventies, Kovner evaluated both traditional Judaism and the Haskalah more positively. It was thanks to tradition that the Jews had survived centuries of persecution; and traditionalism had not prevented them from keeping in touch with the ideas of the times. Their inability fully to enter the mainstream of human progress was due to their estrangement from other peoples, a situation they could not be held responsible for. See Grossman, *Ispoved*, pp. 66–68.

56. The italics are mine. The personalities named by Kovner were prominent in the field of finance, industry and the railroads. He was, of course, indulging in a bit of rhetoric. While it is, by and large, true that Dostoyevsky in his *Diary* consistently attacked the Jewish bankers and railroad magnates (they did, in fact, play a conspicuous role in these spheres), there is no reason to believe that he held their Russian counterparts in any greater esteem. Thus, in the October 1876 issue of *The Diary* (chapter 2, section 4: 11: 436–

442), he severely criticized the new class of Russian millionaires, singling out Ovsyannikov (who had been banished to Siberia) for his complete lack of scruples. It nevertheless remains true that Dostoyevsky put greater emphasis on the misdeeds committed by Jewish exploiters than by Russians.

In quoting Kovner's letter in the March 1877 issue of *The Diary* (12: 76–78), Dostoyevsky deleted the names, replacing the sentence in question by another that read: "In what way is the one better than the other?" and adding: "(At this point, my honorable correspondent compares several Russian kulaks with Jewish ones, implying that the Russians are just as bad. But what does that prove? After all, we don't hold our kulaks in esteem, we don't set them up as a paragon, on the contrary, we wholeheartedly agree that both are equally no good.)"

57. Again, the italics are mine. Dostoyevsky deleted all the names except Goldstein's under the following pretext: "I feel it would be improper for me to print [the names of those persons] because some of them might be unhappy to read that they are of Jewish extraction." In the best anti-Semitic tradition, Dostoyevsky here played Jew against Jew: not even Portugalov, who had no liking for Judaism, made any secret of the fact that he was born a Jew. The brief biographical notices (all taken from the *Yevreiskaya entsiklopediya*) that follow will throw light on the question:

—Portugalov, Venyamin Osipovich (1835–1896): born in Poltava; doctor, publicist, philanthropist, civic leader; resolute adversary of Orthodox Judaism, estranged from the Jewish community until the pogroms of the eighties but prominent thereafter in the Judeo-Christian movement [vol. 12, pp. 761–762].

—Kaufman, Ilarion Ignatyevich (1855– ?): economist, then professor on the Faculty of Law, University of St. Petersburg; prior to his conversion, active in the Society for the Propagation of Education among the Jews in Russia, a progressive reform group working for Jewish emancipation and civic equality [vol. 9, p. 389].

—Shapiro, Konstantin Aleksandrovich (1840–1900): born in Grodno; a convert; poet and court photographer (and Dostoyevsky's photographer); profoundly affected by the growth of anti-Semitism in the seventies, underwent a spiritual crisis and became the bard of his people [vol. 15, pp. 914–915].

—Orshansky, Ilya Grigoryevich (1846–1875): born in Yekaterino-slav; jurist and journalist and recognized authority on the legal situation of the Jews in Russia; refused an appointment to the Faculty of Law of the University of Novorosiisk that was made conditional on his conversion to Greek Orthodoxy [vol. 12, pp. 140–144].

—Goldstein, D. A.: Jewish volunteer in the Russo-Turkish War, cited for heroism by Army Commander General Chernyayev, who wrote: "In my long military career, I have rarely come across such a sterling example of courage and sangfroid as that displayed by Goldstein in the face of the greatest danger, and I consider it my sacred duty by this declaration to honor the memory of the deceased" [vol. 3, p. 166].

—Vyvodtsev, David Ilich (1837–1896): doctor and writer; during the Russo-Turkish War, attached to the headquarters of Grand Duke Nikolai Nikolayevich; toward the end of his life, one of the few Jews to become a member of the Privy Council [vol. 5, p. 850].

58. Whatever they lack in originality, the arguments advanced by Kovner to substantiate his doctrine of atheism indicate how much intellectual ground he had covered since he left the Vilno ghetto some fifteen years before.

59. Grossman, *Ispoved odnovo yevreya*, pp. 113–115 (*Die Beichte eines Juden*, pp. 110–116). This particular passage exasperated Dostoyevsky, an element that Grossman seems to have overlooked. There is an understandable tendency to be obnubilated by the fact that Dostoyevsky deigned to honor his unknown correspondent not only with a personal reply but also with an article in his *Diary*. And there is the further fact that he was unstinting in his esteem for the rare intelligence and erudition of his interlocutor. But was he sincere? One is less inclined to think so after reading the first chapter of the March 1877 issue of *The Diary*, which precedes the chapter on "The 'Jewish Question.'" There is no doubt that it was inspired, in part, by Kovner's disenchanted, even disparaging remarks about the religious feelings of the masses, as will be seen from the following passage (12: 70; italics mine):

"Even though this mass always called itself Christian (*krestyan-stvo*), it still doesn't have the faintest idea either about religion or even about Christ. . . . " This is what is usually said about our people. Who says so? Some German pastor—is that what you are

thinking— . . . or some European traveler . . . or *some educated,
upper-class Jew from among those who don't believe in God and
who suddenly these days have become so plentiful in our midst,*
or, finally, one of those Russians who have settled abroad . . . ? Oh,
no, that is what a huge part of Russian society—and its cream—
thinks. . . .

60. The allusion is to a long letter, dated February 6, 1877, signed with
the initials "T.B." For more information on this young correspondent, see chapter 7, note 18.

61. While the 1874 statute on compulsory military service made no
distinction between the Jews and other subjects of the empire, in
practice the rights of Jewish soldiers were limited by a series of
special ordinances and regulations (*Yevreiskaya entsiklopediya,*
vol. 5, pp. 703–710).

62. Dostoyevsky persists in believing—or pretends to believe—that the
Jewish communities continued to enjoy some legal autonomy, an
allusion to the *kahal.*

63. Of the various people who are known to have visited Dostoyevsky,
there was only one Jew among them, a young girl by the name of
Sofya Lurye, whom I shall have occasion to speak about in the
next chapter. It is, therefore, unclear to what other Jews he is referring. The likelihood is that he felt the need, perhaps subcon-
sciously, to justify his extravagant allegations by exaggerating the
extent of the personal relationships he entertained with the Jews.

64. *Pisma,* vol. 3, pp. 255–258.

65. The magnitude of the legislation limiting the rights of Jews can
be judged from the fact that of all restrictive laws singled out for
abrogation by the Provisional Government in March 1917, 140 per-
tained specifically to the Jews.

The most important restrictions concerned the right of residence and freedom of movement. According to the 1897 census,
94 percent of all Russian Jewry (5,450,000) was concentrated in the
Pale of Jewish Settlement. Established in 1804 by Alexander I, the
Jewish Pale consisted of twenty-five provinces (*guberniya*), which
represented 1/23 of the total area of the Russian empire. Its boun-
daries remained unchanged until 1915. Jews were constrained by
law to reside in the Pale. The right of residence outside the Pale
was extended to certain categories of Jews after 1861 (see chapter
3), but this privilege was severely limited (cf. above, note 43).

Other laws restricted the access of Jews to educational estab-
lishments, participation in commerce and industry, admission to

the civil service, professions and so forth. (See *Yevreiskaya entsiklopediya*, vol. 7, pp. 590–596; also, in *Kniga o russkom yevreistve* [New York, 1960], the articles by A. A. Goldenweiser [pp. 111–138], I. M. Dijur [pp. 155–182] and J. Lestchinsky [pp. 183–206].)

66. Chapter 3, entitled "The Funeral of a 'Citizen of the World,'" was inspired by Dostoyevsky's correspondence with Sofya Lurye.

67. At this place in the letter, Dostoyevsky made the following marginal notation: "Self-defense is permissible, after all the Jews won't change their [one word illegible], so knowing that in advance you limit their rights in part. Why, you can't let the Gypsies in everywhere" (Nechayeva, *Opisaniye rukopisei F. M. Dostoyevskovo*, p. 84). This remark reveals the spirit in which Dostoyevsky drafted his article for *The Diary*.

68. The fragment "it is above all necessary . . . native-born population" is quoted by Dostoyevsky in chapter 2, section 2, of the March 1877 issue of *The Diary* (12: 79).

69. Grossman, *Die Beichte eines Juden*, pp. 122–132.

7. The "Jewish Question"

1. The italics are mine. Here as elsewhere *yevrei* is translated as "Jew" and *zhid* as "Yid."

2. Vladimir Solovyov, *Yevreistvo i khristianskii vopros* (Moscow, 1884), p. 32.

3. In this regard, the critic A. Z. Steinberg, "Dostoyevsky i yevreistvo" (*Vyorsty*, no. 3 [Paris, 1928]: 95–96) has written:

At the moment Dostoyevsky made his entrance on the Russian literary scene, a battle for supremacy was already being waged, in Russian literature and language in general, between "Yid" and "Jew." These terms were now no longer synonymous: in Pushkin and Lermontov, the deep gulf separating the "accursed Yid" from the "Jew" and his "Jewish melodies" was clearly discernible. Dostoyevsky knew perfectly well that as a Russian writer, responsible for the destiny of his native language and his own people, he had to make a choice, but, instead of that, until the end of his life and speaking in his own name, he continually vacillated. . . . To be convinced of the extent to which he weighed all the nuances of the decent and indecent potentialities [of the terms], one has only to recall two lines from his description of the elder Karamazov's stay in Odessa: "At the beginning, he made the acquaintance of, in his own words, 'a bunch of Yids, Yidels, Yiddishers and Yid-lings,' but ended up, eventually, being received not only by the Yids but 'by the Jews as well' ". . . . "In his own words"—you can't help smiling, knowing that the very same gamut, in a variety of combinations, also crops up repeatedly in letters written by Dos-toyevsky "in his own hand" to his wife. . . . No, in the given in-stance, Dostoyevsky is not transcribing the words of Karamazov, on the contrary, it is Karamazov who is echoing him, who is using Dostoyevsky's own lexicon. . . .

The aversion inspired by the term *zhid* can be seen from the following two accounts, the first by Leonid Andreyev (*Shchit— Literaturnyi sbornik* [Moscow, 1915], p. 6):

I remember once spending a whole night talking with an ex-tremely gifted Jewish writer. . . . I tried to convince him of his rare talent, that he ought to write, but he stubbornly maintained that despite the heartfelt love he had as an artist for the Russian lan-guage, he could not write in it—in a language where the word *zhid* existed.

The second is by the late Kornei Chukovsky, the eminent writer and philologist (*Zhivoi kak zhizn* [Moscow, 1962], p. 29):

Soviet people take the greatest pride in remembering the re-markable way in which the Revolution renovated our language. It cleansed it of such repugnant words as *zhid, maloross* [Little Russian], *inorodets* [alien]. . . .

For the anti-Semite, things were crystal-clear. Thus, for Grinevich (*O tletvornom vliyanii Yevreyev na ekonomicheskii byt Rossii i o sisteme yevreiskoi eksploatatsii* [St. Petersburg, 1876], p. 7):

In ancient Russia the Jews were principally known by the name of *zhidy*. Nowadays, that appellation has acquired such meaning, such force and expressiveness that no better term could be found.

4. An attempt was made to construe the image in that sense by Orest Miller in his closing speech at the meeting of the St. Petersburg Section of the Slav Philanthropic Society on February 14, 1881, convened in honor of Dostoyevsky's memory. In reference to a pas-sage from the August 1880 issue of *The Diary of a Writer* ("Two Halves," ch. 3, sect. 3) where Dostoyevsky prophesied the coming

of an apocalypse from which the "Yids" would emerge triumphant, Miller declared (*Biografiya, pisma i zametki iz zapisnoi knizhki F. M. Dostoyevskovo* [St. Petersburg, 1883], pp. 77–78, third pagination):

> And that, of course, served as a "stumbling block," perceived as some sort of deformation of a great talent, a deformation, even, that was not quite human—because, as it happened, the *Yids* were implicated. But Dostoyevsky knew very well that they by no means constituted *a nationality*—that *Yids* could be found amongst *non-Jews* of all nationalities. Reasonable Jews (the intelligentsia, as they are wont to call themselves) did not feel offended and even wrote Dostoyevsky warm and heartfelt letters.

5. See further, chapter 8.
6. The violence of Dostoyevsky's reaction has nothing to do with Kovner's letter of January 26, the one he is commenting on here. That letter was devoid of any trace of the animosity that Dostoyevsky saw as proof of the feelings harbored by the Jews toward the Russians and that he used as a pretext to intensify his attack against them. But since his entire case and argumentation are built on this alleged hostility of the Jews, it is worth inquiring into the real causes of his indignation. As already noted, in his first reply to Kovner (February 14), Dostoyevsky accused him of hating the Russians. Why? "Because you are a Jew" (cf. above, ch. 6). But this was not all. In his second letter (January 28), Kovner had the audacity to call into question the sincerity of the Russians' belief in Christianity—an unthinkable and unforgivable "sin" on the part of a Jew.
7. See my analysis in chapter 2.
8. See above, chapter 6, note 27, concerning the various editions of *Kniga kagala*. All references are to the 1882 edition (part 1).
9. The truth of this statement, verified by my own research, was further corroborated by Léon Poliakov, the noted French historian of anti-Semitism (personal letter of April 15, 1961).
10. *Kniga kagala*, pp. 1–7. The juxtaposition of Dostoyevsky's "quotation" with the verses of the Old Testament quoted by Brafman shows a striking concordance of language.
11. Ibid., pp. 3–4.
12. N. Berdyayev, *Khristianstvo i antisemitizm* (Paris, n.d.), p. 5.
13. How is this thought, devoid of all hatred or malice, to be explained in the context? Dostoyevsky introduces it *on two occasions*: the first time, shortly before the "quotation" that completely demolishes

it; the second time, it is nullified by the remarks that follow it. Is it, perhaps, evidence that Dostoyevsky was torn by some inner struggle? Or was it not simply a literary device to soften the virulence of his subsequent judgments or, on the contrary, by the law of contrasts, to lend them greater weight?

14. L. P. Grossman, *Zhizn i trudy F. M. Dostoyevskovo* (Moscow-Leningrad, 1935), p. 35.

15. Instead of *svet* (light), Dostoyevsky put *luch* (ray), instead of *organ* (organ)—*kimval* (cymbal). Cf. Nestor Kukolnik, *Sochineniya*, 10 vols. (St. Petersburg, 1852), vol. 2, pp. 415–416.

16. Thus, Vyacheslav Ivanov attributed decisive importance to this statement: " . . . no matter how complex the scores of the Russian soul with the Jewish people may be, let no one forget . . . the final and irrevocable verdict of the alleged 'anti-Semite' Dostoyevsky regarding the Russian-Jewish dispute" (*Shchit—Literaturnyi sbornik* [Moscow, 1915], p. 86).

17. Similar views were espoused by Karl Marx in *Zur Judenfrage* (1844). Among other things, he wrote: "The Jew has emancipated himself in the Jewish way, not only by appropriating the power of money but also by the fact that, with him and without him, *money* has become a world force and the Jewish practical spirit, the practical spirit of the Christian peoples. The Jews have emancipated themselves to the extent that the Christians have become Jews" (Karl Marx, *A propos de la question juive* [*Zur Judenfrage*], bilingual edition [Paris, 1971], p. 132).

18. Who was this "generous and educated young Jewish girl" [*blagorodneishaya i obrazovannaya yevreiskaya devochka*]? Very little is known about her. Her name was Tatyana Vasilyevna Braude and she lived in Petersburg. She wrote two long letters (unpublished) to Dostoyevsky on the Jewish question: one, her letter of February 6, 1877 (cited by Dostoyevsky), ran to fifteen pages; the other, dated April 8 and containing twenty-eight pages, was undoubtedly a comment on the March essay, which had appeared on April 2. It is by no means certain, however, that Dostoyevsky held her in such high esteem: he noted on her first letter: "A Jewess— anonymity unnecessary"; and on her second: "A Jewess—take into consideration." (Cf. V. S. Nechayeva, *Opisaniye rukopisei F. M. Dostoyevskovo* [Moscow, 1957], pp. 340–341.) Dostoyevsky, apparently, never replied to Tatyana Braude.

19. *Yevreiskaya entsiklopediya*, vol. 2, pp. 742–743.

20. Beginning in 1878, Dostoyevsky met regularly with Grand Duke Sergei, the fourth son of Alexander II. See Grossman's article "Dos-

toyevsky i pravitelstvennyye krugi 70-kh godov," *Literaturnoye nasledstvo*, no. 15 (Moscow, 1934): 90, 159 (note 2). For information on the expulsion, see Louis Greenberg, *The Jews in Russia*, 2 vols. (New Haven, 1951), vol. 2, pp. 41–44.

21. I. Anosov, *Yevreiskii vopros v osveshchenii F. M. Dostoyevskovo*, 2nd ed. (Kharkov, 1908). Declaring that it was his intention "to recall or, perhaps, even make known Dostoyevsky's opinion about that people [the Jews] and their role in the history of Russia" (p. 4), Anosov reproduced large extracts from *The Diary of a Writer*, especially from the article of March 1877. His comments are devoid of all interest except for one that clearly reveals the incendiary purpose of his pamphlet. Speaking of the defects of the Jewish people, he calls on the Russians "to combat them [the defects] with all their might, not only for their own security but also in the name of justice. Only by standing firm and on guard can we help save one another. Our force, our salvation are in the people in union with the tsar" (p. 16).

22. *Delo Beilisa—Stenograficheskii otchot*, 3 vols. (Kiev, 1913), vol. 3, p. 234.

23. Grossman, who was the first to call attention to the chief prosecutor's reference to Dostoyevsky, noted at the same time the fallaciousness of the quotation. But he implies—and wrongly so, in my opinion—that it betrayed Dostoyevsky's thought (see *Ispoved odnovo yevreya* [Moscow-Leningrad, 1924], pp. 165–166). Numerous passages in *The Diary* and elsewhere contain similar affirmations and reflect the same apocalyptic vision.

24. This lacuna will be filled by the publication (for the first time since 1929) of *The Diary of a Writer* in the new thirty-volume collection of Dostoyevsky's *Complete Works* (but, apparently, in an edition of 50,000 as compared with 200,000 for the works of fiction). It is likewise interesting to note that in one of the rare instances when Soviet literary criticism has dealt at length with *The Diary*, "The 'Jewish Question'" is passed over in silence (cf. V. A. Tunimanov, "Publitsistika Dostoyevskovo: 'Dnevnik pisatelya,'" in *Dostoyevsky—Khudozhnik i myslitel* [Moscow, 1972], pp. 165–209).

25. See David I. Goldstein, "Rewriting Dostoevsky's Letters," *American Slavic and East European Review*, no. 2 (New York, 1961): 279–288; also, "Peredelka pisem Dostoyevskovo," *Novyi zhurnal*, no. 65 (New York, 1961): 111–120. In the light of information that has become known since the publication of that article, the conclusion ascribing sole responsibility to the editor A. S. Dolinin no

longer seems fully warranted. During a visit to Leningrad in December 1973, I learned from a leading young Dostoyevsky scholar and former student of Dolinin that the latter, shortly before his death in 1968, acknowledged to him that he had been compelled to yield to the demands of the censorship and make the deletions in question and, furthermore, that all derogatory references to the Jews would be expunged from the new edition of the *Letters* scheduled for publication in the thirty-volume edition of Dostoyevsky's *Complete Works* (vols. xxv–xxx), the sole difference being that this time the cuts would be indicated by editorial ellipses. (Even in "complete" works, obscenities or words prejudicial to a national minority are, apparently, excised by the censors.)

Twelve years elapsed before there was any public Soviet critical reaction to "Rewriting Dostoevsky's Letters" (with no mention being made of the article, however). In his study "Newly Discovered and Forgotten Letters of Dostoyevsky" (*Literaturnoye nasledstvo*, no. 86 [Moscow, 1973]: 114–152), I. S. Zilbershtein, the eminent literary critic, repeated (unfortunately) the argumentation of the article and drew the same erroneous conclusion, attributing the blame to Dolinin and not to the Soviet censors. He wrote: "Although the deletions were made to spare the writer from being reproached for his reactionary, chauvinistic views, there is no justification for such an arbitrary act on the part of an editor" (p. 115). It is sad to note that Ilya Samoilovich Zilbershtein in 1973—like Arkady Semyonovich Dolinin (Iskos) some fifteen years before—finds himself compelled by the censors "to limit the damage." Who would suspect that Zilbershtein's prudish and prudent descriptions of Dostoyevsky's views as "reactionary" and "chauvinistic" are simply euphemisms for "anti-Semitic"?

26. S. V. Belov and V. A. Tunimanov (eds.), *F. M. Dostoyevsky–A. G. Dostoyevskaya: Perepiska* (Leningrad, 1976). In their Comments, the editors note: "Several of F. M. Dostoyevsky's letters in this edition are printed with omissions designated by ellipses enclosed in angle brackets" (p. 389). Actually, sixteen letters have been expurgated, including two of Anna Grigoryevna's, to wit: nos. 5: p. 11; 16: 26, 27; 22: 39; 49: 75; 130: 201; 141: 213; 143: 218; 144: 219; 145: 220; 189: 278; 194: 286; 196: 289; 198: 292, 293; 200: 296, 297; 202: 299, 300; 207: 308.

27. Berdyayev, *Khristianstvo i antisemitizm* (Paris, n.d.), p. 9.

28. L. P. Grossman, *Die Beichte eines Juden* (Munich, 1927), pp. 160–168.

29. Ibid., pp. 161–162; Kovner is referring to chapter 3 of the March issue, which will be examined below.

30. An interesting question that Dostoyevsky never dealt with.
31. Grossman, *Die Beichte eines Juden,* pp. 168–170, 178–182.
32. Although falling outside of the framework of this study, the subsequent biography of Kovner is not without interest. His last letter to Dostoyevsky was already written from Siberia, where he remained until 1900, enjoying a rather large degree of freedom. In the early nineties, he got married (for the third time) to a young girl, a student of the well-known Siberian educator Kremyansky, with whom he struck up a firm friendship. Two weeks before his marriage, he converted to Orthodoxy—"out of necessity," as he later wrote his friend Rozanov in 1901. After leaving Siberia and wandering about for some time, he finally settled in Lomza, where he died in 1909.
    The Jewish question remained in the forefront of his concerns. In 1897, he submitted a memorandum to Muravyov, the Minister of Justice, drawing to his attention the catastrophic situation of the Jews in Russia. In 1901, he began corresponding with Rozanov on two major themes: the Jews and atheism. He assured him that man could live very well without religion and a belief in immortality; what was really important was to live by the golden rule: "Do unto others as you would have them do unto you." Thus, Kovner wrote to Rozanov on December 31, 1902, a letter which made a deep impression on the latter, who jotted down the following in the margin: "I am in complete agreement with all of this. It was Dostoyevsky who calumniated man by saying that 'without God and faith in the afterlife, men would begin to tear each other apart.' First of all, with their 'belief' both 'in God and the afterlife,' they burned each other up—which is hardly better than tearing each other apart; and they burned up each other for centuries, not individually but on orders from the church." (See Grossman, *Ispoved odnovo yevreya,* pp. 130–156.)
33. As mentioned in the Introduction (note 25), our request for copies of these and other unpublished letters was turned down by the then director of Pushkin House, where they are conserved.
34. Nechayeva, *Opisaniye rukopisei F. M. Dostoyevskovo,* p. 523.
35. Ibid., pp. 491–492.
36. Ibid., p. 413; for a biography of Kulisher, see *Yevreiskaya entsiklopediya,* vol. 9, pp. 904–905.
37. Nechayeva, *Opisaniye rukopisei F. M. Dostoyevskovo,* p. 412.
38. Ibid., pp. 328, 427–432, 449–453, 462–470.
39. See Introduction, notes 14 and 15.
40. The reference is, undoubtedly, to a letter of June 6, 1876, that bore this signature; it, therefore, antedated the publication of "The

'Jewish Question.'" In her letter to Dostoyevsky of July 12, 1876, Anna Grigoryevna wrote: "There have been no letters at all, except from one Muscovite who thanks you on behalf of all Muscovites for touching upon <the Yids>" (*Perepiska* [Moscow, 1976], no. 145, p. 220; see above, note 26). See also Nechayeva, *Opisaniye rukopisei F. M. Dostoyevskovo*, p. 521.

41. *Pisma*, vol. 3, p. 6.

42. *Zvenya* (Moscow-Leningrad, 1932), vol. 1, pp. 464–465.

43. Many press organs of the period commented regularly on *The Diary of a Writer*, among them the following: *Birzhevyye vedomosti, Golos, Molva, Novoye vremya, Odesskii vestnik, Russkii mir, Russkiye vedomosti*. Not having been able to consult such journals, which are not readily accessible in the West, I note here, simply by way of example, a few articles that dealt with *The Diary* (without knowing whether they are directly concerned with the March 1877 issue): *Birzhevye vedomosti*, nos. 239 and 267, 1877; *Novoye vremya*, no. 681, January 20, 1878 (article by V. Burenin). We do know, however, that the March issue (and those of January and February) was reviewed in *Golos*, vol. 11, no. 6 (June 1877): 61–64. As for Dostoyevsky's position on the Jewish question in general, the following articles may be cited: "Voskresnyye besedy—Mysli Dostoyevskovo o yevreyakh—Gde vsevo menshe govoryat o Dostoyevskom. *Alpha*—Dostoyevsky o yevreyakh," *Novorosiiskii telegraf*, no. 1822 (February 15, 1881); "Yevrei o yevreyakh. Z i K⁰," *Novoye vremya*, no. 8975 (February 21, 1901). (See A. G. Dostoyevskaya, *Bibliograficheskii ukazatel sochinenii i proizvedenii iskusstva, otnosyashchikhsya k zhizni i deyatelnosti F. M. Dostoyevskovo . . . 1846–1903* [St. Petersburg, 1906], pp. 76–77, 108, 198.)

44. The documentation is limited to three letters from Dostoyevsky (*Pisma*, vol. 3, pp. 209, 260–261, 263–265) and nine letters from Lurye, only one of which, that of February 13, 1877, is known from brief published fragments (see Nechayeva, *Opisaniye rukopisei*, pp. 418–419). Unfortunately, Sofya Lurye left no memoirs. Nothing is known about her life after 1877. She must have been known among the Jewish intelligentsia since Gornfeld mentions her briefly as having been one of Dostoyevsky's Jewish correspondents: "*Sara* Lurye, who died recently," that is, around 1910 (*Yevreiskaya entsiklopediya*, vol. 7, p. 312). But, according to Anna Dostoyevskaya, *Sofya* Lurye was "the daughter of a rich Minsk banker" who "died young in the nineties of the last century" (Grossman, *Seminarii po Dostoyevskomu* [Moscow-Petrograd, 1923], p. 65).

In her letter to Dostoyevsky of July 9, 1876, Anna Grigoryevna wrote that "a subscription had come in from Saul Solomonovich Lurye, <a Yid> from Minsk, a banker, I think, judging from the seal on the envelope" (*Perepiska* [Moscow, 1976], no. 144, p. 219; see above, note 26). Evidently, Sofya Yefimovna had Russianized both her name and patronymic, her real name being Sara Saulovna Lurye.

45. In the first of the three known letters from Dostoyevsky to Sofya Lurye, dated April 16, 1876, he invited her to come by to see him: "Even though I am busy, for you I will find a few minutes because I appreciate the extreme confidence you place in me" (*Pisma*, vol. 3, p. 209). For a long time there was some doubt about the year of the letter, but not about the day and month. While the year 1876 is now definitely established, the date of April 16 appears questionable to me. For it was in her first *known* letter of April 25, 1876, that Sofya asked for an appointment with Dostoyevsky (see Nechayeva, *Opisaniye rukopisei*, p. 418). Could she have written him earlier?

46. Sofya Lurye explained the reasons why in her letter (unpublished) to Dostoyevsky of August 25, 1876 (cf. Nechayeva, *Opisaniye rukopisei*, p. 418).

47. *Pisma*, vol. 3, p. 385 (Comments).

48. Ibid., p. 260.

49. Ibid., p. 261.

50. The Marxist literary critic Vladimir Desnitsky drew a parallel between Dostoyevsky's views on the Jewish question and those of the Decembrist Pestel, who, "in the *Russian Truth*, suggested that the Jews renounce their national 'essence' . . . and, in case of their 'refusal,' he offered them the state aid of his democratic republic in the noble endeavor of restoring the Jewish kingdom in Palestine. To be sure, Dostoyevsky did not go so far in his thinking as to suggest the mass expulsion, a new exodus, of the Jews to Palestine, but he did introduce into Russian 'Christian' [*nravstvennyi*] socialism that trait of anti-Semitism that is dissimulated by the personal benevolence of the petty bourgeois to the 'good' and 'honest' Jew" (11: xxii).

51. It is interesting to note—without overstating the point—the absence of a Russian Orthodox priest at the grave, inasmuch as Dostoyevsky was forever contrasting the religious tolerance of the Russians with the inflexibility and particularism of the Jews. This may have been the reason why Dostoyevsky stressed the tolling of the bells in "*all* the churches."

52. The use of the terms *yevreichik* and *zhidok* requires some explana-

tion. Dostoyevsky is careful to use the first himself, while placing the second in the mouth of the doctor. Would the doctor have expressed himself in this way? Probably not. But by attributing it to him, Dostoyevsky implies that there was nothing pejorative about the term.

53. See chapter 6, note 57 (concerning D. A. Goldstein).
54. *Pisma*, vol. 3, pp. 263–265.
55. Nikolai Maksimovich Minsky (1855–1937)—a Yiddish poet. On him, see *Yevreiskaya entsiklopediya*, vol. 11, pp. 82–83, and *Kniga o russkom yevreistve* (New York, 1960), pp. 367–368.
56. Nechayeva, *Opisaniye rukopisei*, pp. 418–419.

8. *Dostoyevsky's Last Years: The Anti-Jewish Theme in His* Diary—*His Letters*—*His* Notebook—The Brothers Karamazov

1. In September 1877, the War Minister, General Dmitry Milyutin, advocated the retreat of the Russian forces to the east of the Danube pending the launching of the spring offensive the following year. Even Pobedonostsev, who was a vigorous supporter of the war, and the future Alexander III became disillusioned and feared that the Panslav movement might turn against the government. See Robert F. Byrnes, "Dostoevskii and Pobedonostsev," in John S. Curtiss (ed.), *Essays in Russian and Soviet History* (New York, 1963), p. 99.
2. L. P. Grossman, *Zhizn i trudy F. M. Dostoyevskovo* (Moscow-Leningrad, 1935), pp. 268, 349. A week earlier, in his letter of December 17, 1877, to his old friend Dr. Yanovsky, Dostoyevsky mentioned for the first time his plans for publishing such a journal (see *Pisma*, vol. 3, p. 284).
3. See above, chapter 6, note 24.
4. He didn't go there in 1877, 1878 and 1880.
5. See S. V. Belov and V. A. Tunimanov (eds.), *F. M. Dostoyevsky–A. G. Dostoyevskaya: Perepiska* (Leningrad, 1976)—hereafter cited as *Perepiska*—and my comments thereto (above, chapter 7, note 26); cf. *Pisma*, vols. 3 and 4.
6. Occasionally he did so without any particular malice. Thus, describing his journey from St. Petersburg to Berlin enroute to Ems in July 1876, he wrote the following to his wife (*Pisma*, vol. 3, p. 216; cf. *Perepiska*, p. 213, where the passage enclosed in angle brackets has been suppressed):

As for me, my trip here was pleasant enough and without incident and I managed to get some sleep during the two-day journey. Incidentally, the Russian and the German cars were both cramped, in fact packed full, but the people were bearable. <But just as we were nearing Eydtkuhnen, a Yid who had boarded the train at Vilno latched on to me, one of those higher-class Yids, you might say, who is rich and has two sons in Petersburg—one a doctor, the other a lawyer. He had a terrible cough and kept on spitting and spitting in the car and spat up whole lakes. Endowed with these capacities, he took a seat opposite me and began telling me an interminable story about how he was on his way to Karlsbad to cure his hemorrhoids, what type of hemorrhoids he had, when they had healed over, what kind of swellings and so forth and so on; and out of courtesy I had no choice but to listen to the whole story, there was just no way out, so he harassed me for a good four hours.>

7. V. F. Pereverzev (ed.), *Pisma F. M. Dostoyevskovo k zhene* (Moscow-Leningrad, 1926), pp. 251–252—hereafter cited as Pereverzev —cf. *Pisma*, vol. 4, p. 78, and *Perepiska*, p. 286, for the expurgated versions of this letter; see also chapter 7, note 25. (*N.B.* In this and other letters cited further on, the passages enclosed in angle brackets have been deleted from both *Pisma*, vol. 4, and *Perepiska*.)

It is curious to compare this letter with another written from Ems three years earlier (July 9/21, 1876), where Dostoyevsky tells much the same story, the only difference being that it concerned a Greek mother and her daughter (*Pisma*, vol. 3, p. 220; cf. *Perepiska*, p. 218, where the word "Yids" has been expunged):

The room next to mine . . . has just been occupied by two ladies, a mother and daughter, coming from Greece, I think. They speak Greek and French—they never stop talking, especially the mother; it's not their talking so much, but rather the fact that they shout, literally shout, and what's more without letup, without a moment's respite. In my whole life I've never encountered such tireless loquacity, and with all that I'll have to be working, reading, writing—how can I manage amidst such an endless stream of chatter? . . .

I bought a copy of the Visitors' List: Russians galore, but they're all either *Strogonoff* or *Golitzin* or *Kobyline chambellan de la cour* [in French in the text] . . . or Russian Yids and German bankers and moneylenders. Not a single familiar face.

8. Pereverzev, p. 254 (cf. *Pisma*, vol. 4, p. 82, and *Perepiska*, p. 289).

9. Pereverzev, pp. 258–259 (cf. *Pisma*, vol. 4, pp. 86–87, and *Perepiska*, p. 292).

10. Pereverzev, p. 262 (cf. *Pisma*, vol. 4, p. 90, and *Perepiska*, p. 297).

11. *Pisma*, vol. 4, pp. 88–89. This was one of the few references to the "Yids" that escaped the notice of the censors of volume 4, but this oversight has been "remedied" by the editors of *Perepiska* (p. 296). Furthermore, the allegation was unfounded. In his letter to his wife of July 22/August 3, 1879, Dostoyevsky appeared to be very satisfied with that rate of exchange, which was more advantageous than the one he had been offered in St. Petersburg (200 marks for 100 rubles). See *Pisma*, vol. 4, p. 70.

12. Pereverzev, pp. 263–264 (cf. *Pisma*, vol. 4, pp. 95–96, and *Perepiska*, pp. 299–300).

13. Pereverzev, p. 270 (cf. *Pisma*, vol. 4, p. 102, and *Perepiska*, p. 308).

14. A theme echoed by Pobedonostsev in his letter to Dostoyevsky of August 19/31, 1879: see chapter 6, note 25.

15. Grossman pointed out the existence of this letter in his invaluable reference work *Zhizn i trudy F. M. Dostoyevskovo* (p. 270). No mention of it is to be found in Nechayeva's *Opisaniye rukopisei F. M. Dostoyevskovo*, which does, however, list Grishchenko's letter (p. 363) and Dostoyevsky's annotation thereto: "Reply."

16. L. Deich, *Rol yevreyev v russkom revolyutsionnom dvizhenii* (Berlin, 1923), pp. 51–68, *passim*.

17. *Pisma*, vol. 4, pp. 50–52, and Notes, p. 377.

18. *Pisma*, vol. 4, p. 356 (Notes).

19. To wit, Novakovsky, Felitsiya Sheftel and Aleksandr Bibergal: Novakovsky, recently arrived from Kiev, just happened to be in Kazan Square at the time of the events; sentenced to Siberia with confiscation of property; Felitsiya Sheftel, a young girl of eighteen from Zhitomir, for the last two years residing in St. Petersburg; took an active part in the demonstration, carried the red flag of the Land and Liberty group; exiled to Siberia; Aleksandr Bibergal, third-year student at the Army Medical Academy, involved in the demonstration quite by accident; defended himself with courage; sentenced to fifteen years at hard labor. See Deich, *Rol yevreyev v russkom revolyutsionnom dvizhenii*, pp. 153–191.

20. Ibid., p. 53.

21. *Pisma*, vol. 4, pp. 16–19.

22. *Pisma*, vol. 4, p. 356 (Notes).

23. Dostoyevsky's attempt to "resolve" in his own way the contradiction between Jew–incarnation of international capitalism and Jew–gravedigger of the capitalist order would only come later.

24. *Moskovskii sbornik*, no. 2 (1887): 8 (cf. *Pisma*, vol. 4, pp. 35–36).
25. It is sad to note how narrowly Dostoyevsky construes the term "all humanity," expressly limiting it to "all the families of the great Aryan race" (*vse plemeni velikovo Ariiskovo roda*; 12: 389). Unfortunately, it was quite in the logic of things. How he felt about the Jews is no longer a secret. But other texts are significant. Thus, in one of his very last articles (January 1881) written shortly before his death—"Geok-Tepe. What Does Asia Mean to Us?"—Dostoyevsky celebrated the victory of Russian arms in Turkestan while bitterly flaying Europe for its failure to understand Russia and its civilizing mission. The Europeans, he wrote, had nothing but disdain for the Russians, whom they regarded as "thieves who robbed them of their culture and disguised themselves in their raiment. The Turks, the Semites are spiritually closer to them than we Aryans" (12: 452).
26. O. F. Miller and N. N. Strakhov, *Biografiya, pisma i zametki iz zapisnoi knizhki F. M. Dostoyevskovo* (St. Petersburg, 1883), p. 358 (second pagination).
27. Ibid., p. 357 (second pagination). It will be recalled that Pobedonostsev expressed himself in a similar vein in his letter of August 19, 1879. But Dostoyevsky seems to go even further. What kind of "illiberal misfortune" did he have in mind?
28. The Russian is, undoubtedly, more expressive: *so mnogimi zhidami, zhidkami, zhidishkami i zhidenyatami*; the variations on the word *zhid* are not readily translatable.
29. The only other instance of Dostoyevsky's use of the word *Geschäft* is found in his letter to his wife of June 21/July 3, 1875 (*Pisma*, vol. 3, p 190; cf. *Perepiska*, p. 201), which I cited earlier.
30. For example, the following: Rakitin speaking to Alyosha—"As your brother [Ivan] sees it, that tinge of socialism won't hinder me from laying by the proceeds and investing them, as the occasion arises, under the guidance of some clever Yidel. . . . " (XIV: 77); Dmitry to Alyosha—"I won't keep you on tenterhooks like a Yid" (XIV: 98); Dmitry, short of money, sells his watch to a Jewish [*yevrei*] watchmaker for six rubles—"That's more than I ever expected!" (XIV: 337); Mrs. Khokhlakova to Dmitry, about a loan she promised to make him—"that money is as good as in your pocket, and not three thousand but three million . . . in no time at all! I'll let you in on the idea: you'll discover some [gold] mines, you'll make millions, you'll come back, become a man of action and lead us to better things. We don't have to leave it all to the Yids, do we?" (XIV: 348); the fair at Mokroye, Yid fiddlers and cymbalists, revelry and merriment, a new song is sung: the protago-

nists—a landowner, a gypsy, a soldier, a merchant—all vying with each other to win the favors of the girls; the merchant wins; Kalganov is indignant—"It's a brand new song . . . who writes such songs for them!? It's got everything except a railroad magnate or a Yid trying his luck with the girls: they would have won out over all the others" (XIV: 374, 384, 390, 392–393).

31. Surprising as it may seem, this passage has aroused little interest among the literary critics. Maksim Gorky is a notable exception. In an article written in 1913 entitled "Yeshcho o 'karamazov-shchine,'" he excoriated Dostoyevsky for his "slanderous" treatment of his characters. Even Liza, for all of her pathological tendencies, could never have told the story of a ritual murder: "the reader sees that the young girl has been slandered: she did not say, she could not have said, such a vile and odious thing." As for Alyosha's "I don't know," Gorky wrote: "the reader realizes that Alyosha could not have replied as he did; Alyosha cannot 'not know'; given the manner in which he has been portrayed, he simply does not believe in that shameful legend, even though he is a Karamazov, organically he cannot believe in it." And Gorky continued: "And if the reader can be shown that Alyosha in his youth really 'did not know' whether Jews drank the blood of Christians, then the reader will say that Alyosha is by no means the 'modest hero' the author makes him out to be but rather the notorious figure still alive today and making a profession of cynicism under the pseudonym of 'V. Rozanov.'" See *F. M. Dostoyevsky v russkoi kritike* (Moscow, 1956), pp. 395–396.

32. Dostoyevsky criticized Tolstoy for having violated that law, reproaching him for having "used" Levin (in *Anna Karenina*) to give expression to "his own convictions and views, thrusting them into Levin's mouth almost forcibly and, at times, even clearly to the detriment of artistic quality" (12: 201).

33. "Dostoyevsky i pravitelstvenyye krugi 70-kh godov" *Literaturnoye nasledstvo*, no. 15 (Moscow, 1934): 110–114.

34. *Yevreiskaya entsiklopediya*, vol. 9, pp. 938–940. (There is no mention in the "Notebooks" for *The Brothers Karamazov* of either the Kutaisi affair or the dialogue between Liza and Alyosha.)

35. *Upotreblyayut-li yevrei khristianskuyu krov?* (St. Petersburg, 1879).

36. Ibid., pp. 21, 31.

37. "Dostoyevsky," *Literaturnoye nasledstvo*, no. 15: 113. The article in the *Citizen* was actually the reprint of the memorandum prepared by V. I. Dahl (better known for his famous dictionary) in 1844 at the request of the Ministry of the Interior. See D. V.

Grishin, *Dostoyevsky—chelovek, pisatel i mify* (Melbourne, 1971), p. 154.

38. "Dostoyevsky," *Literaturnoye nasledstvo*, no. 15: 113.

39. Ibid.

Conclusion

1. Dmitry Merezhkovsky, *Polnoye sobraniye sochinenii*, 24 vols. (Moscow, 1914), vol. 14 (*Prorok russkoi revolyutsii*), pp. 208–209.

2. Martin Buber, *Israel and the World*, 2nd ed. (New York, 1963), p. 189.

Index

Abaza, Yu. F., 192 n. 11
Aksakov, Ivan, xxvi, 35, 134, 176
 n. 21, 177 n. 22, 177 n. 23; as
 editor of *Day*, 33, 38, 39, 41, 47,
 48, 178 n. 25; as Slavophile, 91,
 92, 93; "Why Should the Jews
 in Russia Enjoy the Equality of
 Rights Denied to Our Schismat-
 ics?" 48
Aksakov, Konstantin, 35
Aksakov, Sergei, 35
Aleksandrinsky Theater, 127, 167
 n. 7
Aleksandrov, A., "A Few Words
 about the Talmud," 41
Alekseyev, M. P., 3, 4, 8
Alexander I, 202 n. 65
Alexander II, 33, 34, 69, 90, 169
 n. 5, 174 n. 6, 206 n. 20; assassination of, 96, 130, 150
Alexander III, 94, 193 n. 26; as tsarevich, 90, 93, 191 n. 10, 212 n. 1
Alonkin's House, 184 n. 14
Altman, M. S., 188 n. 12
Andreyev, Leonid, 204 n. 3
Annenkov, P. V., 35, 175 n. 14
Anosov, I., 131, 207 n. 21
Antichrist, 87, 105, 153, 163
Anti-Semitism, 123, 131, 163, 185
 n. 22, 204 n. 3; in nineteenth-
 century Russia, 30, 92, 95, 96, 97,
 98, 109, 130, 176 n. 17, 193 n. 21,
 200 n. 57; in Russian press, 33,
 34, 35, 47, 148. *See also* Dostoyevsky, Fyodor Mikhailovich:
 anti-Semitism of, invoked by anti-
 Semites

Antonovich, M. A., 43, 45, 180
 n. 44
Armenians, 151, 189 n. 14
Atenei. See Athenaeum
Athenaeum (Atenei), 35, 175 n. 10

Babel, Tower of, 65
Bach, Mme. (landlady), 146
Baden, 58, 59, 61
Bakhtin, Mikhail, xxiv
Bakunin, M. A., 70
Balkans, 92
Balzac, Honoré de, 5, 7, 8; *Eugénie
 Grandet*, 3, 7; Gobseck, 5; Gran-
 det, 7; Nuncingen, 5
Banking. *See* Dostoyevsky, Fyodor
 Mikhailovich: on capitalism
Beilis, Mendel, 131
Belinsky, V. G., xxi, xxvi, 50, 71
Bely, Andrei, 94; Senator Ableu-
 khov, 94
Bender (moneylender), 61
Berdyayev, N. A., 55, 125, 132, 182
 n. 10
Berlin, P. A., xxii, 15, 16, 17
Berlin, 57, 58, 95, 212 n. 6
Berlioz, Hector, 12, 169 n. 23
Bessarabia, 33, 34
Bibergal, Aleksandr, 214 n. 19
Bismarck, 153, 192 n. 17
Black Hundreds, 66
Blagoobraziye, 64
Blas (musician), 169 n. 23
Blok, Aleksandr, "Retaliation," 94
Bludov (chairman of Jewish Com-
 mittee), 34
Boborykin, P. D., 35